THE
LOCKDOWN
PAPERS:

Social and Political Essays

John Dillon

KATOUNIA
PRESS

The Lockdown Papers

1st Edition Published by
Katounia Press, Dublin, 2020
www.KatouniaPress.com

ISBN: 978-1-5272487-7-9

ABOUT THE AUTHOR

John Dillon is Regius Professor of Greek (Emeritus) in Trinity College Dublin, having returned there in 1980 from a period in the University of California, Berkeley, where he was a member of the Classics Department from 1969 onwards. Prior to that, after graduating from Oxford, he spent some yvears in Ethiopia, teaching English in Addis Ababa. His chief area of interest is the philosophy of Plato and the tradition deriving from him, but he has always had an interest in more popular forms of writing as well, together with a weakness for practical politics, which he does his best to resist. The present volume contains a selection of the results of these journalistic tendencies. A second edition of his novel, *A Scent of Eucalyptus*, came out in 2019.

See more at: www.JohnDillon.ie

Acknowledgements:

These collected letters, esssays and articles
first appeared in *The Irish Times, The Irish Independent*
and *The Sunday Independent*
from the 1960s until the first decade of the twenty-first century.

Contents

Preface   11

Introduction   13

Irish Times: Articles and Interviews   17
  Hyenas at Harar   19
  A talk with Jomo Kenyatta   22
  Bombing the priceless past out of Yugoslavia   25
  An Irishman's Diary   27
  Heart Attack: Walking back to a whole new life   30
  IRISH TIMES Letters to the Editor   33

Irish Independent: Articles   43
  Worker participation urged   44
  Nine-year backlog in High Court   46
  Is there a right to life?   49
  Bruton's thoughts: who listens to an original thinker?   52
  Let's hope Beckman has got it wrong   54
  A moving sign of the times   57
  A misguided heroism   59
  Inertia and arrogance to blame   62
  The Danish analogy revisited   65
  Taking the gun out of Gaelic Games   69

Sunday Independent: Articles   73
  "Oblivious to any danger": a week in Moscow   75
  Scandal and the national psyche   78
  Time right for "license to thrill"   81
  We don't pay Charlie enough!   83
  Immortality and infallibility   86
  Talking shop and a flight of fancy   89
  Free money and our dependency   92
  Treaty through the looking-glass   96

Sunday Independent: Articles (cntd)

Maastricht Shmaastricht!	98
Joys of pessimism	102
The essential civil servant	106
The PDs in purgatory	109
Provo terror tactics backfire	112
Trinity's ambiguous role	115
How black is the black economy?	117
The Maastricht morass	120
The Bishop and the Lady	123
A rumour machine lubricated by clerical errors	125
Churchill and the purity of the race	127
Help our emigrants go	130
Justice for the rich and the poor	133
What is all this stuff about 'life'?	135
Can we pump fresh heir into this vacuum?	138
Over that rainbow	140
Pushing a 'vow of poverty' a bit rich	143
Sex and scandal diet is inedible to foreigners	146
A raw deal for our young	149
What is a poor old university to do?	151
Alms and the man	154
Consigned to the dustbin of history	157
We need to put Saint Patrick to work!	160
Parallels of an Easter's mad decline	163
Health Police handcuffed our national fun	166
Democracy Could Make History Yet	169
Paradise Island, of Corse	172
It's criminal to neglect our own	175
Labour takes a leap from Albert's book	178
Performing without a safety-net	181
High IQs and the cow's tail	184
A slow case of liberal burnout	187
Time to look into our hearts	190
Ulster has great potential as a theme park	193
Getting off this merry-go-round	196

Sunday Independent: Articles (contd)

Insurance war needs a 'plan of campaign'   199
Charged a whopping €25 for a single transaction   201
We need to encourage dropping-out   203
Apocalypse now, or at least soon   206
Europeans are wimps, long live America   209
Sinn Fein would have made us into a Burma   212
Organised religion has truly wrong-footed Him   215
Left Google-eyed by my alter ego as raunchy guitarist   218
Nation's favourite Hobbs is skating on thick ice   220
For true happiness, philosophers advise less is more   223
Come back Fr. Mathew, we need help to drink sensibly   226
How Charlie cast his spell   228
Beginning to look a lot like Armageddon?   231
It's just dandy, I feel I can be a yankee doodle again   234
Supreme beings must work in the real world   237
Opposition parties need to think outside their own box   240
Would Enda put the Shinners in Cabinet?   243
Bertie's chief sins are now cast in bricks and mortar   246
Sinn Fein at heart of the anti-Lisbon lunatic menagerie   249
Americans feeling the chill wind of anxiety   252
A sacrifice for the benefit of education   255
Athens at war: could Greek mob rule take root Ireland?   257
It's 10% off everything in recession escape plan   260
Can we survive our awful greedy binge?   262
Save the Green Coalition baby   264
Greeks must be brave and get history to repeat itself   266

Preface

This is a book of surprises, offering the perspectives on life and society of a learned mind infused with humour, anger, irony, irreverence and much that is wise over forty years of a richly lived life.

John Dillon, former Professor of Greek at Trinity College Dublin, and a member of one of the country's most distinguished political families, provides us, in *The Lockdown Papers*, with a book of essays, letters and newspaper articles that span from his African years to his most recent reflections on twenty-first century events.

The greater part of the book is taken up with a running commentary on the main political, social and cultural events in the changing Ireland of the 1970s to recent times. Hindsight often deals harshly with judgements and predictions handed down on an almost weekly basis and John Dillon often got it wrong – with the evidence here for all to read. But more often than not he is on the ball, and clearly he has good material to work with, as he takes us through the Haughey years and the scandals of those frenetic times.

Rumours, often of a most lurid kind, are revisited, and more than once the reality proved even more lurid. We meet again Bishop Casey and Larry Goodman, the Kerry babies, the various tribunals, Brendan Smyth and the missing files, political heaves and coups that were and predicted coups that never were. We follow the emerging sex scandals in the Catholic Church and the arrogance and complacency of a hierarchy accustomed to unquestioning obedience.

It offers us commentary on events as they happened – as the country argued with itself over the hitherto taboo topics of contraception, abortion and divorce. Gay rights were still far in the future, but on these issues we get the robust, informed and often acerbic views made without fear or the benefit of hindsight. For most people of a certain age, their own memories will be awakened, and not always comfortably.

And of course, the North is never far away. John Dillon's views here are those of an old-fashioned constitutionalist. He is hard on Sinn Fein, but as John Dillon's grandson he is equally alert to the wiles and treachery of perfidious Albion. And like most of us at the time, he had no idea how it would all work out. Or indeed if it would.

On the question of his political predictions and whether he got most of them right: more often than not, not, as I say; but consider this example from 2007, when he counselled Enda Kenny and Pat Rabbitte not to seek to form a coalition when such seemed possible:

> *'On the other hand, Enda and Pat, it is better if you stay on your high horses and let Bertie back in for a bit. There is undoubtedly something of a bust-up coming in the economy and it really would not be good for democracy if it could all be blamed on the foostherings of a ramshackle coalition government which would collapse after one and a half years and allow Fianna Fail to coast back in. Better to let Bertie clear up his own mess.'*

He got that one right.

John Dillon does not dwell much on his own experience as an election candidate. Perhaps just as well, because if he had followed the family route into politics we would not have had this book – a delightful pot pourri, at times idiosyncratic but written with old-style elegance, pungent and direct where it needs to be, and always with a refreshing absence of humbug, and always with honesty.

Maurice Manning

Introduction

I always wanted to be a 'writer' – that is to say, a rather louche character with long, straggly hair, a mauve smoking jacket, a cigarette holder, and perhaps a sultry mistress, based preferably somewhere on the Riviera, or possibly one of the smaller islands of the West Indies. Fate – along with some discreet nudging by my father – decreed that I become an academic instead. Nonetheless, over the years I have from time to time, either provoked or unprovoked, indulged in literary or journalistic experiments of one sort or another, and I thought, at this late stage of my career, that it might be worth gathering some of them together, if only for my own amusement.

In a way, this may be seen as a gentle riposte to my father. I can recall him declaring, when, in 1961, in my early twenties, on the heels of a rather expensive and elaborate education, I declared my preference for turning to creative writing, that it was a very precarious and stressful calling, and that I might well end up "like that poor fellow Joyce" (he had had occasion to call on James Joyce when he was in Paris as a post-doctoral student of Indo-European philology in the mid-1920s, and had found Joyce's life-style and living conditions rather depressing, as indeed they were). This, it must be said, coexisted in his mind with a certain regard for Joyce's writings. He preserved a first edition of Ulysses, which he had picked up in Paris when he was there, and he liked to take down his copy of *Finnegans Wake* from time to time, and read portions of it out loud. He was also, however, an old friend of Oliver St. John Gogarty, and shared the latter's scepticism as to the ultimate value of what Joyce was trying to accomplish in the Wake. And he liked to remind people that the famous Tower was not Joyce's at all, but *Gogarty's*.

I also remember him, in that same year, as a desperate device to discourage me, inviting the distinguished journalist Ulick O'Connor out to dinner at the house, with the express remit of describing to me the precariousness of the life of a freelance writer, which Ulick duly did. I remember him emphasising how one is completely at the mercy of one's editor, and only as good as your last article; in fact, he dutifully laid it on with a trowel, and fully earned his dinner. Slightly sobered by that, I went off instead to teach English in a private school in Addis Ababa, Ethiopia.

But I am wandering from the point. There is in fact every chance that I should not have succeeded as a creative writer, and would have ended up in a garret somewhere in Dublin, propping up the bar in Neary's, and grumbling to anyone who would listen about the lack of discernment and irremediable philistinism of the general public, which had failed to accord me due recognition. As it is, I have been able to disregard the general public to a very large extent, and to concentrate, from a series of safe havens, on a reasonably appreciative 'elite' (a much abused term, in my view!) of sympathizers with Plato and Platonism, while attaining a modest level of recognition and security, and I really cannot quarrel with that.

As far back as my time in Addis Ababa, however, I toyed with the composition of a rather avant-garde novel, entitled *The Game of Chess*, but it never came to very much. The novel I finally composed about my time there, *The Scent of Eucalyptus*, came to fruition much later, in 2006. It took a heart attack, in early 1995, and the subsequent recuperation from that, for me to complete it. The titzle was published by a small academic press, the University Press of the South, in New Orleans and in 2019, a revised second edition was published by 451 Editions in Dublin. The new edition is now available by order from most Irish bookshops, and online from all major book retailing websites.

I have also, however, been fortunate enough to be able to indulge my penchant for what might be called creative journalism from time to time. This I did in Oxford, when I was an undergraduate there in the late 1950s and early 1960s, and in the U.S., when I was teaching in the University of California at Berkeley during the 1970s.

In Oxford, it happened that my old friend Auberon Waugh (with whom I had also been at school in Downside) became involved in 1960 in the Oxford literary magazine *Isis* whereat he roped me in to contribute occasional short stories and other squibs. I also, in the same period, wrote a number of stories for the university newspaper, *Cherwell* then edited by my friend Nicholas Leonard, who was beginning his distinguished career in journalism.

In Berkeley, where I taught Classics in the University of California from 1966 to 1980, I became quite friendly with the novelist and short-story writer Leonard Michaels, who taught at the time in the English Department, and wrote a column for *The San Francisco Review of Books*, entitled 'The Western Spy'. When Lenny got tired of this column, he bequeathed it to me, and I carried it on for a few years, till I in turn got tired of it. I also wrote for a Berkeley journal, *University Publishing*, chiefly about books.

For these "lockdown papers", however, I have selected predominantly journalistic work published after I returned to Ireland, from the 1980s onwards. The exception to this is a couple of articles that I wrote when in Ethiopia during the years 1961–63. One is an interview I had with Jomo Kenyatta (then, as I recall, Minister without Portfolio in a sort of interim administration), when on a visit to Kenya with a friend in the summer of 1962. The second is an account of a visit to the exotic city of Harar, once home to the poet Rimbaud.

Back in Dublin in the 1980s, after returning to Trinity College to take up the position of Regius Professor of Greek, I was introduced by my friend, Nicholas Leonard (see above), who was furthering his career as an journalist at the time as London editor of the *Irish Independent*, to his boss, Aengus Fanning, and Aengus got me to write a few feature articles for him on various topics of the day. When Aengus was promoted in 1984 to be editor of the *Sunday Independent* (in which capacity he became, in my view, one of the great Irish newspaper editors of recent times), he took me along with him, again as an occasional contributor of generally satirical pieces on issues of the day.

This relationship continued, on and off, for a period of over twenty years until his much-lamented death in January 2012, and produced quite a body of work. I would have preferred to have had a regular column (even a monthly one, perhaps), but he was never quite prepared to give me that. Instead, Aengus would phone up, at irregular intervals, generally on a Thursday night, and philosophise at me for a while down the phone, before asking if I could do him 'a thousand words or so' on whatever was on his mind – this having then to be composed in something under twenty-four hours, a good discipline for an academic!

The results of this are inevitably a series of somewhat ephemeral pieces, but since they are always reflections on subjects of the day, they can be seen as a sort of commentary on the history of the period, and, as such, may still be of some interest. The headings are uniformly the work of a sub-editor (even when I ventured to suggest one, it was gently brushed aside), but I have left them in, as they are generally pertinent, and often witty. I toyed with the provision of short headings or footnotes to elucidate the obscurities of some of the characters and incidents dwelt on in many of the pieces. On reflection, I decided that any sort of background details would be in danger of taking up almost as much space as the essays themselves, and the interested reader can always have recourse, in this day and age, to Google or Wikipedia.

I note, with a certain grim satisfaction, that while my articles offered a series of solutions over the years to certain chronic ills of our state, virtually none have been acted on, leaving the problems I adverted to still remaining to be solved. I think particularly of the scandal of insurance claims and legal costs generally, about which I have something of a bee in my bonnet. The peak of my activity occurred in the late 1980s and early nineties, when the late C.J. Haughey was dominating the political scene, and heading for a fall, only to be succeeded, after some upheavals, by the inimitable Bertie Ahern, so that many pieces reflect the excitements of that era. I also, however, did book reviews for the paper at an earlier period, mainly in the area of international politics, which are excluded from the present collection.

I have also included a small selection of letters written to the Editor of *The Irish Times* over the years that have survived the ravages of time, and also seem to me to touch on issues of lasting importance.

The title of this collection derives simply from the fact that the COVID-19 lockdowns of the Spring and Winter of 2020, while in many ways tedious and depressing, also provided time for going through archives and attempting to put some shape on one's life. I realised suddenly that I had time to compile the paperwork for a collection of these essays, which, as a journalist friend once remarked to me, sadly, would otherwise simply provide wrapping for tomorrow's fish and chips. As it is, given the unexpected opportunity to compile them into a book in 2020, they may live to see another day.

John Dillon

Irish Times:
Articles and Interviews

Hyenas at Harar

May 31, 1963

'When you are a Moslem, I will consider you my master', replied Abdulahi bin Mohamed. the last Emir of Harar, to the demand of Menelik II that Harar submit to incorporation in the Ethiopian Reich. He enclosed with the message a robe, a turban and a prayer-mat. It was the end of 1886, and the Egyptian troops, with their British 'advisers' had just pulled out of the ancient city, having decided that they had after all no real interest in it. They left Abdulahi in command of a feeble defence force, inadequate even to control the surrounding Galla tribes. The British here came in for some bitter criticism from Arthur Rimbaud, who had been in Harar for some years as agent for a merchant in Aden. 'It is precisely the British with their absurd policy', he complained, 'who have undermined and continue to undermine all the trade along the coast. They wished to improve everything and they have done more damage than the Egyptians whom they have successfully ruined. Their Gordon is an idiot and their Wolseley is an ass. Everything they touch is a never ending progression of absurdities and waste.'

But Rimbaud got out in good time. Menelik's reply was direct and uncompromising: 'I will come to Harar and replace the mosque by a Christian church. Await me!' On January 7th, 1887, his forces crushed the army of Abdulahi at Chalenco, and Menelik entered Harar. And now the Cathedral of Medhanie Alem (Saviour of the World) dominates the Faras Magala (the Horse Market) the main square of the city. The mosque, however, still stands. Harar had been closed to infidels until Sir Richard Burton won through to it in 1855. Exaggerated reports had spread of its wealth and power, which Burton was able to deflate a good deal. Still, it remained a mysterious city, and even in 1963 I hoped to find some aura remaining.

The drive up from Dire Dawa is magnificent. Dire Dawa, the midway stop on the Djibouti-Addis Ababa railway, is down in the Rift Valley, but Harar is in the hills, 5,500 ft. up. It is on the first (or last) section of the Ethiopian plateau, which rises out of the flat deserts of

Dankalia and the Ogaden. Historically, it is more closely connected with the mediaeval Somali kingdom of Adal, from which Ahmed Grañ̃ launched his devastating invasion of Ethiopia in the fourteenth century.

The approach from the north is dominated by a magnificent boulevard, flanked by the various buildings of the Harar Military Academy, the Sandhurst of Africa, but this obscures the entrance to the Old City. One has to drive round to the south to see the city spread out on its hill, as Burton must have seen it. The old walls are breached and crumbling, but still confine the city within them. There is one street in the city along which a car may be driven, and it runs from north to south, opening into the Faras Magala in the middle. Otherwise one must go on foot through tiny, winding streets with dilapidated old Arab houses on either side. There is not really much to see, when one gets down to it. The mosque is of venerable age, but completely plain, and Rimbaud's house is not of great interest. The market is colourful, but then so are all markets in Ethiopia. Besides old coins and suchlike relics, one can buy basketwork of elaborate and colourful design. Harar also produces, in small quantities, some of the best coffee in the world.

The only other thing the old city is now noted for is its hyenas. Nowhere else in the world, perhaps, is the hyena such an accepted institution. They roam round the walls at night and walk the streets, quite at peace with the inhabitants, if not with the inhabitants' dogs. The only disturbing aspect of their presence is their constant whooping. There is, in the shadow of the south wall, an old gentleman who lives with the hyenas, and he is now becoming something of a tourist attraction. Every night he holds court, summons his friends by name, talks to them, and distributes bones. He has become a bit stingy of late, though, and the bones looked dry and unappetising. The hyenas accept the bones out of politeness, while their sad, nervous eyes look around for something better. We concluded, since the new bones so closely resembled the old, that the poor hyenas had to dodge round behind the wall after being dismissed and give the bones back. They were certainly a tyrannised and depressed company.

But it is the military academy and the rapidly-expanding teachers' training college that constitute Harar's real contribution to contemporary Ethiopia. We were shown round the former, and generally splendidly entertained, by an Indian colonel we had known from Addis, and saw enough to realise that it is a very businesslike place. It is modelled consciously on Sandhurst and turns out a very high class of graduate. The policy has been to go around the secondary schools of the empire in the summer term and select all the most promising pupils, and pack them off to Harar. This results in excellent standards, but also, it seems to me, will tend to create a 'young officer' class, as exemplified by one young lieutenant I met.

'The problem is,' he said to me over coffee, his face creased in a tense frown, 'are we going to have enough time to get Ethiopia fixed in the twentieth century? If there were to be a revolution now, there would not be enough of us to ensure that the country will move forward and not back. As things are now, it will sink back into darkness, dragging us with it.' The conclusion was that the Old Man must hold on a while longer, until a few more young men have established themselves.

The teachers' training college is not nearly so impressive a place, and the standards have been low, but this year it doubled in size and acquired a new director, a Canadian Jesuit of volcanic enthusiasm, who is determined to raise standards and expand still further. Also, the Army has agreed to stop taking all the best students for the military academy.

Harar is a favoured place, being not only almost perfect climatically, but also the birthplace of Haile Selassie (his father, Ras Makonnen, was governor here). The Emperor visits it at least once a year, for the pilgrimage to Kulubi on St. Gabriel's Day, and usually more often than that. It is also of considerable strategic importance as the gateway to the Ogaden, and a number of army divisions are stationed in the area, in case the Somali Republic should be so foolish at any time as to launch an attack.

A talk with Jomo Kenyatta

December 14, 1963

Only once, so far, I think, have I had the feeling that I was in the presence of a great man, and that was when I met Jomo Kenyatta in Nairobi on Sept. 12th, 1962. In the midst of the thronging friends and petitioners who besieged his office in the Ministry of Finance, he consented to discuss with me briefly the future of Kenya, or Africa, and of the world.

I had gone along to Solar House, his personal headquarters, one of the new blocks of flats that are steadily rising up on the south side of the city, on the off-chance of being granted an interview. Since I could not claim to belong to any newspaper, or even to be contemplating an article, I did not expect too much.

I was presented to Achieng Oneko, his personal secretary (now Minister of Information), who had been sentenced along with Jomo for the founding of Mau Mau, and asked him if there was any possibility of the Old Man sparing me a moment. When he heard that I was from Ethiopia, he was extremely friendly, and promised to do what he could. And he did, because when I returned a few days later, he told me that the Mzee (the 'Old Man') would see me next morning at eleven o'clock. I went off in confusion to try and think up some intelligent questions.

Next morning I returned to Solar House, and then walked over with Achieng Oneko to the Ministry of Finance, where Jomo was holding down the rather formal job of Minister of State for Constitutional Affairs in a suite of offices on the second floor. On the way over, we talked about Ethiopia, where Mr Oneko had been the previous autumn with Jomo, on a very successful semi-official visit. During his stay, Jomo had given a talk at the university, to which I had brought down my senior English class, from the school where I was teaching.

I had heard the Mzee addressing his people at Bahati location the previous Sunday, and I had been overwhelmed by his presence and the control that he had over the crowd. This was a meeting held to effect a reconciliation between Tom Mboya and Oginga Odinga, his two chief and ever-quarrelling lieutenants. The English reporters that I was with were in great excitement in expectation of a riot, but Odinga, in fact wisely, failed to show up (Nairobi is a solid Mboya stronghold). When the car carrying the leaders appeared, however, there was great excitement amongst the crowd, and the KANU Youth Wing had a lot of trouble holding them back. As the leaders mounted the platform, there was still much shouting and cheering, but when Jomo turned to face them and raised his arms, a silence fell. Then he told them to sit down, and, like a field of corn bent by the wind, the whole assembly sat down. He then addressed them for two hours.

Now, as I entered the room, the vast grizzled figure in the chair a few feet away was too much for me. He sprang up, however, leaned across his desk with a broad smile to grasp my hand, and offered me a seat. He was apparently delighted at this intrusion. There were a number of other people in the room, all of whom clustered round us, smiling expectantly. I confessed that I was not really writing for any newspaper, but had just wanted to meet him.

'All right', he said, cheerfully. His English was not as good as I had expected from a past student of the London School of Economics, and author of *Facing Mount Kenya*, but his years of imprisonment must have taken the edge off his fluency. 'All right', for instance, he used to mean 'fine' or 'not at all'.

All during the interview he toyed with the great flywhisk of black horsehair that lay in front of him on his desk, which, along with his massive walking-stick and his red fez, has become a symbol of the man. I first turned to the problem of preserving traditional customs in a modern environment.

'Do you think', I asked, 'that traditional African customs and habits can be fitted into a modern society' – and I gestured at modern Nairobi through the window – 'or must they inevitably be abandoned? I mean, for instance, the initiation rites, and the family system.'

He scratched his beard. 'No', he said, 'I don't see that. You Europeans assume that your way is the only way. We Africans think that you have forgotten what life is for. You are always rushing about. We will fit our customs and ideas into any situation.'

I said that I thought that young people in Europe missed a lot through having no proper initiation ceremonies into adulthood, and he agreed, saying that it was a cause of confusion and uncertainty for the young. He agreed that family loyalties must be reconciled with the claims of the general public, say in a government department, but defended the close personal relationships that members of a clan have.

We turned then to politics. I avoided mentioning controversial issues, most of which would inevitably be embarrassing, and on which Jomo could give only guarded, formal answers, but asked whether he thought that there was any reason for opposition parties in a newly-born African state.

'Surely', he said, spreading out his hands, 'if we are honest, we are all in favour of the same things. We are all African nationalists, we are all socialists, we are all democrats, we are all against imperialism. There are no classes that need parties to represent them. In our country, opposition should come from within the party. There is no excuse for an opposition party.'

He smiled at me like a lion after the midday meal. We agreed that an opposition party could only represent personal, tribal or regional interests, and/or the interests of the retreating imperialists. I turned to economic issues.

'Doesn't it make you uneasy, sir, that such a large proportion of the country's business should be in the hands of foreigners? Are you taking any steps to change that? I notice that Mr Odinga has organised the small traders of Nyanza...'

He gazed out of the window at the teeming office blocks and bustling streets of this booming capital that he had inherited, and once again spread his hands. 'We will see. Gradually it will come, gradually ...'

It was obvious that the subject disturbed him, as well it might. Even if one peeled off the big British firms at the top, one would still be left with the small shopkeepers in the little stores and shacks all over the country, from Nairobi down to the smallest settlements, and almost all were either Indians or Arabs.

I rose to leave, thanking him for receiving me. Again, he leaned across the table, and grasped my hand as I bowed myself out.

'All right', he said, 'All right!' and the eyes twinkled over the grizzled beard.

Bombing the Priceless Past out of Yugoslavia

November 14, 1991

It is a callous and unfeeling reaction, I suppose, but as I read of the bombs and shells falling on the seaside resorts of Croatia, my mind turns not so much to the unfortunate citizens, who are facing ruin and death there, as to the priceless antiquities, both from Roman times and from later periods, which are being reduced to rubble because of the monstrous mutual hatred of two kindred peoples.

This area covers the coastal portion of the former Roman province of Dalmatia. The Romans first stuck their noses in about 200 BC, although they only conquered the place thoroughly in AD 9, after which it became a province. Roman domination lasted till the fifth century, although in 395 the emperor Theodosius took the momentous step of running the boundary between the eastern and western empires along a line that still divides Serbia from Croatia, destining these two areas to different cultural development, specifically as Greek Orthodox. and Roman Catholic, respectively.

At any rate, more than four hundred years of Roman influence have left their mark, although the chief relics of it are fortunately rather further north along the coast than the main centre of destruction at the moment, the grand old city of Dubrovnik. Dubrovnik (the former Ragusa, which was for centuries a seafaring city-state, rivalling Venice) is in fact not a Roman but a medieval foundation, though none the less splendid and valuable for that. The old city, with its walls still in place, dates from the 13th to 18th centuries, a fine mixture of Gothic and Renaissance architecture (its main glory, perhaps, being the 15th-century Rector's Palace), and it seems to be this that is receiving the brunt of the present bombardment.

The main glories of the Roman era, however, are further up the coast, and not touched, I think, as yet, though no doubt, if obstinacy prevails, the destruction will get to them. First, we have Split (Spalatum), where the Emperor Diocletian built himself a massive palace for his retirement in 295-300 AD. He came from this area, being born at nearby Solin (Salona), also a fine Classical site.

The palace is still well preserved and is of dimensions that eclipse most surviving Roman antiquities in Italy. It should make a fine target. Somewhat further up the coast again, one finds the lovely old towns of Zadar and Rab (although the surroundings of Zadar are somewhat disfigured by modern urban sprawl, which could well be bombed), both with Roman and early Christian antiquities as well as later adornment. Sibenik, somewhat further south, is a lovely medieval town with fine Venetian monuments.

The part of Yugoslavia I know best, however, is the north-west corner of Croatia, currently furthest from the fighting, the beautiful peninsula of Istria. In this part of the world one is struck first by a patina of *fin-de-siecle* charm derived from the Austro-Hungarian Empire, which ruled here from 1797 to 1918, and which even fifty years of communism have not managed to dispel; and then by the influence of the Venetians, who dominated the area for over five hundred years before that.

A series of little ports on the west coast – Koper, Piran, Porec and Rovinj – are endowed with piazzas and palazzi which would not be out of place in Venice itself. Down at the tip of the peninsula, at Pula, one is brought further back in time by the sight of the massive and excellently preserved amphitheatre, which actually far surpasses the Coliseum in Rome. This would make an excellent target for Serbian bombers. Similarly, the magnificent Basilica of Euphrasius in Porec, dating back to the sixth century, one of the most perfectly preserved early Christian churches in Europe and one of the most important monuments of Byzantine art on the Adriatic, positively cries out for shelling.

Contemplating these treasures, and many others, I am moved to suggest that there is a case for a pan-European or UN force being sent in at least to the coastal area of Croatia, to ensure that we preserve this part of our common European heritage. If Serbs and Croats are determined to massacre each other to the last man, then it is probably foolish to stand in their way, but at least we could insist that they go and do it somewhere else.

An Irishman's Diary

(Some reflections on the fall of communism)
February 3, 1992

It is already becoming a little embarrassing to cast our minds back to the preposterous state of euphoria that possessed more or less everybody in Europe just two years ago, as walls, guard towers, barbed-wire fences, statues of Lenin, and the regimes that erected them, all came tumbling down in eastern Europe. One recalls scenes of fatuously dancing and embracing crowds, of champagne corks popping, and of random revellers saying how very overjoyed they were. If anyone at all was thinking of the future, they were not in evidence at the time.

The Polish elections of last autumn form a nice contrast to those scenes of revelry. This was the first free election since before the Second World War, when they were not all that free either. Just about 40 per cent of the electorate bothered to turn out, and the largest party, by a short head (in a field of about 70, including the Beer Drinkers' Party) was the former Communist Party, now called the Liberal Democratic Party, or some nonsense like that. The Beer Drinkers' Party actually pulled in about the same percentage of votes (5 per cent) as does our own Workers' Party. It took some months for a government to be formed.

This is not just a Polish joke. It is actually quite serious, and an important sign of things to come. What we have all come to realise with horror over the last year is that the peoples of Eastern Europe had been held in a sort of time warp for fifty years or so. They were not purified or ennobled by their dreadful experiences. They seem to have learned nothing and forgotten nothing. They have simply awoken, as from a bad dream, and have gone back to being themselves.

This is unfortunate, because they really never liked each other. This may be a tribute to their perspicacity, but it does not make for a peaceful world. The Croats, as we all know, abhor the Serbs, a sentiment which is cordially returned by the latter. They both have historical atrocities to remember against each other, and they have both been adding to these in recent months. It seems impossible that they

27

should ever be at peace with one another. And wait until the Bosnians, Herzegovinians, Montenegrins, Macedonians and Albanians get in on the act! In particular, the Albanians in Kosovo yearn to be reunited to their motherland, incredible though that may seem in present circumstances, and the Serbs are determined that they shall not be. The Bulgarians have a claim to Macedonia, and the Macedonians in turn cherish an ambition to seize much of northern Greece (the historical Macedonia).

Then the Hungarians do not like the Romanians, nor the Romanians the Hungarians. And this is unfortunate, since there is a large Hungarian minority in Romania, particularly in Transylvania.

The same is true of Poles in Lithuania, and Russians in Moldova (which wishes to be reunited with Romania). As for the Bulgarians, they are being beastly to their Turkish minority. Not even Czechoslovakia, the most advanced and rational of these countries, is free from the canker of nationalism. The Slovaks are now feeling that they do not really like the Czechs, although neither is subordinated to the other in what is (one would have thought) a rather satisfactory federation. But nevertheless there are moves to break up even that.

I leave out of account in all this the pullulating mass of conflicting nationalities which has arisen from the rotting corpse of the Soviet Union. One must wish the new Commonwealth of Independent States the best of luck, but one must also reserve the right to be sceptical. Certainly, the same forces that are at work in Eastern Europe are present there, too, with knobs on.

In the face of all this, I can foresee something almost unimaginable at the moment – the growth of a certain degree of nostalgia for the admittedly grey certainties of communism. I don't seriously want to suggest that there will, or ought to be, any significant body of thought that would advocate the return of Stalinism, but I do believe that it will begin to occur to many serious people throughout the East before very much longer, as they come increasingly up against the seamier side of capitalism, that perhaps they should not have thrown out the baby with the bathwater.

There was a baby, then, somewhere in that very murky bathwater? Yes. I think that there was. Let us call it, not the infant Jesus, but the infant Karl. Communism, after all, is a dream about creating the objective conditions for the ultimate *liberation* of the individual. All the oppression and enslavement of so many people for so many years was just a regrettable means to a glorious end, necessitated by the refractoriness of human nature – and by the constant seductive allure of a superficially more attractive way of life represented by the United States and Western Europe.

Even now, the idealised view which so many people in the East have of the Western way of life is sad to see. They believed nothing of what their own rulers told them, and everything which they managed to see or hear from Western sources – books, films, magazines, radio broadcasts, music, fashions. Nothing about unemployment, homelessness or crime impinged upon their consciousness.

The 'baby', then was the ideal that, as a condition of true freedom, everyone should have a right to free education and health care, to take them as far as their talents would reach, followed by the guarantee of a job, and a place to live at a price they could afford. The basic necessities of life were to be cheap enough to be comfortably within the reach of everyone. These included the obvious foods, essential (if not fashionable) clothing, public transport, and access to culture, such as drama, music, art and film (provided, of course, that it was not such as would undermine the effort to achieve this better life), and to sporting facilities.

That was the dream, and a good deal of it was actually realised, if only at a rather dismal level. The pity of it was that it was all achieved only at the cost of grinding oppression, the fostering of a class of time-serving and place-hunting toadies and bullies, and reckless financial and environmental practices, unchecked by anything resembling independent criticism, which ultimately brought the whole system to bankruptcy.

It is that dream, however, which, after a few more years of reckless stampede towards a will-o'-the-wisp capitalist paradise, will, I think, begin to reassert itself. However, I fear that much nastier things will be happening by that time, of which we are only now beginning to have an inkling, and the dream will have little chance of realisation.

Heart Attack:
Walking back to a whole new life
October 26, 1998

It wasn't anything like I expected it to be. I was walking down Westland Row to the train, after presiding at a lecture in Trinity and having taken the visiting lecturer for a drink in the Pavilion. It was early January and about 11 p.m. at night, and I was actually walking rather fast, aiming to catch the second-last train back to Howth. The street, I recall, was more or less deserted. Suddenly, about half way to the station, I was struck by what seemed to me to be a ferocious dose of heartburn. It ran all up and down my windpipe and settled somewhere at the back of my throat. Stopped abruptly in my tracks, I cursed the pint of ale I had drunk.

After resting for a while against some railings, I managed to creep on the rest of the way and got myself on to the train. The pain eased somewhat during the half-hour journey to Howth and, having got there, I managed to creep to my car and drive myself up the hill. Once in my bedroom, though, it became clear that this pain was not going to go away. As I lay rolling about on the floor and groaning, my wife phoned the emergency services and was told – wisely, as it turned out – if I could move at all, to get me into the car and drive me to Beaumont Hospital herself, rather than waiting for an ambulance, which might take some time. So that is what she did.

At Beaumont, a young doctor lost no time in injecting me with something. I was by this time barely conscious, but still babbling about suffering from indigestion. I remember him looking down at me humorously, needle in hand, and saying: 'Now you don't really believe that, do you?' That quietened me. Once I had had my injection, I was really in a fairly beatific state. The pain had receded (though apparently the period of danger lasted till the next morning), and I remember no longer caring much what happened to me. If I died, that was perfectly all right with me. It was not that I was in great pain, or anything. It was just that I was tired, enormously tired. My whole past life did not pass before my eyes. I just remember contemplating my end with surprising equanimity – and something of that feeling, I am glad to say, stays with me still. I hope that I will be able to hold that thought when I need it.

For the next six weeks, I was an inmate of the cardiac unit at Beaumont, before being transferred to the Blackrock Clinic for my bypass. There are still only two places in the Republic where bypasses can be carried out, the Blackrock Clinic and the Mater Private Hospital, and I belong to an organisation which is raising money for a third such centre. I was fortunate not to have to go on a waiting list. After the operation, I experienced, like other heart surgery patients, curious hallucinations (somewhat later, Brendan Kennelly told me that he, after a similar operation, was visited at his bedside by a man whose face was made of rain!). Jesus Christ appeared to me – but he was, somehow, dressed up as Bugs Bunny. He capered about wildly, and made a variety of silly noises, though without conveying any coherent message. I got the feeling that the Second Coming, if it occurs, will be a pretty zany affair.

After the bypass, you must be up and walking within a few days in order to prevent a build-up of fluid on the lungs. After a week I was sent home to recuperate, and ten weeks after that, I was fortunate to begin a rehabilitation programme at Beaumont Hospital. The programme developed by Dr John Horgan constitutes a model for the whole nation. For an hour three times a week, we performed a carefully planned sequence of exercises on various machines. There were also weekly sessions with the dietician and the psychologist – who gave useful talks on recognition of stress and the avoidance of depression. I had thought that my life was not particularly stressed, but I now realise the degree to which in fact I had been stressed. The tell-tale sign is that one feels one is indispensable – but watch out! No one is indispensable.

I have returned to work, and an essential part of my routine is my daily, brisk walk of no less than 40 minutes. It has become the most important feature of my day, to which anything which arises in the office must take second place. I hope I have learned from this whole experience, three years on, that no aspect of one's job or profession is worth killing oneself for.

IRISH TIMES Letters to the Editor

a selection

The Other Congo, Aug. 27, 1963

Sir, Dr. Conor Cruise O'Brien's recent letter (August 19th) in your columns prompts me to certain reflections. Dr. O'Brien has incurred widespread disapproval of a very basic kind as a result of his revelations about the Congo, and this letter shows that his spirit is not rebuked, nor his eye dimmed. There he took the lid off British methods; here he has lifted the curtain that protects French neo-colonialism.

I know nothing of West Africa, but I have travelled enough recently in East Africa to see that what is really going on in, say, Tanganyika is radically different from what is said to be going on there. I refer to the amount of freedom that the country really enjoys. In reality, none of the new nations of Africa, except perhaps Ghana, has achieved any solid freedom. They are all as thoroughly dominated and as efficiently exploited as they were ten years ago, and I see no probability of a change in their status in the near future.

Dr. O'Brien, I think, went out, like myself, a liberal, heartened by the new awakening of Africa, ready to observe this great continent at last coming into its heritage. And look at Dr. O'Brien now!

But why has he aroused such resentment? Simply because he has touched on one of the nerves of Western Democracy. Our traditions of free speech allow us to criticize and attack nearly every aspect of our situation, but there are certain things that must not be revealed, and the true state of affairs in Africa is apparently one of them. We may belabour the little lies as vigorously as we wish, but the great lies, the basic deceptions, we must leave alone. And herein lies Dr. O'Brien's sinfulness.

Yours etc.

Role of the T.D., May 24, 1964

Sir, Mr Basil Chubb, in his examination of the role of the T.D. in Irish life, is not, of course, concerned with the historical origins of this situation, though he did mention the alien character of British rule as a cause. But it is possible that the Irish attitude to the T.D. may have roots much further back, and that the T.D. may be for the many the modern equivalent of the ancient rí of the tribe. A quotation from the *Cáin Aigillne (Ancient Laws of Ireland,* Vol. II, p. 279) may be relevant:

'The head of every tribe should be the man of the tribe who is the most experienced, the most noble, the most wealthy, the wisest, the most learned, the most truly popular, *the most powerful to oppose, the most steadfast to sue for profit, and to be sued for losses.'* (my italics)

Attention is particularly drawn to the last two qualifications. To these ancient principles the modern Irish electorate has added what seems to me the rather decadent belief that these same powers reside equally in the widow or orphan of the hero originally chosen. Otherwise, nothing much has changed.

Yours, etc.

Irish, July 14, 1972

Sir, My father, Myles Dillon (who died on 18th June last), appears to have become involved posthumously in the sort of controversy he least of all liked; one about the unfortunate Irish language. I do not wish to prolong the argument unnecessarily, but there is one phrase of Mr O'Conchúir's letter (July 5th), which really needs correction: 'Professor Dillon expressed his satisfaction that so many young Bretons were insisting on learning their own language despite the full weight of the French murder machine.'

Apart from the fact that my father was not inclined to borrow Pearsian formulations, his point was quite the opposite from what Mr O'Conchúir seems to imply. It was rather the following:

(1) He hoped that membership of a large unit such as a United Europe would actually make Irishmen more proud and protective of their heritage, including the language. He cited

the recent growth of Breton studies in France, despite lack of official encouragement, as evidence in support of this thesis.

(2) He made it clear, to me at least, that there was no hope of such a happy development taking place in Ireland unless compulsion was dropped and encouragement substituted. Somehow the language had to become a thing of joy instead of drudgery and be left to those who really loved it for itself, in the hope that their number would grow. If the Irish people then rejected the language, that would be their free decision, which he would regret profoundly. He believed, however, that they would not do so.

My father indeed loved Ireland and her culture deeply, and was optimistic about our future, but I'm afraid that Mr O'Conchúir cannot legitimately claim him for his particular dreary dogma.

Yours, etc.

A Certain Symmetry. April 26, 1983

Sir, The SDLP, as we know, will not enter the Stormont Assembly, because they do not approve of the purposes for which it was set up. Now we learn from the Alliance Party that *they* will not attend the All-Ireland Forum, because they do not approve of the purposes for which it was set up.

I discern a certain symmetry in the pig-headed futility of these positions, and find it particularly disheartening that they should be taken up by the two organisations in whose hands, one would think, most of the hope for future positive developments must rest.

Why cannot the SDLP say to the Alliance Party: 'We will attend your wretched Assembly if you will attend our lousy Forum. Let us see what each of us can do to make the deliberations of either body more meaningful. If we can do nothing, then we can always walk out again.'

Such a move would certainly put the ball in the court of the Alliance Party, and call their bluff as a party open to change and new ideas. As it is, both of these organisations are revealed as being just as closed and hard-line as their respective extremists.

Yours, etc.

An Taisce, July 14, 1983

Sir, Mr Bobby Molloy, in a speech in Dáil Eireann yesterday (July 5th), made the damaging accusation that An Taisce was a predominantly middle-class organisation. He also hinted darkly that it had close links to Fine Gael. Tact presumably forbade him to mention what was also, doubtless, in his mind, that the organisation has a fairly large *Protestant* membership. The point he was making, obviously, is that a concern for the preservation of the environment is un-Irish, since it is not a concern of the Plain People of Ireland, represented by Fianna Fáil.

In this he is probably correct. It is also a fact, though, that the preservation of wild life is not a concern of African tribes. Their only interest in the elephant is his tusks, the rhino his horn, the colobus monkey its coat. Would Mr Molloy therefore hold that, since wild life conservation is solely a fantasy of over-fed, over-developed Western democracies (and worse, of the *middle classes* thereof!), it is an illegitimate activity, and should be condemned as interfering with the aspirations of the local tribesmen?

Or is it just that a somewhat broader view of what we owe to future generations of humanity is, on the whole, characteristic of those who are comparatively well-educated and comfortably off?

Yours, etc.

Jury Awards, June 26, 1985

Sir, It is to be expected that the Bar Council would bring considerable rhetorical resources to its defence of the jury system in civil cases, but there was one argument in particular that I found quite breathtaking in its sophistry.

It was admitted that, in the 'more rigid' English system, the loss of one eye, for example, would get you £15,000 to £17,000, whereas here one might be awarded as much as £50,000. The Council, however, felt that the UK system could not fairly be compared with Ireland's arrangement, since *it could not be assumed that Irish views of what was just would conform to those of the British.*

The magnificent effrontery of this point, I think, deserves

celebration. 'We Irish think differently', as Bishop Berkeley would say. The stone-faced British reckon one eye at no more than £17,000, but we Irish ask ourselves, 'How can we put a value on an eye? Every eye is unique!' For a compassionate group of twelve Irish people, gathered together as a jury, its value might be anything!

The concern of the Bar Council for the preservation of the distinctive Irish sense of justice is admirable, but, as they admit themselves, there are banal 'economic considerations' to be taken into account. Partly, at least, because of the maudlin compassion of Irish juries, this country is rapidly becoming uninsurable, at any reasonable rates. And that means, since insurance companies are not charitable institutions, that we will become an *uninsured society*. Then perhaps we will be prepared to get into line with the rest of Europe in the matter of the expert and impartial assessment of damages.

Yours, etc.

John Dillon's Motives, April 9, 1986

Sir, Nollaig Ó'Gadhra, in his otherwise interesting article of April 2nd on 1916, makes what seems to me an unnecessarily snide and ungenerous reference to the motives of my grandfather in opposing the executions of the 1916 leaders. Dillon, he says, deplored the British backlash "not only because of its inherent distastefulness, but, more especially, because he feared what such reaction might do to his political fortunes."

It is undeniable that John Dillon saw, with stark clarity, that the executions, and then the decision to introduce conscription in 1918, spelled ruin for a process of constitutional development to which he had devoted almost forty years of struggle, and would give the country over to violent courses, of which he could see no good end.

This is not the same, I submit, as a selfish concern for his own survival. He, along with Redmond, was the leader of the Irish Nation (so far as anyone could judge). He had a right to be concerned about his survival.

There lies behind Mr Ó'Gadhra's remarks the extraordinary and offensive assumption still abroad among people of the Sinn Féin persuasion that the Home Rule Act of 1914 conferred immeasurably less than they gained by all their shenanigans. This is absurd. The Home Rule Act, like the Treaty, conferred 'freedom to achieve freedom', and a much more substantial and balanced freedom for the whole island than was in fact achieved. My grandfather was quite right to seek to preserve it.

Yours, etc.

Holiday Value, August 8, 1986

Sir, I write, on the eve of departure for a low-budget holiday in the south of France to comment on Mr John Bruton's gallant attempt (reported in your columns of August 4th) to rally the nation to take its holidays at home. He speaks of the attractions and the *value* of holidays in Ireland.

Now I am not one of those who blame the present Government for the weather (actually I believe it to be retribution upon us for our appalling behaviour in the recent referendum), but I would suggest that Mr Bruton *could* do something about the prices of hotels and restaurants.

While in France, I expect to sleep (a family of three) in charming old inns for no more than 100 francs a night (*avec douche!*), and to dine superbly for not much more than 60 francs a head (*vin compris*). I may be disappointed (I am a year out of date), but I doubt it. Where could I stay comparably in this country for less than £35 a night, or dine for less than £15-20?

I don't wish to ignore the efforts of Mr Bruton, for whom I have the greatest admiration. He has reduced the appalling rate of VAT. But we are still not competitive. Why should anyone either come here, or stay here, to be rained on and swindled? I have heard the oft-repeated lamentations of hoteliers and inn-keepers, but I am not impressed by them. They have simply pitched their expectations too high, and someone, either the Minister or the market itself, must bring them down to earth.

I know what such radical social reformers as Genghis Khan or Idi Amin would have done with them, but in a modern democracy I recognise that one must proceed more circumspectly. Nevertheless, the Minister *could* act, for instance, by setting up a chain of Parador-like inns and restaurants, which would pitch their prices deliberately to compete with the Continental average. Such action would force the inefficient and the rapacious either to get their act together or to get out of business.

Yours, etc.

Talking to men of violence, January 31, 1994

Sir, It has long been a mystery to me why, when so much emphasis is placed upon the close links between Sinn Fein and the IRA, that virtually nothing is made of the almost equally close links between the DUP and Protestant paramilitary extremists, the UDA and the UFF. Mr Sammy Wilson of the DUP has now provided a welcome reminder of the closeness of those links by his warm endorsement of the genocidal proposals of the UDA for the creation of an "ethnic" homeland within the area of Ulster, with its schemes for ethnic cleansing and the "nullification" of those Catholics who refuse to be displaced from their homes.

It is not clear to me why Sinn Fein should be required to renounce violence absolutely and forever before they are to be allowed to approach the conference table, whereas the ageing warriors of the DUP should be allowed to posture before the cameras as staunch upholders of "democracy", while exhibiting by every sort of nod, wink and verbal code-language their total support of their own military wing, whose actions are in general more mindlessly savage than those of the IRA.

It is high time the British and Irish political establishments ceased posturing about 'not talking to men of violence'. In the long and inglorious history of their disengagement from empire, the British have rarely talked to anyone else.

The only consideration, surely, is whether Mr Adams and his colleagues represent a factor of any significance in the Northern Ireland situation. If they are deemed to do so, talk to them; if not, ignore them, and get on with the job without them.

Yours, etc.,

Semperit Pulls Out, September 25, 1996

Sir, *Semper it*, how are ye? *Semper non* bloody it. The arrogance of the German masters of Semperit, Continental AG, surpasses all understanding. They are backing out of the enterprise themselves, in order to batten on the cheap labour force of Eastern Europe, and they refuse to consider the sale of their physical plant to any of their possible competitors – that is, to anyone who knows how to build and market a tyre!

These, let us remember, are people to whom the IDA recently gave a grant of £12 million to upgrade their plant in Ballyfermot. Could I urge Richard Bruton simply to regard their assets in Ballyfermot as sequestered, and to sell them to the most competent tyre manufacturer he can find, whether American or Asian? Let us give them a run for their money. *Semper eamus!*

Yours etc.,

Dracula on Stamps, Thursday, October 9, 1997

Sir, I am most edified to see that An Post has issued a set of four stamps to celebrate Dracula. I only regret that this imaginative move has to be set against its decision, which I ascertained recently, not to celebrate in any way the 150th anniversary of the 1848 Young Ireland Rising, which occurs next July.

I wonder what the priorities are. Dracula was (and is?) a bloodsucker, of Romanian origin, with extensive offshore interests. As such, he is doubtless a suitable role-model for the present generation of fun-loving Irish entrepreneurs, but it is a pity that no thought is to be given to a group of decent, honourable men, led by William Smith O'Brien, who made a noble, if hopeless, effort to keep alive Ireland's sense of nationhood and self-respect in very dismal times.

As we pass blithely from the era of the family rosary round the fire to that of the strawberry-flavoured condom, there is a danger of our consigning to oblivion much that was good.

Yours, etc.,

The Answer to Marching, June 5, 1998

Sir, Would it not be a great triumph of the spirit, as well as a tactical move, if on the occasion of the next Orange march in the North, the Catholic population came out, not to shout protests, and hurl missiles, but rather to cheer the marchers on with evident good humour, showering them, perhaps, with rose petals, sweets, and confetti? That should surely be the proper reaction to these unfortunate benighted creatures for whom this demented marching is, apparently, an indispensable symbol of identity.

Such marching, after all, is really quite a minor disruption in itself to a given neighbourhood. It is usually over and done with in a quarter of an hour or less. Its noxiousness lies, as it is intended to lie, in the offence it causes to the (previously) subject population. If that population now decided to show its moral and intellectual superiority by welcoming such manifestations in a true spirit of Christian charity and brotherly love, I suspect that it would spoil the fun of them so thoroughly that provocative marching would wither away. But, sadly, the obtuseness of one side in that part of the world can still rely on being fed and fostered by the other.

Yours etc.,

Philosophy in Schools? October 29, 2014

Sir, The real reason why proposals for the introduction of philosophy into the school curriculum have consistently failed, despite being repeatedly advanced over the last few decades by such groups as the Committee on Philosophy of the Royal Irish Academy, has simply been the opposition of the Catholic Church, which felt that its proper domain was being encroached upon. The power of such a veto is now much lessened, I think, and the remaining problems would now be how to select a course of study that would be neutral as between the various schools of philosophical thought, and how to prevent such a course from being mind-numbingly boring.

A solution would be to employ a process of Socratic-style questioning, presenting a series of propositions, in ethics or metaphysics, and encouraging students to question them, and provoking students in

41

turn to advance their own opinions, which would then be subjected to the same process. This would train the students in a basic philosophic method which could be applied to the whole of their curriculum, which would in turn produce a more open-minded and inquiring younger generation.

It is such a programme that we are currently developing in the Platonic Centre in Trinity College Dublin, and which we hope to be able soon to present to the second-level teaching unions for their feedback. We do feel that such a module would be a most beneficial component of at least the last few years of the secondary school curriculum.

Yours, etc,

The Vulture Charities, Saturday, Feb. 4, 2017

Sir, I must say that I am (grimly) amused by the imaginative names that the distinguished Dublin law firm Matheson has selected for the 'charities' that they have created for the various vulture funds on their books: Eurydice, Medb and Badb – the first from Greek mythology, the latter two from Irish. Eurydice, wife of Orpheus, was an unfortunate lady, more sinned against than sinning, whose only fault was to inadvertently cause her husband to look back when he should have been going forward; Medb and Badb, on the other hand, were both formidable ladies, the former a queen, the latter a war goddess. Both had strong predatory instincts and very little pity on their victims.

I note that Matheson, under pressure from recent untoward publicity, are now conducting a review of these entities, with a view to reconstituting them. If they need new names for them, could I tentatively suggest Medusa, Scylla, and Charybdis?

Yours, etc,

Irish Independent: Articles

Worker participation urged
March 1, 1983

In recent days, against the background of an alarming deterioration in the industrial relations climate, we have heard eminent people once again suggesting that there should be some serious moves made in the direction of worker participation in industry. Among them was Mr Harold O'Sullivan, former ICTU President and present General Secretary of the Local Government and Public Service Union. Even as he was speaking, Ranks workers, sitting in at their closed flour mills, were being hauled off to jail. Then, last weekend, on being released from Mountjoy in the early hours of Saturday morning, they immediately resumed their sit-in. Meanwhile, in another part of the industrial scene, the Clondalkin Paper Mills workers, backed by the Trade Union movement as a whole, managed to force the Government to honour its predecessor's commitment to take over the mills.

I find it disturbing that the Ranks workers are willing to submit themselves to the ordeal of a prolonged sit-in, and undergo a term in jail, not because they wish to save their jobs, but because they want bigger redundancy payments. Mr O'Sullivan's thoughts were directed in a totally different direction, towards the concept of giving workers some real involvement in the management of the firms in which they are employed.

What I would like to see would be bands of socially-conscious workers, aided and abetted by a far-seeing and statesmanlike Mr Harold O'Sullivan, demanding from employers and government alike that they be allowed to take over concerns such as Clondalkin, Carrigaline and Ranks (Ireland), and run them themselves – with, at most, an initial period of government subsidy and provision of managerial expertise. The sad thing is that, unenthusiastic as employers would be about this prospect, workers are even more so. 'Take over control of the factory?' they say, 'No bloody fear. Let the bosses worry about running the business. Just give us our money every Friday, and don't talk about recession, competitiveness, productivity and marketing. That's not our problem.'

This is an attitude we have inherited from the British Trade Union movement, and it is an attitude we can ill afford. British Trade Unions rejected Marxism and all that stuff about worker's control of the means of production way back around the First World War, and they have never looked forward since. Here at home, we have been experimenting tentatively for some time with worker directors on the boards of semi-State bodies, much of this due to the efforts of Michael O'Leary, when he was Minister of Labour in the 1973 – '77 Government), and with giving workers the opportunity to buy shares in the company (as Guinness's have been doing recently), but this can too easily end up as window-dressing. One or two workers on a board are virtually powerless, and are continually in danger of being co-opted into a management consensus, while a few shares in Guinness's are not going to result in any real transfer of authority. Indeed workers are justified in seeing such granting of shares and odd seats on boards as a trap, to bind them more closely to the company's fortunes, without giving them any say in the running of it.

Something more, then, is needed than this. There have, admittedly, been some isolated instances of firms actually handing over power to their workers (I can think of only, two, Crannac Furniture of Navan and Bewley's Cafes; there may be more), but in none of the recent cases of a firm's going out of business can I recall the workforce saying, 'All right, hand it over to us. We'll run it!' The Trade Union movement of this country has a duty to move forward from the stagnant British model, and with the help of its parliamentary representatives in the Labour Party, to take its proper share in the running of the economy.

Nine-year backlog in High Court
April 12, 1983

There is now a backlog of up to nine years in the processing of High Court injury claims awaiting a jury trial. The saddest aspect of this sad situation is that it is only the tip of a very large iceberg. There are currently immense delays in getting any kind of case to trial in the High Court, and, much less excusably, there have been considerable delays in getting the judge to hand down the verdict once the trial has been held (up to five years, in some recent instances), though this latter situation, it must be said, has recently improved. A person who is knocked down and seriously injured today may well be a full decade older before any compensation is received through the legal process. When the case finally comes up, many of the witnesses may be dead or vanished, and the firm being sued may have long since gone into liquidation. All these things have happened in one case or another in recent years.

Of course, nine years is an extreme possibility, but at least a couple of years is the norm. At present, on average, it takes about one year to settle pleadings. This means that, from the date of service of the High Court writ, the entry of appearance, the service of statement of claim, the notice of particulars, the entry of defence, the reply to the defence, and the notice of trial, if you will pardon all this jargon, takes one year. From this point there is least a two-year delay to the hearing. And then – if there is no postponement, for any of myriad reasons – the hearing goes ahead. Even then, though, the pace is that of the tortoise. The dominant feature of the Irish legal scene is the clogging of the legal calendar with a vast backlog of cases. One major cause of this, which can and should be done away with, is the insistence on a jury trial for accident cases. In most other countries of Europe (on both sides of the Iron Curtain, let it be said!) these cases are tried by a court of (usually three) expert assessors, who are experienced jurists of proven probity.

In this country, a simple car accident requires a full-dress jury trial – a major production, with junior counsel, senior counsel and expert witnesses. What must be realised is that this, though it seems to be for the benefit of the ordinary citizen, is really for the benefit of the legal profession. There is no evidence that a jury produces a fairer result than would a court of assessors. The inordinate damages occasionally awarded do not further the cause of justice: they simply raise the cost of car insurance, and increase lawyer's fees. There are further absurdities built into the system, all designed to increase costs and delay verdicts. Expert witnesses must be called to assess injury. In most cases, an ordinary G.P. who had attended the victim would serve perfectly well, but a specialist is invariably insisted on. The specialist will possibly not have attended the victim at the time, and will often simply have examined him or her for the purpose of giving evidence in court. His time is valuable, and he is only intermittently available.

In England there is now an agreed procedure where each side exchanges full medical information, and where possible the medical evidence is agreed before the case is heard, thus making it unnecessary for the doctors to be called to give formal evidence. A short agreed report is simply read out. If there is an irresolvable dispute, the evidence is referred to a medical assessor, and if even this procedure fails, the doctors must come to court, but this is a last resort and relatively infrequent. Why cannot this happen here? I have already stated the reason. It is not in the interests of the legal profession that it should happen, and governments are made up, to a remarkable extent, of members of the legal profession. In this case, there is also the superficial plausibility of the argument that a jury trial is the sacred right of the citizen.

But superfluous jury trials are not the only problem. There is also the extraordinary under-utilisation, and downright misuse, of High Court judges. No doubt we need a few more of these, but there is no need that they should sit only from 11 a.m. to 1 p.m. and from 1 p.m. to 4 p.m. on the days when they sit, and that they should not sit at all for the whole of August and September. Why should our court system take the summer off? Hospitals don't, Police stations don't. And above all, criminals don't. There is actually no need for individual judges to sit longer hours (though they well might): it would be quite possible to stagger their hours, and even their terms, so as to get a day-long, year-round court system.

Then there is the curious custom that a High Court judge is deputed, fairly frequently, to go through the non-jury list and to call each case. There may be a few hundred of these cases, and thus a day in the life of a valuable, highly-paid High Court judge is wasted, doing a chore that some minor functionary could perfectly well perform. And there is more. Strange as it may seem, judges do their work in truly Dickensian conditions. They have no proper secretarial backup. They have no aides to help them in their research (as in the US for example). They have never heard, it seems, of such a thing as a word-processor or a computer. All these things should be supplied to them, and they should be taught how to use them.

Is there a right to life?
April 23, 1983

In the midst of the vast outpouring of views concerning the proposed Amendment on Abortion, one basic question has not, so far as I can see, received the attention it deserves, and that is the question of the status of a 'human right', such as is the Right to Life now being talked of. The doctors and the lawyers have had a good deal to say from their particular perspectives; perhaps it is not unreasonable that a philosopher should also say a word or two.

The supporters of this Amendment have unhesitatingly assumed that there is such a thing as a human right floating about in the atmosphere, as it were, like a Platonic Idea, independent of the decision of any society to establish it in law, and their opponents have not, I think, challenged this assumption. But this assumption should not go unchallenged. We have become hypnotised, in the modern world, by the concept of civil, or human rights, ranging from the rights to life, freedom and the pursuit of happiness, through freedoms of speech, assembly, education and information, and going on, in the minds of an ever-increasing number of citizens, to the notion of various forms of free lunch. There is nothing much wrong with that, perhaps, as long as it is recognised that these rights are in the nature of man-made social contracts, drawing what validity they possess from the will of the group, organised or otherwise, who propounded them, and that they do not subsist in and of themselves.

It is helpful, I think, to trace back all this talk of human rights to its origins. This leads us back, at least as far as the modern world is concerned, to the heady days of the French Revolution, in the years immediately before and after 1789, when the basic rights of life, liberty and the pursuit of happiness were launched upon the world. These were taken up by the framers of the American Constitution (mediated by such influential works as Thomas Paine's *The Rights of Man*), and quickly became a cornerstone of modern progressive thought – in which connection one should not omit to mention Theobald Wolfe Tone and the United Irishmen.

However, even at the outset of the campaign for human rights in the 1780s, a systematic ambiguity was introduced by proponents of the concept, and this has persisted. The French, as we know, are a nation prone to rhetorical flourishes, and they indulged in language which suggested that these rights subsisted in the nature of things, and that all that any assembly of people was doing when it propounded a set of rights was to give expression to them. Even Tom Paine, when he declared, in 1791, that 'the end of all political associations is the preservation of the natural and imprescriptible rights of Man; and these rights are liberty, property, security and resistance of oppression' (*The Rights of Man*, Part 1, p.110), is inclined to elevate these rights onto the transcendental plane. He is claiming to contemplate the genus Man, and derive from it, with logical rigour, a series of attributes inherent in it; but in fact he is indulging in what philosophers, nowadays, would call a 'persuasive definition', seeking to attach a new meaning to a given concept by purporting to define it.

Similarly, the 'pro-life' lobby (an offensively self-righteous term, which I therefore consign to inverted commas) appears to assume that the unconditional right to life of an embryo is a fact independent of any human decision to grant it, and prior to, and independent of, the dogmas of any religion or sect. If they were prepared to admit that they are simply seeking to enshrine the current doctrine of the Catholic Church in the Irish Constitution, their position, though more objectionable, would at least be coherent. But since the Irish Constitution is ostensibly a non-sectarian document, that would not look very good. So, they are driven to assert that this right to life transcends all religious dogma, and somehow inheres in Nature.

But this, I submit, is nonsense, and dangerous nonsense. Neither the born nor the unborn can have any rights whatever which some body of citizens, formally gathered together, have not resolved to give them, and no such rights have as yet been explicitly granted by the Irish nation to embryos, any more than to future generations as yet unconceived. If the Irish nation resolves to grant this new right to Irish embryos, then it will become a right which Irish embryos will have; but let us not imagine that this right inheres in them, and that it is only for us to recognise it.

For this reason, if there must be a Referendum, the new wording proposed by the Government is very much less offensive than the old, since it allows the present generation of Irish citizens to do all that it has any right to do, which is to lay down laws and principles of conduct for its own contemporaries, while preventing it from imposing absolute rules on future generations, who must be allowed to decide these things for themselves.

Bruton's thoughts: who listens to an original thinker?

October 12, 1983

Mr John Bruton is in grave danger of becoming one of our most innovative and far-sighted statesmen, without anybody, it seems, paying much attention. Indeed it is a grim index of the generally negative tone of Irish political commentary that much more attention is given to his supposed political ambitions or setbacks (Why is he not still Minister for Finance? Is he a possible successor for Garret?) than to the continual stream of ideas which he puts out for the solution of our major problems.

John Bruton is only 36, and not even yet, presumably, at the height of his powers. Already, however, he has shown, for someone with a comfortable farming and legal background, a remarkable grasp of the essentials of finance and industrial policy. He demonstrates here much greater powers of 'lateral thinking' (such as is now so desperately needed) than certain of his distinguished senior colleagues – perhaps precisely because they are trained economists and he is not. A concern for *Dáil* reform has been one of his interests, revealing a characteristic impatience with the waste of talent and energy represented by ill-prepared and ill-attended non-debates on the floor of the House, and his establishment of the new committee system is a significant step in the right direction. In his main area of interest, though, industrial and social policy, he has yet to make a comparable impact.

Bruton has been putting out original ideas for some years now, but this article is provoked by his recent contribution, in a speech delivered in Co. Wicklow on September 8. For some time Bruton has been fascinated, and rightly so, by the phenomenon of Japan. (Indeed, I would not be surprised to learn that he had something to do with the President's recent tour of that country, in order to focus our attention upon it better.) He has pointed repeatedly to the superior ways the

Japanese organise their industry and commerce, and on this occasion he returned to the theme, with special reference to our unemployment problem. In Japan, it would seem, it is customary for the top third of a worker's wages to be related to the profits of the firm, in such a way that, if the profits fall, their wages fall proportionally – down, presumably to the extreme case of a seriously loss-making enterprise, where the workforce (and, I trust, the management as well), would only be receiving two-thirds of their 'normal' salary. On the other hand, none (or very few) are laid off.

It is this that is the great virtue of such a scheme for a country in our present state. Unless we are prepared to consider some such scheme, Bruton says, we are plainly headed for a situation where we have a substantial majority of the work-force unemployed, while a minority of active workers, on uneconomically high salaries, constitute a sort of 'aristocracy of labour', unwilling to let any of their less fortunate brethren in on the action, and increasingly coming to begrudge the high taxes they will have to pay to keep the non-working majority at some sort of subsistence level.

'Is this the way we want to live?' asks Bruton. 'What sort of society do we imagine will result from this?' Of course, John Carroll and friends in the ICTU will simply sidestep such an awkward question and take refuge in various forms of well-worn claptrap. What this claptrap sidesteps are the unpalatable facts that a) there is not a great deal more work than at present available for anyone to do, and, b) there is very little wealth lying about in a form that is readily distributable. The great problem that advanced industrial countries face even at the best of times is that the actual amount of work requiring to be done by individuals gets progressively less as efficiency and automation take hold. And yet, as the Japanese have shown, even in such circumstances, one can keep a much larger proportion of people working than we are doing.

John Bruton is putting a challenge starkly to this society: either be prepared by one method or another to share out the work available more equitably, or, be prepared for the progressive disintegration of society. The sad thing is, as I say, that no one appears to be paying much attention, even to the extent of bothering to denounce his ideas. To the square-headed men who dominate our public life, Bruton's ideas must not seem to be practical politics at all.

Let's hope Beckman has got it wrong
March 4, 1984

The volume of optimistic noises about the world economy is growing almost daily. Recovery is in the air. The U.S. is booming again. So is Japan. The European economies are beginning, it seems, to pick themselves off the floor. Even Ireland is to expect some growth in 1984. It seems obstinately perverse, then, amidst such bullishness, to assert that we have in fact hardly yet entered the real depression which awaits us, and that the present upswing is simply the last small hillock, obscuring the ultimate precipitous descent.

Such, however, is the thesis of a most stimulating and disquieting book published recently by the economist and investment analyst Robert Beckman, an American who has lived in London since 1963. He came over to Dublin some months ago and gave a seminar to a group of businessmen, setting out his theories, but caused only a minor ripple in the news media at the time, though he greatly impressed those who heard him. His thesis is based on the following considerations. Back in the 1930s, the great Russian economist Kondratiev identified a long-term (approximately 54-year) business cycle, which seemed to him to have been operating in Western society ever since accurate records were obtainable, and certainly since the early eighteenth century. There was, for instance, an economic collapse in the 1720s, preceded by a protracted period of boom from 1700 or so – the period of the 'Mississippi Bubble'.

Then another upswing. followed by a depression in the 1780s. Then an upswing from 1790 or so, all through the Napoleonic Wars, followed by collapse from 1815 on into the 1820s. Then an upswing from 1840 to 1870 or so (the Great Famine in Ireland was a purely local phenomenon!), fuelled mainly by the growth of railways, followed by a collapse at the end of the 1870s, which was reflected here in widespread rural unrest arising from falling agricultural prices, and caused the growth of the Land League. Another upswing occurred in the 1890s and continued through the First World War to the end of 1920s. And we all know what happened after that. Any of us who are under 50 have only lived through the latest upswing, which began in the Second World War, and carried through the fifties and sixties, fuelled by cheap energy from oil, and the growth of computers and automation, until the oil crisis of 1973. And now here we are in the 1980s.

What we have undoubtedly seen, over the last 250 years, is a series of approximately 50-year waves of prosperity, leading to overproduction and speculative frenzy, followed by a slump lasting about ten years, which in turn leads to another up-wave. Kondratiev's theory does not invalidate the shorter business cycles, of 40 months and 8–10 years, associated with the names of Kitchin and Juglar (a Kondratiev cycle coincides, in fact, with every sixth Juglar cycle), but it does impose a larger pattern upon them.

It is noticeable, also, that shortly before the big collapse there normally occurs a minor crisis, coinciding with the fifth in a series of Juglar cycles. There was one such in 1864–6; another in 1920–2; and, most recently, there was one in 1974–6. In each case the economy struggled back to a degree of prosperity, only to sink more drastically 8–10 years later.

So then, if Beckman is right (and his historical accuracy, at least, seems unassailable), where does that leave us? Either we must argue that we have, through our superior economic wisdom, broken out of this historical cycle, or we are plainly now on the brink of the precipice. Some would take consolation from the fact that the stock exchanges of the world have been made proof against the sort of collapse that occurred in 1929 by the enforcement of much stricter regulations, but the stock exchange is only one part of the picture. As Beckman points out, the recklessness that characterised the stock exchanges in the 1920s is now a feature of the world banking system.

What has happened, especially since 1973, when Arab money flooded back into the European and American banks, is that these banks have recklessly lent enormous sums to such countries as Mexico, Brazil, Argentina, Nigeria, Poland and Romania (not to mention such tadpoles as Ireland), and now these countries are in effect on the verge of defaulting, or actually defaulting. Only fear of the psychological consequences has dictated that Brazil, for example, be not held in default, but only 'rescheduled'. If the price of oil were to fall much further, the Arabs would come looking for their money, to shore up their economies, and their money would not be there. And then things would become very interesting indeed. The other area where irresponsibility has been shown is in property speculation. In this country we are seeing the results of the gross inflation of the price of agricultural land, and we have seen already the demise of the Gallagher empire. Certain other 'empires' are being only held together by banks who do not dare to call in their debts.

But let us not despair. Depression is not all bad. Beckman has amusing passages on the way that fashions change, society becomes more orderly and conservative, and community spirit grows during a depression. Two things there will be much less of are strikes and inflation. Above all, if Beckman is right, there is no point in blaming either ourselves or the unions or the government. The whole process is inevitable, and must simply be lived with. It is a sort of cleansing process which human society must periodically go through.

A moving sign of the times
September 22, 1985

1879 was a very bad year. The summer was the wettest and coldest on record. During the six months from March to September, cold rain fell on 125 days out of 183, that is, on about two days out of every three. The potato crop, ravaged by blight, was down to a third of normal, and turnips and other green crops to about a half; the turf harvest also was reduced by over half. On top of that, there had been an economic depression for a number of years.

Sound familiar? Well, read on. Mayo was perhaps the worst hit area in the country. On August 21, in the small village of. Knock, the Virgin Mary appeared to a number of people, perched on the gable of the local church, and started a stream of pilgrims which has not ceased up to the present. Now, 106 years later, Our Lady of Knock has been joined, it would seem, by Our Lady of Ballinspittle. The statue of the Virgin 'moved' in Ballinspittle on July 22, and to date many other manifestations have been reported around the country, all attracting crowds of pilgrims. Effete urban intellectuals like myself have been much exercised of late, first in ridiculing these events and then in trying to explain them sociologically. This article is intended as a contribution to the latter activity. My own contact with the phenomena has been minimal, but typical of an increasing number of people.

I have had occasion to drive past the grotto at Ballinspittle twice in the last two weeks, both times during the day. Cars lined the narrow road for a considerable distance in both directions. Crowds of worshippers knelt in prayer before the grotto, while a rather tinny loudspeaker blared out a hymn to the Virgin. The Virgin herself was unmoved.

On the other hand, a lady of my acquaintance who lives not far away, and is French and an agnostic to boot, is in some embarrassment. Out of curiosity she paid a visit to the grotto one evening not long ago, and to her great alarm and annoyance, the statue moved. It distinctly nodded at her. She feels herself to be mildly disgraced by this, but to me she is a privileged being, like one who has seen a ghost, or a flying saucer. If there is something remarkable going on here, she is now part of it.

And there is something remarkable going on, I think. What we are seeing is neither conscious fraud nor yet a visitation of the supernatural. What we are seeing is simply a lot of ordinary minds near the end of their tether. I don't wish to sound too dramatic. I certainly do not wish to imply that large numbers of people are going mad. But I would maintain that the phenomena that we are witnessing can be placed in a certain context which may throw light on them.

To go back a bit further than 1879, perhaps the most terrible disaster to strike Europe until modern times was the Black Death, which raged throughout the middle of the 14th century. One bizarre result of the despair and confusion caused by this was a dancing madness that broke out in Germany in 1374. In that year, to compound everyone's misery, there were heavy spring floods of the Rhine. Large numbers of people were caught up in this enthusiasm. They were convinced that they were possessed by demons. Forming circles in streets and churches, they danced for hours with leaps and screams, calling on demons by name to cease tormenting them, or crying that they saw visions of Christ or the Virgin or the heavens opening. The madness spread to Holland and Flanders, the dancers going about from town to town in groups and proclaiming that the end of the world was at hand.

But is it fair to compare the dancing madness to the present phenomena in Ireland? Not entirely unfair, I think. If up to 12,000 people go out into the open countryside of Co. Sligo and see lights in the sky, which form themselves into the Virgin, Christ and Padre Pio, it does not much matter whether they are wildly dancing or peacefully saying the Rosary. In either case people are in an abnormal state of mind, and for similar reasons.

Of course, I may not be right, but if I am, the rulers of this country had better watch out. 1879 saw the apparition at Knock, but it also saw the birth of a powerful and well-organised agrarian agitation, the National Land League, brainchild of Michael Davitt, but arising out of the crisis conditions which then obtained. The present manifestations indicate to me that, what with the weather and unremitting economic miseries, the national psyche has had just about enough, and the remaining months of the year may see more on the move than statues.

A misguided heroism
April 22, 1984

It is rather curious, and slightly uncomfortable, to be in the position of owing full allegiance to one's native land, and yet not being able to summon up much enthusiasm for the National Myth. This is, I think, by no means a unique situation. Many nations around the world and most post-colonial ones, have gone through multi-stage upheavals which have left a certain proportion of the population 'on the wrong side'. In our case, however, despite revolution and civil war, the victors, on the whole, both in 1922 and 1932 (despite many ominous rumblings and some regrettable incidents) were tolerant and fair-minded enough to allow a diversity of views to flourish. In more modern times, or in less good-natured countries, my family would either have been shot, or at least have been driven into exile, where we would still remain. This is, I think, important to bear in mind.

That said, I will turn to my personal view of the significance of the Easter Rising. I was brought up to believe that the Easter Rising was an unmitigated disaster, which had brought to ruin a constitutional settlement that had taken forty years of hard struggle to arrive at (and which was already on the statute books, as the Home Rule Act of 1914), without bringing any obvious benefits in its place, and I find no compelling reason now to reject that point of view. It did not, after all, unite the country, nor did it Gaelicize it (if that can be accounted a benefit), nor did it even truly free it from Britain. The claim of the Sinn Fein tradition that the 1914 Home Rule Act was of so restricted a nature as not to be worth having is a desperate piece of bluster, no longer supported, I think, by any reputable historian.

It did, certainly, confer an independence which was limited in important ways, but there can be no serious dispute that it qualified for Michael Collins' description of the later Treaty as 'freedom to achieve freedom'. It also had a substantially better chance than any Sinn Fein settlement (which is admittedly, not saying much) of bringing unity to the country. People like Redmond and Dillon, Carson and Craig, did not much like each other, but they had sufficient respect for each other's integrity and experience of affairs to have made possible subsequent contacts. How much such contacts would have led to would have depended, then as now, largely on the attitude of the British Government, and from that quarter not much can ever be expected.

But is there really any point in going over this old ground once again? As we await the report of the New Ireland Forum, I think that there is. What we are being asked to do, as a nation, by Garret Fitzgerald, in the various initiatives that he has taken, is to look at ourselves closely and at our national myths and consider where they have got us. I suggest that we are living a lie which virtually nobody believes any more (except perhaps the faithful at a Fianna Fail Árd-Fheis – and presumably those who provide safe houses for the likes of Dominic McGlinchy). We are not a Gaelic nation; we are a profoundly and blessedly mixed one, and we should celebrate that. We are not a Catholic nation; a mostly Catholic 26-county state, certainly, but that is not Ireland as I imagine it. We are not a neutral nation; our much-vaunted neutrality is humbug, born of a (not unreasonable) technicality introduced by Mr de Valera, and fostered since by the convenience of getting a free ride in matters of defence. Furthermore, it is not clear to me that we have any deeper reason for being outside the Commonwealth (fatuous as that organisation may be) than would India, Nigeria, Canada or Australia – nations which we helped to build and rule. Little thought was given, when we left that organisation in 1949, to the degree to which we were betraying the myriads of Irishmen in the latter two nations, and in Britain itself.

To return to the Easter Rising, I think it is possible to salute the heroism, and admire the characters, of the 1916 leaders, while still regarding their action as a grave error. My grandfather indeed, found himself in that curious position in May, 1916, as the executions went ahead. In the course of an impassioned speech in Parliament on May 11, he said:

"I am proud of these men. They were foolish, they were misled . . . (uproar). I say I am proud of their courage, and if you were not so dense and stupid, as some of you English people are, you could have had these men fighting for you, and they are men

worth having . . . It is not murderers who are being executed,
it is insurgents who have fought a clean fight, a brave fight,
however misguided."

His outburst shocked even many of his own colleagues, but it did provoke Asquith to go over to Ireland that evening and put a stop to further executions. That was remembered, it seems, by many of those who were under arrest at the time. I remember asking my Uncle James (who has never made any secret of his views on the Rising and its consequences, but who nevertheless rose to the leadership of one of the two Sinn Fein parties) how he got on with stalwarts of that tradition, such as Richard Mulcahy or Seán MacEoin, not to mention Cosgrave himself. He maintained that they got on very well, but one factor that helped was that that speech of his father's was remembered.

But I do not wish to drag my uncle into a discussion that he would wish no part of. For me, this is an historical question. I did not live through any of the relevant events, and I am not concerned with the Civil War attitudes that they spawned, except to regret the distortions they have introduced into our political life. However, I do not feel that we should turn our attention away from 1916. Rather, we should study it more closely, and more objectively. We should also dust off the 1914 Act, and study that. We still have a serious identity problem, and such studies might help to resolve it.

Inertia and arrogance to blame

October 12, 1986

About three and a half years ago (April 1, 1983), I wrote an article in the *Irish Independent* highlighting certain gross failings of the Irish court system. I dealt with the up to nine year backlog in the processing of High Court injury claims and the unnecessary delays and expense arising out of our preserving trial by jury in injury cases (unlike any other country in the EEC). This is in addition to the notorious racket of having a Senior Counsel as well as Juniors in attendance on these cases, and calling in superfluous 'experts' at immense cost (e.g. a Harley Street specialist where the local G.P. would do) to authenticate technical details.

I pointed out how long *legal* holidays were greatly contributing to the backlog and how the extraordinarily primitive conditions under which judges are expected to do their work (in respect of, say, word processing facilities or aides to do back-up research) leads in turn to sometimes immense delays in giving verdicts.

Liam Collins' excellent article of September 15 leads me to take another look at this theme, and see whether any changes (for better or worse) have emerged in the interval. In doing this, I have no desire to divert public indignation from the misdeeds of solicitors, which I hope will continue to receive effective coverage. I do it simply to remind us all that every aspect of the system – solicitors, barristers, courts and prisons – needs urgent attention.

Let us take these problems one by one. First of all, what of the backlog in processing injury claims? The 'up to nine year' backlog was a trifle tendentious even then; 3–5 years was always a more realistic figure. But even this is really a grave scandal, if one considers the human problems involved in such delays – victims fall into debt, witnesses die or disappear, the world forgets.

However, there is good news to report on this front. Not only have two more High Court judges been appointed, and a determined effort made to reduce the backlog (the delay is claimed by a lawyer of my acquaintance to be down to nine months, which is actually about right), but just now – coming into operation on October 1 – there has been enacted a new set of High Court rules (the product of a commission sitting for the last few years under Mr Justice Liam Hamilton), which will considerably streamline and rationalise the process of bringing a case to court. The details are too arcane to be expounded here (pleadings, laying of informations, motions and so forth), but the result will be a significant speeding up of the legal process. This is the first updating of the rules since 1961, and it is greatly to be welcomed. Whatever about the reducing of the backlog, however, the very expensive custom of having both senior and junior counsel in attendance in accident cases is still unaltered, as Liam Collins has described, and juries, although on the way out, are not gone yet, and still making awards as if money were water. It is certainly desirable that accident victims, especially those requiring long-term care, should be adequately provided for, but what we are faced with here is a great deal of unnecessary legal expense, and gross anomalies, if not positive injustice, arising out of the wide variation in awards.

The present problem, however, is that we are rapidly becoming a society where insurance is unavailable at any reasonable rate, and thus an uninsured society, with all the misery which that entails. Of course, juries are not entirely to blame for that (crime, vandalism and drunkenness must take their share of credit as well), but they certainly have not helped.

As to the third main complaint I recorded in April, 1983, the primitive conditions under which judges have to operate in the Four Courts, nothing, I fear, has changed. A judge still has to write up his judgement, and get it typed, with very inadequate secretarial or research facilities. There are computer programmes in existence which would make the checking out of relevant cases a matter of moments, but they are not available to our judges. They do not even have the benefit of word-processors. If they make a mistake in their text, the whole passage has to be typed again, and there are never enough secretaries available. The bright young aides available in other jurisdictions, especially the American, to do back-up research, such as the assembly of precedents, are unknown here. It is little wonder that many judgements are monstrously delayed – though the foibles of certain justices, such as dropping all work for the duration of Wimbledon, are a significant factor also. A little investment here, both in hardware and personnel, would improve things greatly.

A final word. I would not wish to seem to advocate rapidity in the judicial process as an end in itself. No doubt the process of trial and condemnation is remarkably swift in such places as Iran or Uganda (though I don't know how they are on running-down claims), but one would not want to change our system, with all its faults, for theirs. Due process of law takes time, quite properly. However, a good deal of unnecessary delay does result from the inertia and arrogance of a profession which has secured itself virtual immunity from accountability to the public, and that is something which needs to be challenged. I am glad to be able to report some improvements in the last three years, but it is still not much to cheer about.

The Danish analogy revisited:
or, do we need a national strike?
July 14, 1987

Sometimes, just occasionally, one experiences the exhilarating sensation that one is seeing the future, and that it works. The only catch is that, in the case I have in mind, much blood, sweat and tears must flow before any happy outcome can be hoped for. And yet the vision is there. I refer to what we may term the Danish Analogy.

Back in September 1982, a four-party coalition, led by the Conservative Party's Poul Schluter, came to power in Denmark as a minority government, and introduced a package of austerity measures even more severe than those contemplated by the Social Democratic government they had just defeated. The new government faced a foreign debt of DKr. 54 billion, due to rise to 79 billion by 1984, involving a gross borrowing requirement of 132 billion (approx. 10 kroner to the Irish £4, which puts them more or less in line with ourselves).

They faced this in the 1983 budget by taking the following drastic steps: abolishing index-linking of wages and unemployment benefits, imposing a six-month wage freeze, limiting public sector pay increases to 4%, cutting social welfare spending, and introducing national health prescription charges. In spite of all this, they survived till December 1983, being defeated only on some foreign policy and defence issues, which were not of a vital nature. However, the projected budget for 1984 was too much for one of the Coalition partners, and on December 10, it was rejected by Parliament, leading to a general election in January 1984. This was won, in fact, on an 88.4% turnout, by Schluter's Coalition, with the narrowest of majorities (one seat, gained after a recount). A further package of austerity measures was presented in the 1984 Budget - DKr. 1,500 million in public sector spending cuts (with 4 billion promised for 1985), and increases in taxes on beer and cigarettes. Once again, the Danish people took it on the chin, though there were demonstrations outside Parliament during the vote.

Things were starting to come right. Inflation came down to 6%, the current account deficit was halved, the krone was stabilised, interest rates came down from 22% to 13%, exports recovered – but unemployment increased slightly, from 10% to 10.7% The 1985 budget presented more cuts still, and stern wage restraint. At last, the public lost patience. On March 24, a general strike began, led by the private sector, over a collective wage agreement that the Government was pressing for. The Government let the strike proceed for a week, while the country ground to a halt, causing itself immense misery, and then, on March 30, Parliament passed a series of emergency degrees ordering a return to work. The unions had had enough. Everyone went back to work, accepting a 2% and 1½% wage rise respectively over the next two years. The rest, as they say, is history. What we now see is a minor Danish economic miracle: low inflation, flourishing exports, steady reduction of debt, rising real growth. The former comprehensive welfare state has taken some severe knocks, but people have got over that. They have got used now to paying at least something for what they receive, and being glad to have a job, since the alternative is not as comfortable as it used to be. In short, a reasonably healthy, vibrant society has arisen.

The question is, is there anything that we can learn from all this, or is it just an edifying fairy-story about a far-off land? Obviously I think there is a great deal to be learned, or I would not have wasted your time telling it to you. Of course it will be said, correctly, that we cannot compare ourselves too closely to Denmark. For one thing, it is a far more developed country than Ireland. In 1983, for instance, its GNP per head was US $11,490, one of the highest levels among industrialised countries. Their agriculture is immensely more developed than ours, and they have a much sounder industrial base. But on the other hand, their population is about the same (a little over 5 million), and they have no indigenous resources of coal or metals, any more than we have (though they are now drawing on considerable finds of gas, and some of oil, from the North Sea).

But it will be said, they are Danes (Nordic, sober, purposeful, hardworking and thrifty), whereas we are Irish (Celtic, inebriated, feckless, lazy and improvident). I am unwilling to be content with these racial stereotypes. If there is an element of truth in this contrast, it is not that we are simply born that way; it is that somebody or something has not kicked our asses hard enough for us to snap out of it. The fact is that, despite high taxation, direct and indirect, and the high cost of almost everything, if one still has a job in this country, life is not so bad that one has any sense of crisis, whereas if one has lost one's job, one sinks, first into the euphoria of short-term social welfare benefits, and then into dumb despair (and so no longer counts, politically). This government, it must be said (with the support of a responsible opposition, a benefit the late Coalition did not have!), is tackling certain aspects of our problem, but it is still only skirting round the main issue, and the result is that its measures are producing only minimal results, with maximum uproar.

What is needed is the administering of a severe and salutary shock to a group of central significance in society, that group to which I belong myself, the public-sector wage-earner. What further shock, one might ask, do we need? Are we not punch-drunk already? Strangely enough, I think that, despite the relative privations of the last five years, those of us with secure, pensionable employment have really not taken on board the full enormity of the situation. Only when one actually loses the job does that dawn on one with proper force, and then it is too late. For those still with jobs, I would make the following modest proposal: instead of a 3% increase, or even a pay-freeze, let all public service pay be cut 10%.

I am not oblivious to the reaction there would be to such a proposal. Indeed, it would probably provoke a general strike in the public sector, which would bring the country to a halt. However, on the Danish analogy, that may just be what this country needs, and I would accordingly welcome it warmly. So should the Government. Their position is curiously strong, as was Poul Schluter's in 1985. They have really nothing to lose by further austerities, and much to lose by half-measures which will leave them in the same wretched position as the previous coalition. And they have, as I say, a 'loyal' opposition, morally unable to oppose such measures, except verbally.

The benefits of such a drastic cut would, I suggest, be considerable (I am not so mad as simply to wish to renounce 10% of my salary for nothing). First of all, it should produce a considerable decrease in public spending (though also some loss of tax revenue). This in turn should make it possible to contemplate next year some reduction in tax levels, thus stimulating business and relieving the P.A.Y.E. worker. It should also help to minimise the cuts in employment which will otherwise be necessary, thus saving people from being thrown onto the social welfare rolls, with further loss to the exchequer. But above all, after the inevitable knee-jerk reaction of marches, speechifying, and strikes, it would bring it home to a large section of the community that there really is a war on, a war with an insidious enemy, difficult to put a face on or attack in any old-fashioned way, but one which is effectively threatening the whole Western way of life. This enemy is the tendency to live beyond our means, to consume more than we produce, that has led to the world-wide problem of Debt.

It is now a more immediate menace than even over-population or the Bomb, frightful as those are. The defeat of this enemy will entail radical changes in individual life-styles and in the structure of society. In particular, the concept of job-sharing, for so long a term casually bandied about, will have to become the norm - or rather, we must see the progressive abolition of the concept of the nine-to-five job, to be replaced by something like rotating shares in the amount of 'work' available, with a corresponding increase in 'leisure' activities, and rather more modest rewards for all. Defeat of the enemy will thus produce a more balanced, rational society; to lose this war will lead to its swift breakdown.

But this is all becoming rather utopian. All I set out to do was to revive the Danish Analogy, very effectively presented by the *Today Tonight* team on RTE just before the last election, but effectively forgotten since then. There is a model for us to follow. It is not impossibly difficult to emulate. Has this government the will to march us in that direction? On past evidence, probably not. I am used to the eyes of my political friends glazing over when I suggest actual wage cuts. Such talk is simply beyond the range of practical discourse. And yet I wonder why. After all, a 3% wage increase at the moment is in fact a 7% cut at least (such an increment, as a witty friend of mine remarked recently, is really an excrement), and it aggravates the basic problem, whereas a straightforward cut would at least start to alleviate it, while actually producing psychological advantages as well – outrage, and then mental alertness – instead of the dim, grumbling dissatisfaction created by spurious raises such as we have been receiving. It is a pity, therefore, that this proposal will not be acted on. Soon it will be too late.

Taking the gun out of Gaelic games
July 16, 1987

The pulling of a gun by a Garda in plainclothes on a group of unruly hurling fans in Thurles last Sunday is only the latest in a series of such incidents over the last year or so. The firing of a gun by a Garda detective at the Lynagh funeral in Emyvale, Co. Monaghan back in May is one case that comes to mind; another is the semi-comic sequel to the freeing of Miss Evelyn Glenholmes in March, 1986, where a submachine-gun was fired into the air. The last two incidents, however, at least had some connection with dangerous subversives, even if they were not being subversive, but only unruly, at the time. This time, however, we have a gun being pulled on basic yobbos, as they are going about their normal business of wrecking property. What is the world coming to? One young gentleman, a Mr – , almost died of shock, and is contemplating suing the Gardaí, for the mental distress caused to him.

Almost everybody in authority, particularly the GAA, and most conspicuously Fr Pierce Duggan, the chairman of the Semple Stadium Committee, has come strongly to the support of the Garda in question, declaring firmly that 'in the circumstances, it was the only action that could be taken'. No one in the GAA hierarchy, it seems, found this pulling of a gun a worrying development. Perhaps it is a sign of the times, but the last occasion I can recall guns being pulled on a crowd at a Gaelic game was in Croke Park in November, 1920 by the Black and Tans, on the original 'Bloody Sunday'.

Then the guns were actually fired, as we know, with considerable effect. I heard Fr Duggan being asked by David Hanly on *Morning Ireland* last Monday what he thought would have happened if the crowd had not been quelled by the Garda's gesture in pulling his gun. Would he have advocated him firing it? Fr Duggan effectively side-stepped this by reiterating that the action was effective in stopping the riot, but the question still remains: what would the Garda do next? Fire into the air? And if that did not impress anyone, fire at someone's legs? And then what?

We can see, surely, that dangerous waters are being entered here. One cannot get into the habit of drawing one's gun in troublesome situations, unless one is prepared to use it. Hooligans get smart after a while. It is like threatening to put one's children out of the car and leave them on the side of the road this instant unless they stop fighting in the back. Sooner or later you have to deliver on such a threat, or your bluff is called. And then where are we?

Let me make myself clear at this point. I am not disputing the now-established convention that special groups of Gardaí, or individual Gardaí, should carry guns in special situations, and use them if necessary. Unfortunately, the existence of both ruthless political extremists and equally ruthless organised criminals have rendered the noble ideal of an unarmed police force, instituted here by Kevin O'Higgins, inapplicable to all situations. But at least we do not yet have the American or continental situation of large revolvers bouncing on the ample hips of any policeman you happen to meet, and submachine guns casually dandled on the knees of guards at any bank, government building or police station – none of which actually prevents the countries in question from being far more violent places than Ireland, with all its faults.

It is disquieting, therefore, that Fr Duggan and the GAA hierarchy should see nothing strange or untoward in this event. I have no doubt that the sight of a large mob of Cork hooligans trying to knock down a gate is thoroughly alarming, but the acceptable solution to this is a larger force of unarmed Gardaí or stewards, rather than a small number of armed ones. One cannot really blame the individual Garda for doing what he did; he just should not have been put in that position.

The issue is a large one. Once policemen start waving guns about, whether they intend to use them or not, the process of alienation of the community from the police has gone pretty far along, and may be irreversible. I know it is hard, especially in certain areas of our capital city, and in certain fraught situations, to maintain time-honoured standards, but the ideal of the unarmed policeman, interacting with the community, and acting on its behalf, rather than against it, is something worth preserving, and there are precious few countries around the world where this situation still obtains.

Let us not let it slip through our fingers on the assumption that there are easy shortcuts to crowd control, such as spraying them with tear gas or machine gun bullets. Recent events in South Korea, for instance, should remind us that one does not achieve peace and quiet that way, except in the very short run. You can quell a bunch of yobbos once, perhaps, by waving a gun at them, but next time they will be back, and this time a few of them will be toting guns, and then things will really get interesting. It is far better, surely, to confine the firearms to situations where the other side is known to be armed and dangerous, and to deal with ordinary citizens, however rambunctious, by employing more old-fashioned methods of crowd control. It will pay off in the end, even at the cost of the occasional broken turnstile.

Sunday Independent: Articles

"Oblivious to any danger":
Chronicle of a week in Moscow
August 25, 1991

It seems a long time ago now, but last December I had the opportunity to spend a week in Moscow, where I had been invited by the Institute of Philosophy of the Soviet Academy of Sciences to take part in a small symposium. It was my first time to Russia, and it was an exciting time to be there, so my antennae were out for new and stimulating experiences of every sort, and I was not disappointed. I began an article on my adventure when I got back, but dropped it – partly, at least, because even then there were rumours of coups in the air, and I was anxious not to cause trouble for my friends (who could inevitably be identified) if the old ways were suddenly reintroduced. They seemed blithely oblivious of any danger, but I was not so sure. The events of the last week, however, have reactivated me. First, on Monday, it seemed as if I had been privileged to witness life in the Soviet Union during a brief, anomalous flowering of freedom which would soon be only a dim memory, but then, on Wednesday evening, the clouds broke up, and I realised that I had, after all, had a view of the new Russia at a formative stage in its development. I would like to dedicate this brief memoir to my genial hosts of last December, to wish them every future happiness. There will be hard times ahead, but it will be worth it.

I looked round my room in the Higher School of the Communist Party with a mildly sinking feeling. It was late on Saturday night, December 8, and I had had a hard day. I had been lodged here by my hosts, rather than in one of the accepted tourist hotels, on my arrival from Shannon, and I wondered how I would survive a week. The exterior of the Higher School, as we drove up to it through the dismal, potholed streets, was forbidding in the extreme – a series of vast blocks surrounding a central square – but appearances were deceptive: the room I was shown to was bright, clean and warm, and, contrary to the warnings I had received from 'experienced' friends, everything seemed to work.

My host, Yuri Schichalin, had met me at Sheremetyevo airport some hours before, where there was actually very little formality about getting through either passport control or customs. He was accompanied by his wife, Yelena. It turned out, happily, that he owned a car, albeit a rather battered Moskvich, which tended to cut out at every traffic light. But we made it into town along an impressive freeway, which then became Leningrad Avenue as we entered the city.

Only when one gets to Russia, and tries to live, does one realise something of the enormity of the problems that the system faces, if it is ever to become a 'market economy'. Western politicians and 'experts' talk of this transition far too glibly and tend to make unreasonable demands.

The problem, it seems to me, is this. A system has been created where the proper price is not paid for anything. Either it is accounted a necessity of life, and is absurdly cheap, or it is treated as a decadent and possibly subversive luxury, and it is monstrously expensive, or simply unobtainable. For instance, I was given by my hosts, with apologies, a sum of 69 roubles for expenses during the week. The official exchange rate had been reduced from parity with the pound sterling, which was quite absurd, to, I think, ten roubles to the Punt, which was still way below the unofficial rate. At that rate, I was being given about £7.

But I was quite unable to spend this money (forewarned, I had brought a roll of single dollar bills, and some cartons of Marlboro cigarettes, for 'emergencies', but I ultimately gave away the cigarettes, and came home with nearly all the dollars). Our breakfast, of black bread, tea, porridge, or cottage cheese with sugar, cost about 20 kopecks. Lunch (when I was allowed to pay for it) was just over a rouble for three courses – hors d'oeuvres, cabbage soup, and meatballs with pasta. One could, in fact, have three square meals a day, of admittedly undistinguished quality, though generous quantity, for about 50p.

Food, such as bread, vegetables, fruit and meat, is available, when it is available, for virtually nothing. Clothing I did not explore, but what I saw in shop windows was absurdly cheap. Likewise books and records – I bought four fine classical records for 9 roubles, less than a pound, in the big Melodya store on Kalinin Street, and a new collection of Gumilev's poems in a bookshop nearby for two roubles. The monthly rent of a comfortable, three-room apartment in a good area of town, such as my hosts possessed, is 25 roubles a month. Health services, of course, are free. Education is free.

So what is the problem? The problem simply is that one's salary is also absurdly low. A good salary for a skilled worker, or professional, such as a teacher, an architect or an engineer, is between 200 and 250 roubles a month – at current rates of exchange, about £20. The necessities of life are thus not ridiculously cheap; they are about right.

The root of the present crisis is that goods and services are no longer being provided at the prices which were in the past paid to factories and collective farms. Only the iron hand of compulsion could cause this idealistic but economically crazy system to function. With that iron hand removed, it has simply fallen apart. No one is afraid any more, and everyone is out for themselves. Factories will not fulfill orders, but indulge in barter between themselves, and with collective farms; collective farms will not deliver the produce, but sell it themselves on the black market (largely run by an indigenous Mafia).

And yet what is to be done? Any attempt to disrupt the equilibrium between these totally unrealistic prices and these derisory salaries in the direction of introducing a 'market economy' must be attended by extreme hardship and discontent. At a conservative estimate, one would need to increase prices (to the producer and to the consumer) ten times to get them anywhere near a real 'market' value, and then, inevitably, increase salaries by a like figure to match them. The inflationary pressures unleashed by such a move would be explosive, but I see no alternative.

I came away from Moscow, after a week, punch-drunk with new impressions, but with an overall feeling that something wonderful, though at the same time extremely stressful, was happening to a great nation, a warmhearted and immensely civilised people, who profoundly deserve a break. After the events of this past week, and the triumph of Boris Yeltsin, I have renewed hope that they will get that break.

Scandal and the national psyche
October 6, 1991

The nation is in a remarkable mood. To judge, at least, from the news media and from everyone one talks to, we are in a state of high moral indignation, and we are enjoying every minute of it. The notion that all the richest men in the country have combined with each other and with the political leadership of the state, in all the positions of the Kama Sutra, to rip off the taxpayer, and become just a little richer – and have now been caught in the act – fills us all with unseemly glee, however po-faced we may appear in public.

A good deal of our indignation stems, I think, from the fact that we could never be in a position to do anything like this ourselves. Our chances of outwitting the Revenue Commissioners by setting ourselves up in the Cayman Islands or Northern Cyprus, with a company called Darapti or Felapton, with our cleaning lady and office boy as directors, and thus somehow freeing ourselves of the crushing burden of PAYE, are really very small. Even those readers who may be surviving on a mixture of unemployment benefits and nixers can feel a warm glow of begrudgery when they consider how quickly and painlessly you can attain riches if you know the right people.

It may actually be a genuine shock to a lot of people that this sort of thing is going on under their noses, but it shouldn't be. The plain people of the United States, for example, love their country, and are extremely proud of their way of life, but at the same time there is hardly anyone over there who does not believe that the scene in Washington, and indeed in most of the major city administrations, such as New York, Chicago, Boston, Detroit, Philadelphia, or Newark, New Jersey, is irremediably corrupt (in which opinion, I may say, they are confirmed at regular intervals by resounding scandals). The American public are certainly ready to be roused to a state of prurient indignation by a good scandal (preferably there should be sex and drugs in the story as well as money, as in the case of the recently disgraced Mayor of Washington), but are they surprised and shocked? I should say not.

In Britain, France, Italy or Germany the story is the same, with different national emphases, from pederasty to Mafia assassinations, as one moves from north to south. In each case there is a degree of media-fuelled moral indignation, but virtually nobody is surprised or shocked. And the interesting thing is that the same sort of people go on doing the same sorts of things, quite certain that there is no way that they are going to be caught. In this they are actually not unreasonable, since very few of them ever are caught; even as we mull over the few little irregularities that have come to light now, next year's potential scandals are flourishing alongside them, and only a select few of these will ever see the light of day.

Are we really so shocked at all this, then? And if so, from what perspective are we approaching it? If we are coming from the angle of Mr Proinsias De Rossa or Mr Pat Rabbitte, we can be indignant that these overstuffed bloodsuckers are taking the bread from the mouths of the unemployed of Finglas or Ballymun to buy another yacht, racehorse or Yeats painting. But those of us who do not feel so passionately that anything that they deserve is actually being stripped from the inhabitants of Ballymun, etc., have to ask ourselves, what exactly is our gripe? After all, Mr Smurfit, at least, did a great deal of good to the Irish nation by transforming a loss-making economic dinosaur into the extremely profitable and efficient business that a phone company should be. And Mr Comerford did more or less the same for the wretched Sugar Company. So if they can't resist making a little more on the side by using the same skills as got them where they are today, who are we to begrudge them that?

As for myself, I don't think that I would very seriously begrudge a man as effective and hard working as these men, who are creaming a little off the top, if that is what turns him on. But I'm afraid that, in the case of Telecom at least, rather more is at stake. We don't know how much Mr Smurfit actually made on the Johnson Mooney & O'Brien site sale, but it was surely peanuts to a man in his position – a few hundred thousand, perhaps, hardly enough to pay for the construction of one tee at Straffan. I think, however, that Mr Smurfit is interested in bigger things. What he is concerned with is, first, arranging for the privatising, and then acquiring personal control, of the whole Irish telecommunications system. That is something worth planning for.

My guess is that these complicated sales procedures regarding the site had something to do with that, and facilitating Mr Desmond was an essential part of the scenario. We can't know much more about that, however, until we know who really owns this Cypriot company – and that we may never know.

But to get back to the question of shock and surprise: am I surprised at all this? Well, I'm ashamed to say I am, just a little. Not shocked, but surprised. I realise that I should not have been, but what I am a little surprised at is that the peculiar composition of the present government, with a very suspicious and alert PD component, led by Mr O'Malley, breathing down his neck, should not have restrained Mr Haughey from patterns of behaviour which in happier circumstances he might have indulged in without a backward glance. But the truth is that long-established patterns of behaviour do not change that easily, and they have generally in the past worked pretty well. The whole ethos of Fianna Fail dictates that people like Mr Larry Goodman or Mr Dermot Desmond or Mr 'Pino' Harris, if they show themselves to be good men and true when they are needed, may expect in turn to be looked on favourably when some opportunity arises, and will once again not be found wanting when the need arises once more. And so things go on, snowballing quietly all the time.

All that I think I knew. Where I was naive, as it seems to me now, was in supposing that the unwelcome circumstances of a coalition government would in some way inhibit these sorts of arrangement, and that we would get a government characterised by the forcefulness for which Fianna Fail is justly renowned, but without many of the untoward accompaniments of that forcefulness. Not so, it seems. Mr Haughey's contempt for the opposition parties, for his own ministers, and even for his coalition partners, is so complete that he did not feel inhibited at all from proceeding in time-honoured fashion. This may prove to be his ruin, but at the time of writing it is by no means clear that he will not triumph over adversity once again, and go on to enjoy greater glories yet.

Time right for "license to thrill"
October 13, 1991

The recent flurries of excitement, both here and across the water, over distinguished members of society resorting to prostitutes and being triumphantly apprehended, or otherwise unmasked by the forces of law and order, put me in mind of a stimulating discussion I had, some years ago over dinner, and shortly before his death, with Alexis Fitzgerald the Elder. Alexis Fitzgerald was a man of exemplary piety, but also possessed of a most active and enquiring intellect, and he liked a good disputation. So, on this occasion, he put to me, to my great surprise, the proposition that prostitution should be legalised, more or less challenging me to argue against it if I could. I think he had a shrewd idea that I had no inclination to argue against such a proposition. He really wanted to see if I could defend it.

Now I can see no good reason why an overtly secular, modern democracy should have any other concern, in connection with the practice of prostitution (whether through the medium of organised brothels or on a more individualised basis), than to keep the peace. By which I would understand ensuring (a) that no one is being exploited, i.e. being forced into prostitution, or being oppressed by pimps or madams, or terrorised by mentally unstable clients, and (b) that no socially transmittable diseases (e.g. gonorrhoea, VD or AIDS) are being transmitted. Other than that, I really do not see on what basis a state that is not explicitly enforcing the decrees of some branch of Christianity, or, perhaps, of Islam, should find it necessary to criminalise this very ancient activity.

Has it not, at last, become time, prompted by what seems to me these very regrettable and rather childish incidents, to ask ourselves rationally what our position is? 'Kerb-crawling', so-called, such as the wretched Sir Allen Green was indulging in, is offensive insofar as it may embarrass and distress innocent female members of the public. But this activity is a by-product of the illegality attendant upon prostitution itself. Simply visiting an established brothel seems to me to be an entirely inoffensive activity – provided always that the brothel in question is being run on equitable lines, which it should be the business of the State to ensure. It is perfectly monstrous that clients, be they prominent politicians, high officials of the GAA, bishops, or even editors of newspapers, should be molested and blackmailed by the police, or anyone else, for indulging in this practice. The police seem to have behaved particularly badly in this affair, in that they have managed to leak the names of the 'suspects' quite widely, so that certain names have come even to the ears of such unworldly persons as myself. But, then, the police are not really the main culprits. They are committed to pursuing an out-dated and absurd policy, at the behest of politicians who are prepared to look benevolently on the commission of far worse crimes in the financial arena.

We don't pay Charlie enough!
October 20, 1991

As the dust and stench from the political and financial killing-fields grows ever higher, I find myself a prey to strange and paradoxical thoughts. Let me air some of them, to see if they stand up at all.

First of all, a paradoxical thought: can it be that some of the present problems have arisen because our top politicians, specifically the Taoiseach himself and the Minister of Finance, are not being paid enough – indeed, that their salaries are not even in the right ball-park. Before you begin to tear this newspaper up into little pieces, I suggest that you stop and think for a moment. We are now, even in Ireland, in a state of relatively advanced capitalism, where the really top men in the industrial and financial fields are pulling in salaries of over a million pounds a year, together with heaven knows what perks, while even their senior subordinates are in receipt of many hundreds of thousands, again with proportionate perks, share options and so on.

At the same time, senior politicians, who are just as intelligent and highly-trained, and who in most cases work just as hard, are taking home salaries from £75,000 on down (the Taoiseach earns £72,353, the Minister of Finance £57,497). Unlike civil servants, they have no security of tenure (though the ministerial pension – a concept to which I must say I do not object at all – helps a little), and although they are allowed a proportion tax free for expenses (which are very real), they are otherwise subject to the rigours of PAYE.

Now, we have inherited in this country a very exalted and austere concept of public service, inherited largely from Mr De Valera, but also from W. T. Cosgrave (who was no sybarite either), according to which one should be pleased to serve one's country for a modest reward, sufficient to keep body and soul together, and the purchase of an occasional new suit when holes appeared at one's elbows. It is also true that many politicians have come from professions and businesses which can provide them with a substantial subsidiary income, but one cannot assume that, especially if a government of a socialist complexion were to assume power. However, we are now at a stage of our economic and social development where the gap between the income of the men who are meant to be ruling the country and that of those men with whom they inevitably have to deal in the course of their duties is so vast that strains necessarily develop.

In fact, in the case of Mr Haughey, the discrepancy, in so far as there *is* one, is disguised by the relatively expansive life-style he has been able to maintain in Abbeville and Inishvickillaun, but it would have been a little awkward for Garret FitzGerald, say (though Garret might not have noticed it), to entertain Mr Smurfit or Mr Tony O'Reilly to tea or a glass of sherry in his basement flat in Palmerston Road. In either case, though, the fact that these men are earning more in a month then you are earning in a year might be thought to induce a certain sense of awe that is not desirable when one is engaged in dealings with them. It is not necessary to suggest that there is any danger of outright *bribery*; it is just that the gross imbalance in income must produce a degree of strain, and perhaps of excessive respect for their wisdom.

It also, I would suggest, provides evidence of a wrong order of priorities. I do not in fact believe that *anyone* should earn £1,000,000 a year, or even a quarter of that. Indeed, I do not believe, that, in a healthy society, *anyone* should earn more than five times more than anybody else. But we are not at the moment in a position to dismantle the capitalist system. In the meantime, it seems to me arguable that the highest officials of the State should be accorded salaries at least comparable to those of senior executives in major industrial concerns, and that means something not far off £200,000-a-year. Of course, we would expect them to earn it, but I think that normally they *would* earn it, every bit as much as the captains of industry earn theirs. They would certainly spend a great deal less time on the golf course, or on their yachts in the Mediterranean.

That is possibly enough provocation for one week, but my thoughts have also been turning specifically to Mr Haughey. It seems to me that now, like the aged Oedipus at Colonus, his misfortunes (even if self-inflicted), and his stubborn endurance of them, are, beginning to confer on him an almost heroic status. I have no doubt that he will survive these latest pinpricks. But one asks oneself, how might he yet turn the tables on his adversaries, and go down in history as a great statesman?

If it be not thought too impertinent, might I make a suggestion? It is in his power, before he finally bows out, to perform two signal services to the body politic, which, taken together, would paradoxically bring to fruition much of what Garret FitzGerald tried valiantly to do and failed. He could decide to hold two referenda (or, perhaps one composite referendum), (a) on the legalisation of divorce, and (b) on the dropping of Articles Two and Three from the Constitution. Both of these referenda would, in the absence of any significant opposition from the other political parties, be convincingly passed, and they would in turn give a significant stimulus to the solution of the problems of Northern Ireland – though one must not delude oneself that the solution would necessarily include the reunification of the country. Thus might a rather sad end to a distinguished political career turned into a kind of triumph.

In the shorter term, it might also be a smart move to appoint Mr Des O'Malley to be Minister of Finance in succession to the now discredited Mr Reynolds – if that very prudent statesman could be persuaded to accept the portfolio. The country now needs a Minister of Finance who is afraid of no one, and who in turn has the broad respect of the country. Mr O'Malley is, I suggest, one of the few politicians currently practising of whom that can be said, and his hand is needed on the tiller.

And that is *definitely* enough wool-gathering for one week.

Immortality and infallibility

October 27, 1991

It is a solemn and tragic moment in our history. Our Taoiseach, under heaven knows what pressures and strains, has at last intimated to his faithful followers, albeit in rather Delphic terms, that there is some possibility that at some future date he may feel it necessary to lay aside the burdens of his high office. Only he, of course, will be able correctly to judge the moment, but we are all now under notice that some such moment there will be. I am put in mind of a rather nice story about General Franco.

As he lay dying (a fact which, it seems, his doctors had not ventured to explain to him), there could be heard from the square below him, in front of the Palace, a confused shouting or chanting. He asked his aides what the people were saying. His aides were somewhat embarrassed. 'Generalissimo', they explained, 'they are crying, "Goodbye, Franco"'. 'Oh?' said the General, 'Why are they saying that? Where are they going?'

It is indeed a widely observed failing of Great Men (and Women – one thinks, in recent times, of Mrs Thatcher) to believe that one is indispensable and irreplaceable. Any base partiality for the trappings and privileges of office is transmuted and sublimated into a conviction that one is needed by the country; that there is urgent business to be done that no one else can adequately do. There often, it must be said, goes with this a propensity to cut down one's most promising possible successors, and to surround oneself by, or at least favour, relatively second-rate people, thus making one's indispensability something of a self-fulfilling prophecy.

It is interesting, in this connection, that Mr Haughey was recently moved, while marking the centenary of the death of Charles Stewart Parnell, to suggest some comparison between their two cases. There are indeed various aspects of this comparison which might be explored, but one striking similarity is certainly Parnell's firm conviction that no one but he could lead the Irish Nation into the Promised Land. In Parnell's case, this led to a ruinously destructive internecine struggle that set the cause of Irish independence back a full generation, and the cause of Irish unity more than a century. I speak with a certain personal interest, since it seems to me that in fact fully half a dozen of his lieutenants (Parnell did gather good men around him, even if he treated them badly) would have been quite adequate to the job – such men as Michael Davitt, William O'Brien, Tim Healy or my own grandfather, to go no further.

But this pattern recurs widely, after all. Apart from the unwillingness of Mr de Valera, later, in this country, to hand over the reins, and his attempts to cut Mr Lemass down to size by pitting such rivals as Sean MacEntee against him, we have the examples of such old war-horses as Konrad Adenauer in Germany and Charles de Gaulle in France, neither of whom were at all keen to be put out to grass. Mr Haughey has himself made humorous reference to the old men in Peking, but at least in China there is still a traditional belief, however absurd, that wisdom increases with age, almost ad infinitum, which, when combined with the traditional conservatism of communist regimes, does something to explain that extraordinary nest of octogenarians. So I think this conviction of indispensability is something to be struggled against, and when one feels it coming on very strongly, that is probably a good indication in itself that it is time to go.

Another weakness that afflicts the Very Great, and this is to be found in the business world at the moment even more than in the political, is a growing conviction of one's own infallibility. It used to be almost an exclusive characteristic of Popes, but, though still present, it seems more muted and less troublesome these days in that quarter. Where it pops up most conspicuously now is rather among Captains (and Buccaneers) of Industry. One really hardly likes these days to keep harping on Mr Goodman and Mr Smurfit and Mr Desmond, but they do undeniably provide ready illustrations of what I have in mind. All these are undoubtedly men of great business acumen, and their contributions should not be ignored in the present rather fraught circumstances, but what one also notices about them is that, after a series of brilliantly successful projects and coups, their judgment seems to go awry.

In the case of Larry Goodman, he had revolutionised the Irish beef industry, and pointed the way to various new directions in which it must go to survive (we draw for the moment a veil over some of the methods he may have used to achieve this – that is irrelevant to the present point). But what happened? It was not really Saddam Hussein and the Gulf War, we must remember, which brought the Goodman empire to its knees, but a series of ruinously foolish investments in property in London and New York. Mr Goodman was plainly out of his depth in this area, but the conviction had grown on him that he could do nothing wrong, he had the Midas Touch, and anything he threw money at must produce a hundredfold.

Similarly, Mr Smurfit. As long as he stuck to cardboard boxes he was unbeatable. Even the incredible impudence of breaking into the U.S. market as a major player seems to have succeeded handsomely. But then he was tempted to try the property and leisure markets, he was seduced by the charms of Brent Walker and its plausible chairman, and he got badly burned – though he has been able to survive that. Even now, he is involved in what would seem to this unworldly academic, at least, to be a five-star white elephant in the form of the K-Club, about the viability of which rumblings are beginning to be heard, despite Mr Smurfit's rather quaint insistence that anyone who wishes to do business with him should take out a life or corporate membership (a circumstance, I believe, that makes it a rather gloomy place in which to enjoy oneself).

As for Mr Desmond, I prefer not to say too much. He did indeed shake up the rather stuffy stockbroking and financial world of Dublin (though it does seem to be easier to achieve spectacular results in this area if one has access to the right political sources), but the grandiose conception of the Financial Services Centre, which so captivated the mind of the Taoiseach, is now also beginning to look somewhat pale and elephantine. Let us hope for all our sakes that this does not prove to be so.

An obvious stimulus to the conviction of infallibility is if there is no one in your immediate entourage who is prepared to correct or contradict you. Long a problem with Popes, this has also traditionally been a weakness of kings and other potentates, but the evidence indicates that it can become a problem in modern democracies too, when anyone achieves such an ascendancy in either politics or business that no one is any longer prepared to look them in the eye and tell them that they are talking through their hats. If the present upheavals lead to a puncturing of these fantasies of indispensability and infallibility, they will have served a useful purpose, whatever else they achieve.

Talking shop and a flight of fancy
November 3, 1991

I have noticed widespread incomprehension in the circles in which I move at the observation that, despite the pressing national business that is weighing on the nation, the Dail waited until *Wednesday* to reassemble after the Bank Holiday – and this after opposition leaders had been clamouring all summer, it seemed, that the House should be recalled early in September to deliberate upon the grave problems facing us – and, presumably, to propose statesmanlike solutions to them. The rest of us, after all, staggered in on Tuesday morning to face into the rest of the year as best we could.

But this should really have surprised nobody. The members of Dáil Eireann have actually a very accurate view of the importance of their deliberations, and the degree to which anything which transpires on the floor of the House affects the course of events. There was no point at all in toiling back to Dublin on Tuesday morning from one's constituency, still mouldy after the weekend's revelries (and in foul weather to boot), to start the old talking-shop up again. One was still exhausted after the exertions of the previous week, in any case, and it would take some time before the usual gems of invective produced then would assume anything of their pristine lure, so that they could be used once more.

Indeed, a lot of the savagery of the exchanges of the previous week was born of the knowledge that *nothing* that was said in that assembly was of any importance in comparison with what was being transacted off-stage. No amount of eloquence in the Dáil chamber (not that there was much) could affect a single vote when it came to a division. When the Assembly of the Wise did finally gather on the afternoon of last Wednesday, it was once again events somewhere else that were of primary significance. It all depended what Bernie Cahill was going to say at the EGM of Greencore. But Mr Cahill was not giving anything away. The deliberations in the chamber were therefore largely stymied.

It may be worth playing over to ourselves, in that connection, just what we are being asked to believe. It is not the case that the Father of the Nation requested an interview with Mr Cahill. No, it was the other way about. Mr Cahill felt the urgent need to consult the Little Father about the future of the Sugar Company, to solicit his wise advice in face of this great step they were about to take – *privatisation*. He did not just pick up the phone or even get into his Mercedes and drive (so urgent was his need for fatherly advice to be delivered *in person*); he called a *helicopter* (and guess whose helicopter?) to rush him to Kinsealy. When he arrived, there were of course certain things uppermost in his mind – who should we have as brokers for this transaction? What would the Leader think of this bright new firm that is having so much success now, NCB I think its name is? And would the Leader have any views on a good, reliable firm of solicitors? Would that excellent man Mr P.J. O'Connor by any chance be free to take on the job?

But imagine Mr Cahill's disappointment when his inquiries are dismissed with a wave of the hand. He should have known that such matters are beneath the notice of the Leader of the Nation. If he was in any serious doubt on these questions, he should have a word with Mara on the way out. Instead, the Little Father questioned him about the things of primary concern to him - the welfare of the workers, the interests of the sugar beet producers, the problem of finding alternative employment for his faithful people in Tuam, who had always been particularly dear to his heart. A full, frank and wide-ranging discussion took place, covering all these issues comprehensively. It is of course a despicable allegation by the leader of the Labour Party – and a total misunderstanding of the role of the Father of the Nation in a matter of this sort – that he should have made *suggestions* to Mr Cahill as to suitable firms of brokers or solicitors, or should even allow such a topic to be discussed in his presence.

I think that we may take it that this little matter is now laid to rest – unless, that is, Mr Cahill should be deposed from his present position; then he may have another story to tell. In the circumstances, I think his position as Chairman of Greencore is safe for the moment.

For some reason or other, just before I leave you, I am put in mind of poor young Mr Patrick Gallagher, newly out of prison, and presumably still at a loose end. Perhaps a place could be found for him on the board of Aer Lingus or of An Bord Telecom, together with possibly a part-time position on the faculty of the new Michael Smurfit Business School in Carysfort? One should not let his obvious talents be lost to the country once again. It is not going to be easy, after all, in the months ahead, to persuade really *enterprising* people to take on a role in the service of the nation.

Free money and our dependency
November 24, 1991

I was just recently dragged off to see *The Commitments*, and found it immensely enjoyable, not just as simple entertainment, but also as a tract for the times. Roddy Doyle is a teacher, after all, and he cannot help being to some degree didactic. The film (and the book) is a full-blooded celebration of our position as a swaggering third-world nation, with first world pretensions, and at the same time deeply ingrained self-destructive tendencies. That presumably was the message of the rather ill-motivated quarrelsomeness of the band. They seemed to be driven by a compulsion to destroy themselves, even when all external aspects of their situation were positive.

It just happened that my seeing the film coincided with a little story told me by a fearless investigative journalist of my acquaintance, and the things seem to coalesce in my mind. You will remember that some time ago that indefatigable champion of the poor and downtrodden, Mr Pat Rabbitte (no relation of Mr Jimmy Rabbite), made a complaint that the Corporation were being most remiss in attending to repairs to the houses of his constituents in Tallaght.

The places, it seemed, were falling around their ears, and they could not get the attention of the Corpo officials at all. In rebuttal, Mr Noel Carroll of the Corporation remarked plaintively that the houses in question were all relatively new (built in the last 15 years at least), and that his men had been in receipt of complaints as trivial as one about a screw missing from a letter-box. Plainly there was a story here, and my fearless friend (who shall be nameless) did not go forth to investigate on his own, but actually made an appointment with a WP councillor (who shall also be nameless), who undertook to show him around. In this way, he reckoned, he was sure to see the points of maximum distress and need.

The results of this tour were quite astonishing. They had time, it seems, to visit only five houses, in the first three of which the occupants were out. In the fourth house, they were shown, with great indignation, *a leaking tap*. This tap, it seems, had been dripping for weeks and the

Corporation remained callously impervious to all appeals to mend it. The last case was even more remarkable. This house was adorned, it seems, with all the accoutrements of working class comfort – TV, video and stereo CD unit – but the inhabitants were fuming. This time the problem was a large heap of rubble in the back garden, which the Corpo, it seems, had been inexcusably dragging their feet about hauling away. The rubble had been caused by the building of a patio, which the inhabitants had had added on to their humble dwelling, but they were damned if they were going to take away the debris. That was somebody else's business. The WP councillor, to be fair to him, was a little embarrassed at the sum total of their findings, and volunteered the view that, if he had had more time, he could have come up with more striking evidence. My friend wondered, irreverently, if a greater lead time would have given him the chance to knock a few holes in roofs or walls.

His visit had an interesting sequel. A day or so later, he was phoned by a young lady who complained that the mobile home in which she had been living had burned down, and she was now reduced to living in a tent on the side of the road, with an asthmatic child on her hands, while there were houses in the same estate standing empty, but the Corporation would not let her move into one. My friend was full of sympathy, but asked where she was phoning from now. She was phoning from her mam's house. 'But why couldn't you move in with your mother, then, even for a little while?' 'Ah', was the reply, 'me mam's boyfriend won't let me past the door' (this gentleman was presumably out at the time). In other words, good old Uncle Noel and the Corpo can be blamed for not stepping in where one's family is not prepared to do their duty.

There is a lesson here, though, I think (assuming of course, that both Noel Carroll's complaint and my friend's findings are broadly accurate), which should not be swept under the carpet or ignored, since it brings us back to the problem of the national psyche. We are afflicted with two very widespread attitudes, which could be summed up in the phrases 'Somebody ought to do something about it', and 'Sure, they won't miss it'. It is the influence of these twin attitudes to life that gives justification to Brendan Behan's famous remark that, if it was raining soup from heaven, the Irish would be out there with forks.

The first attitude is exemplified by the story just told. It is symptomatic, I'm afraid, of the mentality of dependency spawned by the welfare system, but it is broader than that. The fact is that, although we all recognise with one corner of our brains (a) that any job performed by a public agency costs about three times as much as the same job done by private enterprise, and (b) the bills for such jobs are ultimately paid for by *us*, in the form of taxes, nevertheless we still clamour for the central government or the local authority to come in and do things that we, either as community associations or as individuals, could very well do for ourselves. I wouldn't wish to claim that this attitude is peculiar to the Irish nation, but it is one that we can ill afford.

The other attitude, allied to this one, is manifested in various forms, but I will pick out just two on the present occasion. First of all, are you aware that the annual bill for shoplifting in the Dublin area (coming up to a crescendo in the festive season just ahead of us) is approximately £53 million? No doubt there are elements of real and desperate need here, but mainly, I'm afraid, this stems from an attitude of mind that feels that a few items here and there removed from the large stock of a major store just won't be noticed – 'Ah sure, they won't miss it!'

Well, they miss it all right. It is all added up, and reckoned into the price that is charged to the rest of us – or the firm in question just goes out of business. Either way, the chickens come home to roost. It is part, at least, of the explanation of the sometimes remarkable price discrepancies between the UK and the Republic for many common items.

Another common and disastrous manifestation of this attitude is in the area of insurance claims. Did you observe recently that both the major car rental firms, Hertz and Avis, have withdrawn from the Republic (bequeathing their business to a bunch of optimists from Cork)? Now it happens that I knew the Irish representative for Avis, and I know that he made strong representations to headquarters that he be allowed to continue, since he liked being here, but they showed him statistics to which he had no answer. Our insurance on rented vehicles (as on all others) is the highest in Europe – it was costing them over £2000 a year to insure even the smallest cars. They simply could not make a reasonable profit in those conditions. So they just said 'the hell with it'. Fortunately for them they can do that; the rest of us are stuck here.

The reason, of course, for the high cost of insurance is the frequency of, and exorbitant nature of, insurance claims – many of which, I gather from my friend, in their case were actually put-up jobs involving cars from Hertz or Avis, which then were involved in arranged accidents involving old bangers commandeered for the purpose.

For this I blame, of course, this fatal attitude that there is such a thing as free money, which can be extracted in limitless quantities from insurance companies. But I also lay a good deal of blame on our legal system, and in particular now on our judiciary (and if that's contempt of court, I'm prepared to go to jail for it!). What seems to be happening these days, in the wake of the much-needed abolition of jury trials for ordinary accident claims, is that the judges – who are all, we must remember, former barristers – are deliberately keeping up the level of awards, just to show Dessie O'Malley and the rest of us that abolishing juries wouldn't do any good, and that one shouldn't try to inconvenience the legal profession.

Well, *of course*, abolishing juries will do no good if the judges by themselves are going to be just as reckless about disbursing other people's money as the juries were. What we also need is what the rest of Europe has long since had, a proper fixed scale of compensation for various types of injury to the person, and strict supervision of charges for car repairs.

This is an extremely urgent reform, and it should be accompanied, I would suggest, by some form of no-fault insurance scheme, at least partially funded by a levy on petrol sales, to bring down the cost of insurance, particularly to young people, since they are being put in an impossible position, which in turn leads to their taking the chance of driving without insurance. At the moment, we are becoming a virtually uninsurable nation, and it serves us right. But as long as the notion persists that there is free money about, and that 'they' won't miss it if we cream a little of it off, I see no solution to this problem.

Treaty through the looking-glass
December 1, 1991

Another exercise in high-class historical revisionism is about to grace our screens, in the shape of the four-part series *The Treaty*, the first instalment of which is to be shown next Wednesday by RTE. This series is not a debunking exercise but, like Hugh Leonard's recent excellent study of Parnell, it brings the results of modern scholarship to bear on certain key events in our history. If criticism might be made (and doubtless it will be by strong partisans of "the Chief"), it will likely be that the series constitutes a glorification of Michael Collins, and a hatchet-job on such figures as de Valera, Brugha, and to some extent, Erskine Childers. I do not think such criticism would be fair.

De Valera's behaviour during the Treaty negotiations, as is now generally agreed, was devious in the extreme, and this is well brought out in the series. He had two main concerns, once he realised that an independent Irish Republic was simply not on offer from the British: one was to implicate Michael Collins in the compromise that was inevitable, and the other was to stay in with the "hard men", particularly Cathal Brugha and Austin Stack. Impatient himself of the "straitjacket of the Republic", as he described it, he attempted to square the circle with his subtly scholastic formula of "external association", which was a complete non-starter, and then tried to have things both ways by sending the delegation of Griffith, Collins and the others over to London as "plenipotentiaries", while nevertheless sending them "recommendations", which looked like instructions, from "the Cabinet" – in fact the intransigent rump of the cabinet, since certain key members of the cabinet were after all on the delegation.

A man who comes out of this series even less favourably than Dev is Mr Charles William St. John Burgess, (alias Cathal Brugha). All that I have read of him, I must say, makes him a most unattractive figure – though it gives me no pleasure to say so, since I have a high regard for his son, Ruairi, who is a most civil and broad-minded man, much concerned with the cause of national reconciliation. Brugha was undoubtedly a man of tremendous courage and the highest integrity (though his jealousy of Collins probably coloured his judgement to a certain degree). As Collins remarks in the series, though, "he did not know his arse from his elbow" as regards the IRA's capacity to fight on after August 1921. Nor, it would seem, did he much care. He had fixed in his mind that "the Irish People" had commissioned him and his comrades to establish an Irish Republic and nothing less, and he was going to fight for that to the last drop of everyone else's blood (and, to be fair to him, his own as well).

Now I speak, perhaps, from a somewhat jaundiced perspective, but it seems to me that the Irish People had commissioned no one to fight for anything of the kind, nor had they recently been consulted on the point. The mandate conferred in the 1918 election was certainly superficially overwhelming, but we must remember that it involved only 60 per cent of the electorate (40%, mainly depressed or intimidated Parliamentary Party supporters, stayed at home) and of that 60 per cent, only about two thirds voted Sinn Fein – and this is to exclude the Unionist tradition from "the people" altogether.

Furthermore, the vote in 1918 had mainly been *against* things – conscription, British repression and, perhaps, the perceived political bankruptcy of the Parliamentary Party. It was not necessarily a mandate for a totally independent, Gaelic-speaking, economically isolated Irish Republic. Brugha, Stack, and Childers were largely living in Cloud-Cuckoo-Land, and the main criticism of Dev must be that, though he knew better, he was unwilling to let them, or anyone, occupy 'higher moral ground' than himself.

Maastricht Shmaastricht!

December 8, 1991

Am I entirely out of line, as we approach this much-vaunted summit at Maastricht, in coming to feel just a little queasy at the thought of a United States of Europe? I know I am not alone in this. There has always been dear old Raymond Crotty, shaking his gory locks and warning of the dire fate that awaits us, and my respected colleagues Sean Barrett and Anthony Coughlan have recently been making a number of trenchant points on the same topic, but I can't say that I paid them much mind, until just now.

Like more or less everyone else I know, a sort of vague Europhoria had possessed me, combined with a degree of fatalism. It really doesn't seem, after all, as if we have much choice but to go along, like a little dog being dragged behind a cart, so we might as well try to enjoy it. It is perhaps the succession of rather schoolmarm-ish lectures we have been receiving recently in the media that has concentrated my mind. We have been scolded for not paying more attention, for being too wrapped up in our own national scandals and other problems and neglecting the important developments that are about to take place at the centre. Well, now I'm paying full attention, and I suddenly don't like the look of it at all.

I don't deny for a moment that the supersession of the traditional quarrelling jumble of nation-states that was the old Europe by a rational economic and political community is a good thing, and perhaps even a model for the rest of the world (see, for instance, how the constituent states of the former Soviet Union are looking to us, as we stand now, as a model for their future relations!). But I do not therefore agree that, because some degree of unity is a good thing, therefore an ever-greater degree of unity becomes a better and better thing. From our point of view, indeed, in this small and vulnerable state on the margin of Europe, I think a greater degree of unity will be a very bad thing. Let us stop and consider the prospects for a moment, in the midst of our stampede towards Monsieur Delors' dream of an integrated European empire, ruled from Brussels.

To whose advantage, after all, is a completely integrated political and economic system – a unified currency and banking system, a sovereign central parliament, with majority voting, a unified judicial system, and co-ordination of every sort of commercial and industrial rule and regulation? Surely it is obvious that the major advantage accrues, not to the small and peripheral members of any such organisation, whether nations or individuals, but to the largest and most central.

One does not have to impute any great degree of malice or cynicism to the great panjandrums at the centre of the European bureaucracy to suggest that they have in mind primarily the benefit of themselves and the interests they represent. The Common Market was not created, after all, for the benefit of Ireland, or Portugal, or Greece, and it has never claimed to have been. It would be absurd to think of it as some sort of benevolent organisation. It was created to provide a market in which the major industries and commercial organisations of Germany, France, Italy and later, Britain (and now perhaps even Spain) can expand still further, battling each other, by means of price-wars and take-overs, like ike lords of the jungle, and crushing and absorbing any small indigenous rivals they may come up against, either in their own countries, or in the smaller, peripheral countries.

That is surely the real business of the EEC, and the political developments are designed simply to make that process smoother. As a price for economic domination, they are prepared to assent to hand-outs, in the form of grants to disadvantaged areas, mainly to improve their transport systems and clean up their environments (farm subsidies being now largely a thing of the past) – so that these peripheral areas will become pleasanter places for the hard-working inhabitants of the centre to visit for rest and recreation, when they feel that they have earned a break from their labours.

Is this too pessimistic a view? I think not. It seems to me merely realistic. But if so, what are we to do about it? There is no point, I think, in just resigning from the EEC – unless we want to make a serious effort to become some sort of off-shore tax-haven (and our great army of unemployed wouldn't like that at all). What I would suggest rather is that we stay in and fight, not just for bigger hand-outs, as Mr Haughey is preparing to do, but against the inexorable advance towards centralisation.

There is in fact an alternative, and it is one that it well suits us, as a small nation, to press for. That alternative is a regionalised Europe. This concept has in fact been advanced by many thoughtful people throughout Europe, and in this country has been taken up by such thinkers as Tom Barrington and Richard Kearney. An excellent volume of essays published in 1988, *Across the Frontiers: Ireland in the 1990s*, edited by Kearney, embodies their views. Instead of progressively strengthening the centre, we should strive to break up even the major existing states – Britain, for instance, into Scotland, Wales and England, with Brittany and Provence being split off from the rest of France, and perhaps Catalonia and the Basque country from Spain. Germany, and Italy all lend themselves readily to division also. Instead of making good what is being termed the democratic deficit in the central parliament (a process which would greatly weaken the power of the national parliaments, including our own), we should be advocating the returning of power to even smaller units, such as, perhaps, in this country, provincial assemblies.

All this, of course, will not solve the problem of the ever-increasing concentration of economic power at the centre – as long as we believe that buying a cheaper tube of toothpaste or electric toaster is more important than keeping some of our own sons and daughters in employment in their own country, there is no solution to that – but it will provide some counterweight on the political level. As things are (never mind how they are going to be), what is to prevent a million Dutchmen, say, deciding that they have had enough of being crowded in the Netherlands, moving over to Ireland, and making the Irish serfs and beggars in their own country?

Nothing that I can see, except the weather. More realistically, perhaps, what is to prevent individual wealthy Europeans buying up all our best houses and lands, and putting the ownership of any decent property out of the economic reach of most of the natives? Again, nothing at all. It is happening already. And in a United States of Europe we will have no comeback at all, any more than the State of Montana, or of Maine, or indeed Hawaii, would have in the United States of America. Only a firm resolution to dig our heels in, and a declaration that we now have quite enough unification to be going on with, and should start thinking creatively about quite the opposite process, is going to save a small, marginal nation like ourselves from becoming simply the plaything of the massive super-state that Europe is about to become.

Joys of pessimism
January 5, 1992

The season to be jolly has just passed us by once again, leaving little more than memories of hangovers past and a crop of resolutions for the New Year. 'Tis now the season rather for the Poor Mouth and the Dire Prediction, as we turn to contemplate the future, global, national and personal. The Poor Mouth relates particularly to pre-budgetary manoeuvrings by the various interested parties, and I will return to that topic at a future date. At the moment what interests me particularly is the phenomenon of the Dire Prediction, as uttered by a host of pundits in all the media at around this time each year. I am not here concerned to add any predictions of my own to the pile – I consider myself exempted from that, since I am not an expert in anything relevant. What intrigues me in this connection is rather the question: 'Why is it so very satisfying to make dire predictions?'

Because it is, isn't it, immensely satisfying? I feel the satisfaction of it profoundly myself, when occasionally I indulge. My particular hobby-horse is the world population problem (all the poorest nations breeding like rabbits, progressively overrunning Western Europe, standing room only by the year 2100 or so!), and of course environmental pollution (rivers running black or yellow with chemicals, trees dying of acid rain, tropical rain forests all gone, ozone layer shot full of holes as a tennis net – you know the sort of thing). But the funny thing is, one feels so pleased when one has delivered oneself of one of these diatribes, whether around the New Year or at any other time, so deeply fulfilled. Why should this be?

One obvious, robust answer is simply that these gloomy predictions are entirely justified, and one naturally congratulates oneself on one's perspicacity in uttering them. But that is not the whole story, I think. After all, one is purveying gloom and doom of cosmic proportions. Why should one feel so pleased?

For an explanation, I naturally turn back to the Greeks. A feature one notes about Greek heroes and heroines, both fictional and real, from Homer on down, is a certain tendency to lament their fate over

102

and above what is reasonable. 'Far the best', the playwright Sophocles makes the Chorus say in one of his plays, 'is never to have been born at all; but when a man has once seen the light, this is next best by far, that with all speed he should go back whence he has come.' As for Homer, how often does *Ulysses* during his adventures in *The Odyssey*, for example, express the wish that he had died on the plains of Troy, and foresee only the worst for himself and his companions? The fact that he is largely justified in this is not the point, I think; the point is that *he is hoping and expecting that he is wrong*. The lamentation is intended to be apotropaic – or if that is too long a word, it is an exercise in averting the evil eye. The idea is that if you predict the worst, then you are unlikely to be unpleasantly surprised. Indeed, things will probably work out better than you suggest, and no one will hold it against you when they do.

This is a good strategy, therefore, and explains why it is that the process of getting a gloomy prediction off one's chest makes one feel so much better. What one is really thinking is that one has outwitted fate by anticipating the worst that it can throw at you, and that therefore it might just give up and do something nice for a change. I would even go so far as to suggest that a philosophy such as Existentialism, or the literary nihilism of Beckett, are to be explained in this way. After all, if Jean-Paul Sartre, or old Sam for that matter, really believed their utterances on the nature of the world or the meaninglessness of life, then they should have lost no time about jumping into the Seine and ending it all.

Instead, of course, they both continued into ripe old age, loaded with honours, enjoying themselves hugely, and showing no disposition at all to depart prematurely. This is not necessarily to accuse either of these great men of insincerity (though I do think that Beckett in particular became a bit of a cod in his latter years – *Play Without Words*, how are ye? I must try delivering a lecture without words sometime). It is just to suggest that there is an element of the apotropaic in their strategies for dealing with the world.

So it is, I suspect, with political and economic commentators. It would be an interesting exercise (which I am not inclined to perform) to make a study of New Year predictions on the economy, and on world politics, in this or any other paper, over the last twenty years.

How many times, I wonder, starting with the first oil crisis of 1973, continuing with the second one of 1977, taking in the political and economic uncertainties of 1981–2, right down to the anticipation of the Gulf War in January 1991, could we produce comprehensive jeremiads about the impending end of civilisation as we know it, all of which brought to their authors great kudos as people of clear-sightedness and discernment, but all of which were proved gloriously wrong.

I happened to be reading just recently in the lavatory (as is my wont) a back number of that excellent periodical *The New York Review of Books* from January 1991, containing an article on the Middle East crisis by a well-known expert on the area, one Stanley Hoffman, and I found it most entertaining. Some things the expert got quite right (for instance, he predicted a war, because the U.S. wanted a war), but most other things he got wrong. He thought the U.S. (or U.N.) would probably win, but after heavy and protracted slaughter on both sides, and he naturally assumed that that would mean the demise of Saddam, but the inextricable involvement of the U.S. in policing the area, and severe political repercussions at home.

No one, perhaps, could have foreseen the actual sequence of events, but what happened should really discourage all political crystal-ball gazers, gloomy and otherwise. The great Iraqi war machine collapsed under the Allied assault, with minimal U.N. casualties, but Saddam himself survived, and managed to destroy Kuwait into the bargain. On the other hand, neither the U.S. nor the U.N. is exactly *bogged down* in the Middle East (though opportunities for bogging in that area have not yet been exhausted) but have been instead provoking promising initiatives. Also, though Kuwait and the Gulf are still badly injured, the clean-up and recovery there has been much faster, and the environmental damage less, than the doom-sayers were joyfully prophesying.

But let us come nearer home. What are the current gloomy prophecies facing us? Let's see: first of all, continued world recession, particularly in Britain and the U.S.; 300,000 unemployed at home, and a spate of labour unrest, as the unions strive obstinately for unrealisable goals; virtually no industrial growth and the collapse of the farming sector, in consequence of the dismantling of the CAP. In addition: economic and political disintegration in Eastern Europe resulting in floods of refugees (*or alternatively*, economic revival in Eastern Europe, resulting in serious rivalry for our export industries?).

That's enough to be going on with. One can see the joys of indulging in prophecies of gloom. The only thing to deplore about them is the possibility that someone, either the audience or the prophet himself, might come to believe in them. That could get serious. There is such a thing as 'business confidence' after all. If certain key people actually start believing gloomy economic prophecies, these prophecies are in a strong position to becoming self-fulfilling.

The human race, after all, carries on on the basis of largely irrational optimism. We set out to the office in the morning in the expectation that we will get there (and indeed that the office will still be there), and that we will able to achieve something positive when we do get there. If we began to doubt all that, we might not be inclined to get out of bed at all. The god Prometheus, in Aeschylus' *Prometheus Bound*, proclaims as one of his chief gifts to mankind, on top of all types of science and technology, 'I instilled in them blind hopes.' That is indeed a gift, and should not be cast away lightly.

The essential civil servant

January 19, 1992

My esteemed colleague Liam Collins, in last Sunday's paper, rather went to town on the subject of that ancient whipping boy, the Public Servant. The immediate occasion for his attack was one that I actually am in full agreement with him about - the proposed strike on January 28 – but so intemperate did he become that I was stimulated to cast about and see if there were not anything to be said in favour of the poor beast, especially since (stretching a point) I am one myself.

On all sides, from civil servants, teachers, firemen, Gardaí, health workers, prison officers, we are told that there is an unprecedented level of indignation and radicalisation manifesting itself. I think any sane person must ask, how genuine, and if so, how reasonable, is this indignation? Let us assume it is largely genuine. What does that say about the state of mind of those concerned – such substantial personages as Seán Ó'Riordáin of the Higher Civil Servants, for example, who was sounding off most ominously the other day? These people are surely men of the world. They know perfectly well that in the case of any agreement entered into with a private employer there is always an escape clause, the plea of inability to pay – by reason of a serious downturn in the market, loss of demand for the product, or some more dramatic mishap such as a major fire or flood, or the accountant absconding to South America with the firm's liquid assets.

Well, so it is with governments, whether the public service unions like it or not. Any agreement must be made with the proviso that all continues to go reasonably well in the world. If something unexpected happens, a Third World War, for example, or a rogue comet hitting the earth and knocking it off course, or even a major drought or plague, then all bets are off. One has a vision of Mr Ó'Riordáin and his colleagues standing indignantly in the midst of a nuclear winter landscape, smoking ruins all around them, smouldering remains of their shiny brown suits hanging off them, still demanding that the conditions of the Agreement be honoured in full, or they would have to consider their position *very seriously*.

Of course, nothing like that has happened, but it is nonetheless arguable that things on the wider, global front have not worked out as planned (whether the original presuppositions of the PESP were fatuously optimistic is another matter). God knows that I am no apologist for the present government (in fact I look with unseemly glee on their present predicament, knowing very well what their attitude would be if they were in opposition, and the other lot in power), but I would have to admit that the present situation is really not entirely their fault. The figures do not add up any longer, for reasons quite independent of our control, and presumably men like the higher civil servants, many of whom have a good deal to do with trying to work out the finances of the nation, know this very well. So why are they going on in this obstinately selfish way about their sacred right to more money, when they know that that can only be satisfied at the cost of more borrowing and more unemployment?

But this was not really what I wanted to talk about. I came not to bury the Civil Servant, but to praise him. It is hard, perhaps, to avoid platitude on this subject, but I wonder has Liam Collins ever lived any length of time east of Suez, or in the Third World generally? If he has, as I have, he will surely recognise what a glorious thing it is to have anything approaching a system of public service which is efficient, impartial and honest. We are so used to this, I think, that we either take it for granted, or give out dog's abuse at any behaviour that falls short of this standard.

But it might well not have been that way. Most of the world suffers under systems of public service even more bloated than ours, which are corrupt, partial (in that its members feel it their duty to foster the interests only of their friends and extended families), and hopelessly inefficient. We could easily have gone that way, if we had not been bequeathed by the British (let us admit it), and been prepared to accept, a civil service that observed certain standards of efficiency, honesty and impartiality. And one does not have to go to the Third World to find a contrast to this. Even within the EEC, standards in most of our Mediterranean partners, in particular, fall far short of what we are used to. I have a great affection for the Greek nation, for example, but I do not relish trying to get even a simple form processed in a public office in that country, unless I have a personal introduction to someone.

Certainly there is the other side of the coin: a propensity to caution and conservatism, a certain dullness of demeanour, a liking for forms in quadruplicate, but these are characteristics of public servants everywhere, and if anything are leavened in this country by traces of Hibernian levity. Even a rather grim mandarin like the great J.J. McElligott, Secretary of the Department of Finance for 26 years (from 1929 to 1953), was not without a certain imagination and wit. There is preserved in my Uncle James's papers a most entertaining exchange of letters between him and McElligott during the first Inter-Party Government, where the uncle, in trying to winkle money out of Finance for Agriculture, engaged McElligott in wide-ranging flights of philosophical fancy, to which the Secretary was fully equal (while holding on to the money).

And then a service which fostered the poets Denis Devlin and Valentine Iremonger, or the novelist Séamus Ó'Griana, or the historians P. S. O'Hegarty and Leon Ó'Broin (not to mention Conor Cruise O'Brien and Máire MacEntee), and which put up with the great Brian O'Nolan for so many years, can't be all bad. Bad-mouthing civil servants is rather like abusing politicians: it all sounds great, until you stop to think what you would do without them.

The PDs in purgatory
January 26, 1992

The ancient Greeks (if I may venture to bring them into the discussion once again) had an ethnic joke that was also a logical puzzle, which seems relevant to the present interesting situation. 'Epimenides says that all Cretans are liars. But Epimenides is a Cretan.' I leave you to work it out, as also to work out how it may apply to the issues before us.

The energies of my colleagues will no doubt be concentrated in these stressful days on the problems of Mr Haughey and the Fianna Fail party. As I write this, I see no sign of a clear conclusion to the present fuss. I cling simply to a possibly naive assumption that CJ will come through this somehow once again.

What is to be said, on the other hand, about the PDs? That is the aspect of the situation that particularly intrigues me. Once again the junior partner in government has gone into a huddle, following on yet another malodorous revelation, and emerged with a stern ultimatum to their big brothers, ordering them to get their house in order. We all know the rather bitter political joke about telephoning the Progressive Democrats HQ and getting an answering machine: 'We regret that there is no one available to take your call at the moment. Please leave your name, telephone number and message after the High Moral Tone.'

It is easy to jeer at the PDs and their high moral tone, but I must say that I find such jeering a trifle distasteful. It is all too much like the similar mockery directed against 'Garret the Good' by such people as the late John Healy. It is the tribute that corruption pays to decency and seriousness of purpose. If so, though, there is still a mild aura of absurdity surrounding the public agonisings of the Progressive Democrats on every occasion when some issue like this arises. The problem stems from the fact of having come into politics in the first place 'to break the mould' of existing Irish political life. The annoying thing was, as we know, that the bloody oul' mould refused to break. Fianna Fail and Fine Gael may be hopelessly outdated and dead on their feet, but for some obscure reason the public in general liked having them around (sentimentality, perhaps, combined with a fear of the unknown), and while giving out about them loud and long, persisted in voting for them in large numbers. So there one was left, filled with seriousness of purpose, sitting disconsolately on the edge of the mould, with one's toes in the murky water, emitting at regular intervals a High Moral Tone. It is all very unfair, and a damning indictment of the Irish voting public.

Now one might say that, in view of how bad things turned out to be, the PDs have not done too badly. For a party of six deputies to have three of their number as ministers, and a good deal of their policy in the process of being put into practice, represents a success ratio unequalled, certainly, in the history of this state (I can't be sure about the rest of Europe). Only Clann na Poblachta in 1948-51 would have come near them, and I can't quite remember what the Clann's policy was on anything in particular (leaving aside Noel Browne on the subject of health!).

On the other hand, if one contemplates the future, things do not seem too rosy. One more election, and the unregenerate Irish voter might leave nothing of the intrepid mould-breakers but the High Moral Tone, rather like the smile of the Cheshire Cat. Hence the succession of agonised huddles into which the party goes on occasions like this. Nobody, God knows, can afford an election just at present, but the Progressive Democrats least of all.

I would not, however, wish to be construed as taking pleasure in their predicament. I am actually one of those who would very much like to have seen the mould being broken. I have always agreed with the late John Kelly that the best thing that could happen to the Irish political scene would be for FF and FG to sink their hoary, and largely imaginary, differences, and form a regenerated, rational Sinn Fein party (whatever they would now choose to call it), which would present a coherent approach to the country's problems. I now feel this more than ever, and further that the best leader for such a reunited party would be none other than Desmond O'Malley, who, whatever his minor short-comings, is the only political figure in the country with both acknowledged integrity and leadership qualities.

For the last ten years at least, the chief obstacle to any such development has been the figure of CJ Haughey. Whatever about policy differences, his was a style of doing business that formed a strong contrast to anything that Fine Gael would have found acceptable. But after CJ, with a leader (or leaderene?) of Fianna Fail who recalled a little more clearly the standards of integrity which were characteristic of the earliest generation of the movement (I think, as a good example, of the figure of Toddz Andrews, as revealed in his autobiography), I feel that the continued ritual shadow combat between the two parties would come to seem increasingly absurd.

But this is all Utopian rambling. As I write, CJ is alive and well, and preparing to lead his party into the next century, and the PDs are sitting miserably on the edge of the cesspool, with their little toes in the water.

Provo terror tactics backfire
February 9, 1992

Well, a new dimension was added last Tuesday afternoon to the horrors of Northern Ireland, just when we thought that they had worked their way through everything in that part of the world. A demented policeman breaks loose and shoots down three persons in the Sinn Fein advice centre in the Falls Road, one of whom, a Mr Michael O'Dwyer, was only there as a 'customer', having come in to complain about glue-sniffing in his neighbourhood (the other two were at least connected with Sinn Fein, though in minor capacities), and then drives off into sylvan surroundings and shoots himself.

Various comments have inevitably been called forth by this event over the last few days, depending on what point on the green/orange spectrum one is coming from. What occurs to me, I'm afraid, is a reflection that has been on the minds and lips of many of my acquaintance, and which I think deserves airing, even if it is somewhat short on the traditional charitableness for which our nation is so noted. The thought is, baldly stated: 'Serves them (bloody well) right!' This refers properly rather to the organisation as a whole than to the very minor members of it who were actually cut down (and exempts the unfortunate Mr O'Dwyer altogether), but when its reference is duly delimited, it is not, I think, an unfair comment.

The IRA, after all – and I do not accept for a moment any significant distinction between them and Sinn Fein – have been in these last weeks making a particularly strenuous effort to achieve the psychological destabilisation of the society they are trying to destroy. Quite simply, not knowing where the next bomb is coming from frays the nerves and is designed to do so. In such circumstances, people in positions of stress, or who are otherwise psychologically on the edge, are liable to crack altogether. Officer James Alan Moore was plainly in both these positions, and he cracked with explosive force. An ironic aspect of the tragedy seems to be that the fellow-policeman for whom he was grieving, who was an old and dear friend, had not been killed in an IRA ambush or anything of that sort, but had been the victim of 'a domestic dispute' (not to beat around the bush, his wife has been charged with his shooting). This, however, only points up what I am saying. In the circumstances, for people in positions of stress that Sinn Fein's 'other half' has been striving to create, any little thing may set off a psychological explosion.

The situation is not unlike something that happened in South Africa just a few days before this event, where a young white from a conservative part of the country went on a shooting spree against blacks after being rejected by his girl-friend, killing one person and wounding half a dozen others (he did not have the decency to shoot himself afterwards, however, but was instead wounded by the police). His only explanation of his behaviour, from his hospital bed, was that he felt that his life was over and he wanted to take as many 'kaffirs' with him as he could, and thus do some good to society!

Some motive of this sort was doubtless in the disturbed mind of Officer Moore, as he set out on his mission of death (which, it must be said, he planned with some ingenuity, masquerading as a reporter). What has to be asked, though, is whose fault it was that he was in such a state? And let us not go back to 1690, nor even 1969 - just to the beginning of this year.

It seems to me that, in the short run, the finger must point inexorably at the IRA and Sinn Fein. They are now, of course, whinging and lamenting, seeking for evidence of some conspiracy, and imputing the darkest motives to the RUC for not locking this officer up, but this is simply an attempt to divert the blame from where it rightfully belongs. They have been very successful hitherto, within their chosen constituency, at shuffling off all blame for retaliatory actions from Protestant extremists in response to their regular outrages – as they will no doubt be able to do in respect of the latest appalling massacre on Wednesday. They even succeed, it seems, in getting away with their solemn 'apologies' every time they contrive to blow up or shoot the wrong person within their own community. But now the chickens have come home to roost on their own doorstep, and they cannot expect a vast amount of sympathy from the rest of the country – much though our hearts may go out to the unfortunates who got caught in the line of fire, and to their families.

Having said all that, though, let me go on to infuriate all those that I haven't enraged by my remarks hitherto, by uttering a paradox, provoked by the latest abortion on the constitutional talks front. It seems to me that it should be obvious to any impartial observer that Sinn Fein, despite their ghastliness, must be included in any serious talks that are to take place on the future of Northern Ireland. It is not a question of liking or endorsing what they stand for, or of 'rewarding' them in any way (and what sort of a reward, anyhow, is being allowed to sit across a table from Dr. Ian Paisley for months on end?). It is simply a matter of recognising that they are there, as a genuine part of the grisly scenario, and they cannot be swept under the carpet. That is presumably part of what they are trying to say to us at the moment, in their own inimitable way. And I regret to say that they are quite right.

If the rest of the world confined the list of whom they would talk to, to those parties they liked or approved of, then we would never get anywhere. Indeed, it has been Israel's obstinate refusal to talk to the PLO that has hitherto held up any progress towards peace in the Middle East, and conversely the present degree of progress is very largely the result of their being prepared to bend their own rules to the extent of permitting a face-saving formula to be developed which allows the Palestinians to come to the table. Admittedly, the PLO are the representatives of the Palestinian people to an extent in which the IRA/Sinn Fein are not the representatives of the Nationalists of Northern Ireland, but this is simply a matter of degree. They do represent a significant part of the population, and they should be at the conference table. Supporting violence or renouncing violence has, unfortunately, nothing at all to do with it. Any conference in that miserable part of the world which is confined to the nice guys is simply not going to get anywhere.

And that is perhaps enough iconoclasm for one week.

Trinity's ambiguous role
March 15, 1992

As we sat on the rather uncomfortable chairs of St. Patrick's Cathedral on Friday afternoon, witnessing in those splendid and history-drenched surroundings the impressive ceremony in which honorary degrees were conferred, not only on the First Lady of the country, the first citizen of the city, and one who was until recently first citizen of the world, but also on those two great churchmen, Cardinal Cathal Daly and Archbishop Robin Eames, whom our Public Orator, John Luce, described rather nicely as the twin descendants of St. Patrick, we could not but cast our minds back to how we all got there, and what a wonder it was that we were there at all.

And it is quite a story, after all. On 13th March, 1592, Queen Elizabeth I of England, in response to a petition from the citizens of Dublin, issued a charter establishing in Dublin - or more accurately, 'close by Dublin' (*iuxta Dublinum*) – 'a College for learning, whereby knowledge and civility might be increased by the instruction of our people there'. She went on to specify the desirability of her subjects staying at home to receive a good Protestant and British education, instead of going off, as in the past, to 'foreign universities' in France, Italy or Spain 'whereby they have been infected with Popery and other ill qualities'. The new foundation was to be, called 'the College of the Holy and Undivided Trinity near Dublin', and was established, with an initial enrolment of three Fellows and three Scholars, on the site of the former monastery of All Hallows just downstream from the town – a site rendered vacant by her predecessor, Henry VIII.

The circumstances of the founding of our College are, I think, of more than antiquarian interest. They in fact explain a good deal of the College's subsequent history, and the rather ambiguous role it played in the cultural and political life of the Irish nation until quite recently. Queen Lizzie was no fool. She appreciated that if the Irish were ever to become reconciled to domination from England, their hearts and minds must be captured at an impressionable age through the medium of education. That this ambition was never fully achieved was not really her fault, so much as that of her subordinates. They, by their inordinate rapacity and savage repression, ensured that their presence would never be fully accepted by the great mass of the Irish people. Nevertheless, the College itself flourished well enough, and has now reached its 400th anniversary, in very changed circumstances, in as good a state as it has ever been. It has just last year elected its first Catholic Provost, Thomas Mitchell (though blessedly little was made of that fact at the time) and faces into its fifth century as the most popular destination for Ireland's students, of whatever persuasion.

Last Friday was hardly a time for re-opening old wounds, but the joint presence of the two archbishops with the mention of our first President, Douglas Hyde, an alumnus of the College, as is our seventh, Mary Robinson, conjured up a ridiculous scene in my mind. On July 14, 1949, at the funeral of Hyde in this very Cathedral, the government of the day, led by John A. Costello, huddled outside waiting for the coffin to emerge, unable to take part in the service for ideological reasons. Such an image, so redolent of the attitudes of those days, in turn directed one's thoughts to the notorious ban, imposed by Archbishop John Charles McQuaid all the way up to 1970, which effectively kept Trinity out of the main stream of Irish higher education. Dr. McQuaid was, of course, bothered just as much by the liberal ethic of Trinity as by its Protestant tradition, and it is good to reflect that it is that liberal ethic that has on balance triumphed, to the benefit of our society as a whole.

Trinity is now bulging at the seams, with a huge increase in student numbers, from some 2,000 in 1970, to around 6,000 in 1980, to over 9,000 today. Despite constant budgetary pressures, new buildings are springing up, new programmes are being started (while old traditions are being maintained), and an atmosphere of both scholarship and innovation flourishes. I don't know if Queen Elizabeth would entirely like what she would see now, but she undeniably started something positive way back then.

How black is the black economy?
April 12, 1992

Dear Taoiseach,

An open letter is a curious art form, a little like a prayer, but I'm sure that you will realise that there is nothing personal in this. It is just that you are notionally in a position to make something happen in this area, and so we address our humble prayers to you. I must say that your open and participatory approach to government is a most pleasant and salutary development, and long may it continue! In connection with tackling the scourge of unemployment, it is plainly the sensible and profitable way to go, if only because there is absolutely no party political credit to be gained by anyone in this area, since all have failed equally, and no one has any solution worth a damn. So the smart thing is to get everyone involved in the discussion.

Having conceded the principle of a Jobs Forum, however, it seems foolish to let the opposition parties off the hook by appearing to downgrade the event to a mere Oireachtas Committee, however sensible that might be from the cost point of view, and thus giving them the excuse for pulling out. We certainly don't need another £8,000,000 Mad Hatter's Tea Party like the Goodman Tribunal, just to tell us at the end of the day that we're a hopeless case, and please pay the bill in the office on the way out, but we do need something rather more exciting than an Oireachtas Committee.

No, quite right to keep the lawyers and the accountants out of it! But surely not also the trades unions, the employers and the unemployed themselves – and perhaps even representatives of emigrants' groups? We surely do need a forum, perhaps chaired by a respected public figure who doesn't cost £1,700 a day (the President herself might not be a bad choice), which would be given maximum publicity in the national media, and provoke intensive national debate, not only on specific ideas for creating jobs, but on the wider theoretical questions of the future of the 9-5, 40-hour a week model of job in general, and the notion of 'unemployment' that goes along with that. A lot of garbage will inevitably be talked – the sort of stuff that one is hearing a good deal of these days on Gay Byrne's morning show, as that worthy man conducts his own jobs forum – but we must allow it to be talked, just in order that these many intellectual wind-eggs may be exposed for what they are. All one can hope is that in the process some light may be thrown on the true nature of the problem, and that some sparks of originality may be struck.

I don't propose here to bore you with my views on every aspect of the question, of which I have many, except to say, oracularly, that as long as you persist in chasing the will o' the wisp of full employment in terms of regular 9–5 jobs you will never get anywhere – that model of job is a child of the Industrial Revolution, and is now rapidly becoming obsolete. I just want to concentrate on one topic which particularly interests me, and that is the so-called 'black economy'. The hundreds of millions of pounds allegedly lost to the exchequer through the operations of the 'black economy' is one of the old chestnuts of the unemployment debate which seems to me to symbolise as clearly as anything the wrong thinking that is bedevilling this whole issue. Accurate figures in this area are hard to come by, for obvious reasons, but my economist friends are largely in agreement that earnings in the black economy may amount to up to 15 per cent of the Gross Domestic Product, or approximately £2.5 billion a year.

A figure such as this is guaranteed to set revenue commissioners, trade union leaders and PAYE taxpayers foaming at the mouth, at the thought of what could be done with the tax on all that lovely money, but I want to suggest to them that their indignation is quite misplaced In fact, we should be thanking God for the black economy. If you look at those figures another way, that £2.5. billion (if we reckon on about 20 per cent of this as being paid in wages) translates into the equivalent of 50-60,000 jobs at £200 a week each, which is probably all that is in fact standing between this society and serious social unrest, if not bloody revolution.

The fact is – and let us be frank about it, Taoiseach – that by no means all of those 279,200 'unfortunates' now 'languishing' on the dole are really full-time languishers. In reality, an indeterminate, but not insignificant, number of them are supplementing their income creatively by doing jobs that would otherwise not be done, such as small household repairs, minor construction work, car repairs, gardening and so on. We all know this, I think, and most of us know someone – perhaps have even been helped out by someone – who is in this position. And, instead of agonising about all those imaginary millions in tax that are being lost, I say we should wish them the best of luck. They are simply trying to make sense of a crazy economic system, and are succeeding in some small measure. The main thing to bear in mind is that no tax is being lost to the exchequer, simply because if any attempt were made to collect tax on these earnings, the activity concerned would simply cease, no money would be earned at all, and hence no tax would be payable.

To take one example, who among us could afford to employ a gardener, if we had to pay his PRSI, and he had to pay income tax on his earnings? Mr Smurfit, perhaps, or Mr Tony Ryan, or even yourself, but not me, certainly. In fact, however, many people do manage to employ a gardener for one day a week or so, and to pay him an honorarium which is acceptable when taken in conjunction with a basic dividend from the State, which is what the dole should be regarded as being. It is the way that a whole range of necessary things are done, and decent, industrious people are enabled to put a little something extra on their table for their children. What you should be thinking about is some way of legitimising this activity, while making total inactivity less attractive than it is now. At present we have, because of the operation of outmoded notions of the dichotomy between 'employment' and 'unemployment', the worst of both worlds, where unemployment benefits are in serious competition with many of the lower-paid jobs available, and any attempt to supplement the basic 'dole' with part-time work is penalised to the extent of being rendered impracticable on any legal terms.

The idea of the minimum basic wage for all, as a sort of dividend owing to each citizen, is the formula that I would favour, but I am open to alternative suggestions from authorities more competent than myself. And that is just the sort of thing I would expect to see discussed at a properly constituted Jobs Forum.

Sincerely yours,
John Dillon

The Maastricht morass

May 3, 1992

The campaign for ratification of the Maastricht Treaty has now been well and truly launched, with a clarion call and dire warnings from the Taoiseach and most of the cabinet, and it is plain that the task facing anyone who ventures to raise difficulties about it is going to be a tough one. And yet it seems to me that certain doubts do need to be aired, if only to prevent excessive euphoria about the alleged £6 billion coming our way, and other less tangible benefits that are predicted to flow from ratification.

What concerns me is what I would have thought would be the main issue – the economic aspect, though it seems to be the most difficult for the public to focus on. There are many things to worry about here but let me air just one for the moment. Are you aware that one of the main provisions of the treaty is that we in this country are to bring our ratio of National Debt to Gross Domestic Product down from 100 per cent at present to 60 per cent by 1999, if we are to qualify to join in the unified currency system? This is not just a difficult or challenging goal; it is downright impossible, by any means consistent with democracy. First of all, we would have to stop borrowing *now* – cold turkey! (In fact the current budget projection for borrowing this year is £400 million). Then we would have to embark on a steady series of annual cuts in the debt ratio, from now to the end of the century, of 5.5 per cent. For those to whom figures like this do not mean very much, let me point out that this year's budget hopes to reduce the ratio by 2.4 per cent – and the effects of even that much of a cut are something that we are not going to enjoy. All this, mind you, is planned to take place while the elimination of all tariff and other barriers will be progressively sucking the life out of what remains of our indigenous industries, and pushing our unemployment figures well past the 300,000 mark. The much-vaunted £6 billion which we are to receive, even if it is not a mirage, is not going to save our industries, but will go into beautifying us as a suitable place for Europeans to relax in.

Now I know that in reciting these gloomy facts I become liable to the reasonable riposte, 'So what do you suggest?' What choice, in fact, have we got? After all, it is almost equally absurd that we should go on forever owing around 100 per cent of our Gross Domestic Product. I am not sure that I can answer that question with any confidence, and that is certainly a weakness of the case against Maastricht. My instinct, I must confess, as a non-economist, is to advocate that we should not even attempt to pay back this debt, which now amounts to more than £26 billion – about £7,500 for every man, woman and child in the country. Instead, we should cast about for ways to liberate ourselves from it – or at least from that portion of it which we owe to foreign lenders, which I understand is in the region of £9 billion (owing money to ourselves is somehow less offensive).

That doesn't sound like a very nice thing to do, nor indeed a very effective one, since, if we tried anything like that on our own, the world's bankers would come down on us like a ton of bricks. However, I think that something like this is at last about to happen fairly widely throughout the Third World – and let us not flatter ourselves, we are at least honorary members of the Third World, despite our pretensions to belong to the rich nations' club. After a decade or so of prevaricating, it does at last seem as if such really big debtors as Brazil, Mexico, Argentina, the Philippines, and the Congo are going to pull themselves together and start calling the shots to the bankers. It will be hard for the bankers to intimidate them much longer, after all. They have really very little more to lose. What they must do is what the Irish peasantry did to the landlords over a hundred years ago, in the days of the Land League. not refuse to pay anything, but offer some modest payment that they can afford, and when this is refused – if it is – to withhold all payments, and make contributions instead to a common fighting fund, in order to hold the banks to ransom. And that is something which they could probably succeed in doing – on the sound principle that if you owe your bank manager £1000, you're in trouble, but if you owe him £1 million, he's in trouble.

If such a league of the oppressed is formed, we should not be too proud to join it. We are just as surely victims of the machinations of the world money-lending system as any of the nations above mentioned. Only by concerted action of this sort are we ever going to extricate ourselves from this situation. As to the morality of such a move, I really have no qualms. The old Jewish custom of the jubilee year, with its cancellation of debts, has much to commend it. Other than that rather apocalyptic suggestion, though, I have at present no alternatives to the grim scenario being prepared for us – except, perhaps, to make ourselves into an off-shore tax-haven, a sort of European Hong Kong, to take over from the real Hong Kong!

The Bishop and the Lady:
where did the money come from?
May 10, 1992

Well, talk about a smoking gun! Ms. Annie Murphy seems to have been on a fairly long fuse, but she has finally gone off with stunning effect. As our hearts go out to Bishop Eamonn Casey this weekend, the minds of nasty-minded commentators like myself also inevitably turn to the more disquieting implications of this drama. All this, we must remind ourselves, is very much in the realm of speculation, since (at least as I write) nothing has been said about the details of the matter by either Bishop Casey himself or by the Irish Hierarchy. But that said, let me proceed to speculate. I am not particularly concerned with the moral aspects of this incident; I am primarily intrigued, as are so many others of my acquaintance, with the financial aspects. The monthly payments of $175 a month which Ms. Murphy acknowledges as having been paid over the last 17 years are not, indeed, princely, and well within the episcopal budget, but with the payment of $115,000 in 1990, and the offer of a further $150,000 this year, we are into fairly big bucks.

So the question more or less asks itself – out of whose hide was this to come? It seems to me that there are just three possibilities, two obvious but implausible, one not so obvious, but ultimately more plausible. The first two alternatives are of course (1) Trocaire, of which Bishop Casey has been the mainstay since its inception, and (2) the diocesan funds of Kerry. I think, however, that there are good reasons for discounting both of these possibilities. First of all, Bishop Casey, whatever his indiscretions, is an eminently decent man, and it is unthinkable that he would consider diverting even a pound from the starving masses of the Third World, for such a purpose. Furthermore, we have the assurance of the director of Trocaire that all money donated to it is publicly accounted for, and that there is no way that the bishop could get his hands on it, even if he wanted to. And as I have said, I do not believe that he would have. The diocesan funds might be an easier proposition, but again, Bishop Casey is too decent a man to contemplate such an act. And anyway, for diocesan funds, accounting procedures exist, which would make such activity dangerous, if not impossible.

So, if not these obvious sources of funds in such quantity, then what? The bishop is not, after all, a man of vast private means. No, I can see only one other possibility. Either the Irish Hierarchy as a whole, or, more probably, the Vatican itself, was prepared to bankroll the bishop in this emergency. Now this, just to anticipate my critics (including the Hierarchy itself), is a totally unsupported allegation, and in the nature of things, very difficult to confirm. But one is entitled to ask the question, if sums such as those mentioned are in fact involved, where else can they have come from?

If indeed they have emanated from this source, then interesting consequences follow. We would have to conclude that the Vatican actually knew of this situation for at least the last few years, and was prepared to cover it up, even at considerable cost, to avoid a scandal, and because Bishop Casey is undeniably a valuable man. But if the Vatican is involved, will we ever get to the bottom of this? Ms Murphy has talked of her ambitions to write a book about the whole affair, possibly in novelistic form. An excellent idea! Indeed, if one wanted to go the whole hog, and make a Sidney Sheldon thriller out of it, one could postulate a scenario in which the CIA, for whom, as we know, Eamonn Casey has long been a serious annoyance by reason of his interest in Central America, is rubbing its hands with glee at the present plight of their old enemy.

But I had better stop here, before I go over the top altogether.

A rumour machine lubricated by clerical errors

May 17, 1992

Not for the first time in the last nine months, I am moved to remark that a strange mood is abroad in the land. Once again, the hills and dales are alive with the sound of rumour. Last autumn it was latest deal of CJ and his friends, all the way down to the Pipe at Kinsealy and the Windmill on Inishvickillaun. More recently, there was a brief flurry about further abortion injunctions pending. And now, Lord save us, it is the indiscretions of bishops. A seismic upheaval has passed through the country since last weekend, sending ripples steadily wider and wider. Now that the tribulations of Bishop Eamonn have more or less become old hat (What is to be done with the poor man, by the way? He really can't just go on the missions in the present circumstances, I think. Perhaps room could be found for him on the board of an international company, where his many talents could find a suitable outlet?), a whole new crop of similar scandals is threatening to pop up like mushrooms.

One complete copy-cat case has already hit the headlines, that of Fr Sean Tucker and Mrs Gill Devlin, but that is just the tip of the iceberg, it would seem. It is really very like the moving statues of some years back. More or less every parish in Ireland now seems to have a fornicating clergyman in it, well known to all and sundry. The ladies concerned in the various cases are said to be threatening to found a trades union (all those interested, it seems, should get in touch with that enterprising man, Fr Pat Buckley, in Larne). The newsrooms of the major newspapers are awash with unconfirmed accounts of clerical errors.

It is almost as if all this was lurking just below the surface of the national consciousness for years, and the shock has brought it to the surface. Now everybody wants a scandal in their own parish, even as they once wanted a moving statue or an apparition of the Virgin. It is not quite the same, of course. One cannot really hope to set up a shrine outside the house of the clergyman concerned, with non-stop recitation of the rosary, and watch for apparitions of his mot. A scandal is not a tourist attraction in the same way as a moving statue. But it is plainly deeply satisfying nonetheless.

Perhaps this interminable postal strike has had something to do with it, but it seems to me that we are regressing into the state of mind of an earlier era, where gossip and rumour formed the staple means of spreading the news. It was in such circumstances that miracles and other marvels flourished – always occurring, however, in some neighbouring district (over the mountain, in the next valley), never in one's own. Wild-eyed, whiskery, travel-stained men would tell the tale to an open-mouthed audience at the weekly fair, and the story would be round the parish in no time.

So it seems to be now, even in this age of high technology media. I have heard some pretty strange tales myself, and I would generally be the last to hear anything interesting. The strangest aspect of some of the stories I have heard is the alleged involvement of *prominent* figures from politics and/or industry (and I mean prominent – think of just three of each, and you'll probably get it!) in helping out the clerics concerned. This was allegedly done either by coughing up large sums of money to pay off the ladies in the case, or even by going so far as to provide the keys to luxury apartments where assignations can take place discreetly. One clergyman, for instance, was said to have been spirited abroad after having been facilitated for some time in carrying on a torrid affair in the luxurious surroundings of a certain very well-known club. I will say no more. And, of course, now we hear that *everybody* knew about everything all along – certainly everybody in Kerry! This is the very stuff of mythology (though the ease with which Bishop Eamonn was able, at short notice, to lay his hands on £70,000 plus interest will have fuelled such fantasies), and anthropologically very interesting.

These stories bring together the heroes of our former set of scandals in ingenious ways with this new, previously unthinkable subject of scandal, in a most fruitful and productive mix. It satisfies some deep feeling we all have, that nothing is as it seems, and we are being ripped off and hoodwinked by everyone in authority, political, financial or ecclesiastical. The public world's a stage, and all the men and women merely players. No doubt in the coming weeks most of these ladies will subside, even as most of the moving statues on closer inspection refused to move, but not I trust, before doing a little more to brighten up for us the dreary time between now and the Maastricht Referendum.

Churchill and the purity of the race
July 5, 1992

Well, one would have thought that we had by now received all the revelations that were likely to be vouchsafed to us about that old cod Winston Churchill, but it now seems that we had not. We have long since been apprised of his many personal failings, his military incompetence, his political misjudgements, and so on, to the point where one began to revolt, and to protest, against the rat-pack of sensationalist biographers, that after all he was a Great Man, and his peccadilloes must be placed in proportion. None of us is perfect, after all, not even the most self-righteous of revisionist historians.

However, just as the dust was beginning to settle on the old boy, there comes along Mr Clive Ponting (he of Official Secrets fame – he blew the whistle on the Belgrano outrage, if you recall, during the Falklands War), who is about to publish a new biography of Churchill, and he sets the cat among the pigeons again. Basing himself on papers recently released from the Home Office – papers of so sensitive a nature that they were originally embargoed for a full century – Mr Ponting has produced a remarkable story. It is all, admittedly, pretty ancient history, concerning as it does primarily the years 1910-11, when Churchill, in his mid-thirties, was Home Secretary in the Liberal Government of the time, but it is interesting nonetheless.

To appreciate the situation properly, however, one needs to go back a bit before that. There had been, it seems, a good deal of thought given, in British imperialist circles (as in German and French ones) around the turn of the century, to the preservation, and indeed to the promotion, of racial purity. This was a dotty, and ultimately very sinister, product of late Victorian rationalism, which observed that throughout the animal kingdom the survival of the fittest was the prevailing norm, weak and imperfect specimens being consigned to oblivion (left to die, killed, or even eaten), and even within the range of normal specimens, the privilege of breeding was generally secured by the most powerful, and therefore most perfect, male in the group.

Only among human beings (and amongst the more advanced races of humans), it was pointed out, did these rules no longer apply. Imperfect specimens were foolishly kept alive, and breeding was open indiscriminately to anyone who could persuade a member of the opposite sex to climb into bed with them, irrespective of their genetic suitability. But, argued various earnest persons, should these things not be better regulated, especially amongst those who aspired to rule the world? Indeed, a Royal Commission was set up in 1904 to study the 'Care and Control of the Feeble-Minded' – a broad term, which comprised not only thorough-going imbeciles, but 'the less well-educated, the less intelligent, and those not socially well-adjusted.'

The report of this commission was submitted to the cabinet of which Churchill was a member in 1908, and in due course he read it through. He became wildly excited by it, as often happened when a new idea was presented to him, and when he became Home Secretary in 1910, he turned all his energies to bringing its provisions into law. In fact, he went a good deal farther with these ideas (which, must be said, are actually as old as Plato's *Republic*) than was congenial to most of his colleagues, or to his civil servants, who adopted a very prudent 'Yes, Minister' approach to their volatile chief, and ultimately frustrated his efforts. He had plans both for compulsory sterilisation of mental defectives and deviants, and for the arrest and removal to labour camps of 'tramps and wastrels', and the congenitally unemployable – in both cases to prevent them from propagating their kind, since he was persuaded of the largely hereditary nature of these conditions. Whether wastrels and deviants who were members of the upper class were to be exempted from these provisions is not clear on the evidence, but one presumes that they were.

Now this, as I have said, is all pretty ancient history, and nothing much came of it in the end, so one should not, perhaps, make too much of it, but it's worth, I think, noting the irony that Churchill is here seen as anticipating the views of two other great social theorists of the 20th century, Adolf Hitler and Josef Stalin, both of whom he came later cordially to disapprove of. Hitler, of course, was concerned about Jews as well, but basically he was exercised about the purity of the Aryan race, and in that connection actively pursued the sterilisation and even total elimination of inferior specimens of all sorts, while in Stalin's

Russia any tendency to vagabondage or unemployability got you very quickly consigned to a labour camp, along with all other kinds of social deviants, such as poets and professors of Classics.

So there it is. There is no end, it seems to the ironies of history. Has this episode, though, any current relevance? One lesson one might derive from it, perhaps, is that ideas of this sort were once eminently respectable, and might very well become so again, if social conditions become much worse. It provides an interesting solution to the problem of the long-term unemployed, which is a question exercising our policy-makers a good deal at the present. As for Churchill, he went rather overboard on these ideas at the time, but then what can one expect? He had a very unbalanced father, and the Marlboroughs always were social deviants.

Help our emigrants go
August 9, 1992

It was encouraging recently, just as the Congress of the Wise broke up for its period of summer meditation, to see a first report emanating from the controversial Jobs Committee, presided over by Professor Brian Hillery, that actually provides some food for thought. It may be that Fine Gael are going to end up looking rather foolish owing to their boycott of this entity, but that time, I think, is not yet. We must wait and see whether any of its recommendations, many of them admirable, will have the slightest attention paid to them by the Government (which was what John Bruton profoundly doubted).

However, I am not here concerned with their recommendations, which have been mulled over adequately elsewhere. I was particularly interested, and heartened, by a piece of common sense which they uttered about the ancient problem of emigration – though I am also surprised that they were not given the usual dog's abuse for it. I can only conclude that the usual dog's abusers were on their holidays abroad. What they said, in conclusion, if I recall correctly, was that really no set of solutions that they could propose was going to make much of a dent in the current unemployment figures. The majority of our young people must resolve to look abroad to the rest of Europe if they are seriously interested in gainful employment, and the Government should give them every assistance in doing this.

Of course they are not the first to make this obvious point – indeed dear old Brian Lenihan made it some years ago in Boston, when he was Foreign Minister, and got dog's abuse for it then from a wide range of sanctimonious hypocrites – but it was helpful that they should make it again now, and in this very strategic context. It is, of course, the merest common sense, and the Government should lose no time in acting upon it, even if they drag their feet on all the other recommendations.

What is called for, really, is a series of Government-sponsored employment advice bureaux, both in this country and abroad (attached to our embassies), which would point our young people in the direction of jobs in Europe and provide advice as to how best to go about applying for them. Above all, we need a change of perspective in this area. The image of the emigrant ship, with the sorrowing relatives on the quayside (accompanied, ideally, by 'the girl I left behind me'), and the brave lad with all his possessions in a single battered suitcase, and a shilling or a dime in his pocket, while not, I suppose entirely obsolete, is largely irrelevant to contemporary reality.

Seeking work in Paris, or Frankfurt, or Amsterdam, or Milan, especially in post-1992 Europe, should have no greater emotive connotations to it for young Irish people than would the spectacle of a young lad leaving a small town in Iowa or Minnesota to seek his fortune in Chicago, New York or Los Angeles. There is the language problem, of course, but that is a challenge that can be overcome – once again with well-directed help from the Government. Of course it would be nice if every region, or erstwhile nation, of Europe could provide satisfactory employment for all its citizens, but that is not the situation, and we might as well cop ourselves on. In fact, rather than setting up jobs forums, we would be better employed performing novenas for the economic recovery of Europe. If that should ever come about, our unemployment crisis would resolve itself very quickly, but that is not to say that the Government should not be making plans now to capitalise on that.

In this connection (and perhaps a holiday period is not a bad time to raise the question, since a large consignment of loved ones might be taking the opportunity for a brief trip home), I would like to advert to the proposal of Votes for Emigrants. This is a sort of 'motherhood and apple-pie' issue that has been widely touted by woolly-minded or disingenuous persons, and many who should know better, including many politicians, have been very hesitant about opposing the idea, though being, we may note, less than enthusiastic about acting on it.

Now I think it should be fairly obvious that, much as we might love and honour our emigrés (putting candles in our windows for them, and so on), any scheme that enabled them to vote in home elections would be grossly inappropriate, and open to all sorts of abuses. I know that countries like the US allow American citizens abroad to vote in Presidential elections (and in State and local elections, if they still have a local address), but they are dealing with an almost insignificantly small proportion of the total voting public.

In our case it would not, alas, be so. There is as many Irish in London alone, as we know, as there are left in the whole of Ireland, with Manchester, Birmingham. Glasgow, Boston, Chicago and New York not far behind. Even if you limited the vote to first-generation emigrants, such voters, if properly organised (and we may, be sure that there would be those who would employ traditional Irish political skills to organise them), could effectively determine the result in many constituencies in the country. Some disaffected persons might regard that as a good thing, but in fact it would be a gross absurdity – a sort of 'graveyard vote', such as in the past has elected many a Soldier of Destiny – for elections to be determined by people who no longer have any stake in the country, who pay no taxes, and do not have to accept the consequences of their actions. Strong influxes of votes from Boston or Birmingham, for example, might ensure the return of a half-dozen Sinn Fein candidates in various Border (or even Dublin) constituencies, who might in turn hold the balance of power in a very fragmented government, even as religious extremists tend to do in Israel. There are all sorts of interesting possibilities.

But I may well be flogging a dead donkey here. It is an amusing subject for the silly season, but I do not really believe that any substantial body of politicians are contemplating giving emigrants the vote – except perhaps for presidential elections! That I think I would be prepared to support. We might end up next time with someone even more interesting than Mary Robinson.

Justice for the rich and the poor
September 13, 1992

It is just a year ago this month, I was reflecting recently, that the great season of Irish scandals began, for our entertainment and edification. It seems longer, so great and varied a succession of them did we have.

There was Larry Goodman and the beef (still happily with us). And then there were the goings-on in and around Greencore (Chris Comerford – remember him?). And then there was Dermot Desmond and Michael Smurfit and Telecom and the Johnston Mooney site and the Financial Services Centre and lots of little offshore companies with catchy titles like Bacchantes and Fellatio, and elusive gentlemen with funny names based in the Isle of Man or Cyprus. And then there was Charlie's Pipe and Charlie's Windmill, and finally the Fall of Charlie himself.

And then there was the Bishop and the Lady, and the Diocesan Funds. It is clear that if one has friends like Bishop Eamonn has, one may even come out of one's misfortune with not only unconditional absolution, but a small profit, especially if this great idea of having a whip-around among the clergy of Ireland for £100 a skull works out (there seem to be a few curmudgeons who are baulking at it, but not many). It is heartwarming, indeed, to think that we are all, in our small way, contributing to his Reverence's legal expenses, through the medium of the Sunday collection!

Now of course one wishes none of these gentlemen any ill, but I was made to think of them all, as I say, by this little news item. An unfortunate couple in Coolock, it seems, James and Alice McGrath, were condemned to a week in Mountjoy early last week for non-payment of arrears of £331 owed to Allied Irish Finance. They had incautiously invested in some kitchen renovations, which were being flogged at a stall in their local shopping centre (you know the sort of thing: "Easy monthly repayments!" "Pay nothing now!" "This lovely kitchen unit could be yours for a mere 14p an hour!"), and now they had fallen hopelessly into arrears. One cannot defend their action, of

133

course. They have committed a heinous offence against the Free Market system, and are depriving Allied Irish Banks (which as we all know is struggling hard to make ends meet in these difficult times) of a sum almost equal to that which any of the great men mentioned above might spend in Patrick Guilbaud's of an evening (with perhaps a visit to a boite on Leeson Street to follow). No doubt Allied Irish Finance exhausted all other methods of persuasion to recover their debt. Quite right, therefore, to send them to jail (though the irony of it is that a week in the 'Joy actually costs almost four times what they were in there for – around £1,200, I understand, per person sharing)!

The McGraths have seven children, the youngest of whom is four, but I'm sure the neighbours were very good, or perhaps the unmarried sister was able to step in to mind the little ones, and get them off to school. Coolock is Roddy Doyle country, of course, and I could not help thinking of Jimmy Rabbitte Sr. and Veronica, and how they might react to this humiliating situation. In fact, though, they would be too canny by half to fall for the blandishments of a kitchen renovations stall. But I wouldn't be too sure about Bimbo and the missus, nor many another on that road. And no doubt there are, in real life, many more couples in Coolock in very similar circumstances. There's one born every minute, as they say, and Allied Irish Finance is there to serve them from Monday to Friday, offering very attractive terms.

So what may we conclude from all this? It is one of the oldest clichés in the book that there is one law for the rich and another for the poor. It is good to see these hoary old bits of wisdom illustrated in real life from time to time, or one might cease to believe in them. The couple in Coolock thought too small, and they were quite properly crushed like beetles. If they could have somehow put together a package of borrowing totaling a couple of million, they would have earned our respect, and that of the Bench. A receiver would have to be called in, and proceedings could have continued for years, to the great advantage of accountants and lawyers. But as it was, there was nothing in it for anybody, and the wretches were packed off to jail in half an hour or less.

In fact, we are glad to note they spent only two nights enjoying the hospitality of the State, but the thesis I am advancing is nonetheless valid for that, I think.

What is all this stuff about 'life'?
October 25, 1992

I should have the sense to keep my mouth shut. Look at the bishops! A sensible body of men if ever there was one. Their reverences came out of their bull-session in Maynooth last Wednesday declaring that they were deferring any statement on the proposed Amendment to the Amendment 'because of the complexity of the issues.'

Well, good on them! 'The complexity of the issues!' The issues usen't to be complex when viewed from that quarter, so far as I am aware. They were very simple: there must be no interference with the natural processes of conception and birth for any reason. This perception of 'complexity' is a definite sign of progress. So why can't I too maintain a prudent silence in face of this complexity? Well, I didn't get where I am today by maintaining a prudent silence, I suppose. In fact, the rising tidal wave of nonsense, clap-trap and obfuscation is simply becoming too much for me. I have to put the oar in.

Can it be that Albert has wrong-footed us all? He has managed to produce a form of words that has hard-core SPUCkers and liberals united in opposition to it, while a sufficient mass (48 per cent at the latest count, but it will probably increase) of somewhat confused but basically decent people, together with a bloc of faithful Fianna Fail supporters, are prepared to vote for it as the best possible outcome to a bad job. And even if the wretched thing doesn't pass, it is no matter, because there will be legislation which will embody even more concessions. So no wonder their Lordships are afflicted with a sense of complexity.

My only recourse in face of all the nonsense is to try once again to return to first principles. I did this once before in these columns, and received only a few confused messages from people who were convinced that I was possessed by the Devil, but promised to pray for me (prayers which, I fear, have not been granted). Let me see if we can do any better this time. Hands up out there, I said last time, all those who think that an embryo is possessed from the moment of conception by an immortal soul, which has an individual destiny for all eternity, and which will be gravely inconvenienced (even if Limbo has been abolished!) if it is cut off before birth, or denied the inestimable joys of human existence.

I imagine that there are quite a few readers of this newspaper who do believe that proposition, but there has been remarkably little emphasis laid upon it by supporters of the absolute ban on abortion. There is a good reason for this, of course. It is a proposition that does not commend itself nowadays to an increasing number of people, even in this country, and to assert it would immediately bring the response that a dubious and sectarian theological dogma was being foisted on what is meant to be a non-sectarian, secular state. So instead of that, what we hear are expressions of support for Life In General, and of a determination to resist a threat to the life of 'the unborn'. But what is all this stuff about 'life'? Are Billy Binchy and Des Hanafin and their friends Buddhists, who would not squash a wasp if it got into their marmalade? Or what sort of life are we talking about?

Human life, of course, they reply indignantly, what else? This brings us back to the real issue. Is a potential human life to be taken as being on the same level as an actual human life? That is the question. To take an analogy, let us assume that it is illegal to cut down oak trees in a certain wood. An acorn is a potential oak tree. If left lying where it falls, it will very likely grow into an oak. Is it therefore illegal to gather acorns in the wood? Obviously not – unless, of course, there is another ordinance prohibiting the gathering of acorns! But, if we are not talking about immortal souls here, what is so portentous about a potential human being? At most, such an entity can have potential human rights, which is not going to get it very far. To portray an embryo as somehow a very little baby is a product of the sort of muddled thinking by which we are currently bedevilled.

But in fact I am inclined to doubt whether most of the SPUC people (I will not dignify them with the title 'pro-life') really believe that there is a little person there at all, despite their rhetoric. The curious noun 'the unborn' seems to express the uncertainty at least of those who invented it. If they really believed that there was murder going on every time a pregnancy was terminated, they would not be going along with any of this stuff about 'due regard for the life of the mother' and so on. After all, if a mother's health or life is somehow threatened by the continuing

136

existence of her born child, we do not for a moment condone the idea that the child should be put down. That is just tough luck on the mother.

So abortion is not quite murder, after all, and an embryo is not quite a little baby. In which case, what on earth are we arguing about?

Can we pump fresh heir into this vacuum?

December 6, 1992

Well, the nation waits with bated breath, to see what its fate is to be. What combination of new masters are we to have? And what on earth are they going to do in face of the problems that beset us? We should not neglect, at times like this, to observe how important it is to have a leader, and preferably a leader who can command some respect, however grudging. One may say what one likes about Mrs T and Ronnie and even CJ, but in their prime, at least, they radiated leadership. All we have at the moment is a howling vacuum. There is no lack of advice for our prospective leaders emanating currently from well-meaning persons. The only problem is that it tends to be contradictory.

There are well-respected experts, for example, who tell us that we must certainly devalue, and then there are others, equally substantial, who tell us that that would be a complete disaster. We are urged to raise taxes, and on the other hand to lower them; to raise social welfare payments, and to try and get the PRSI system to pay for itself; to sell off state assets, and to increase state involvement in such assets as Aer Lingus.

In the face of all this, it is hardly to be wondered at that the negotiations to form a new government are taking on a remarkable complexity. In this connection, I was guilty last week of speaking rather disrespectfully of the Labour Party, even quoting against them Sean Lemass's dismissive characterisation of so long ago. "A harmless, decent body of men," indeed! They are actually far from that now. For one thing, a good many of them are women. For another, there is now a fairly substantial group of vigorous young members who would maintain discernibly radical views, and who are certainly in no mood to be taken for granted by Fine Gael or the PDs. Such stalwarts as Emmet Stagg and Michael D. Higgins are no longer alone.

In the face of this development, resulting from Labour's great triumph at the polls, I'm afraid that John Bruton's approach to forming a government can only be described as obtuse. He has been airily

138

planning 'rainbow coalitions' without regard for the intentions of the other prospective partners - apparently oblivious to the fact that he himself has suffered a rout. In view of this, it is hardly surprising that Mr Spring should want to teach him a lesson in etiquette. If he wants to form a government, he must approach Mr Spring in a much humbler frame of mind. Presumably that is part of the message being conveyed by all this intimate manoeuvring with the Democratic Left. There is no reason to doubt, in fact, that many members of the Labour Party are perfectly sincere in their desire to be allied with DL - if only out of a disinclination to leave them out there sniping at them from left field while they flounder around in government, wrestling with intractable economic problems. But overall, these negotiations must surely be regarded as only opening moves in a larger game of chess, the aim of which may rather be to force the two halves of (the original) Sinn Fein party back together – and to remain comfortably in opposition for the moment. No, only the irresistible yearning for the Mercedes could induce any person of leftish persuasions into government at the moment. And so the nation is left on tenterhooks, waiting for a leader to emerge.

Perhaps, after all, we should just allow Albert to carry on. Poetic justice, after all, demands that Bertie Ahern be left to introduce the next budget. It's going to be a lulu.

Over that rainbow

December 27, 1992

Negotiations, we hear, have been going very well between the prospective partners in Government, and a little break over the Christmas constitutes an ideal opportunity to digest each other's proposals and positions, with a view to going hard at it again next week. As the visions of Mercedes fade in the minds of the erstwhile rainbow partners, let me try to console them by suggesting that they are not really missing much. Being in office in partnership with the Labour Party in adverse times is never easy, and, whatever about the £8 billion down the road, the immediate future is pretty much fated to be adverse in the extreme.

Bertie's next Budget (or will they make Michael D. Minister for Finance instead?) has got to take account of a set of preposterous wage increases for public servants under the PESP (postponed from late last year, but still quite unjustifiable), together with the reality of social welfare payments (no doubt to be increased, in deference to Labour's wishes) for nearly 300,000 souls.

At the same time, it will be striving to meet the draconian targets for reduction of the national Borrowing Requirement laid down by the Maastricht regulations. To let Fianna Fail off the hook at this stage would be grossly foolish and unprofitable on the part of the opposition parties. Knowing the normal performance of the Soldiers of Destiny in opposition, they would have any wretched 'Rainbow Coalition' that managed to come together in rags and tatters before spring by virtue of unscrupulous and indiscriminate attacks on every measure taken, with Labour in particular beginning to run for cover. As it is, they are left to carry the can, and a fine can of worms it will prove to be.

But what of the Labour Party? Much attention has reasonably been focussed by commentators in the last week or so on the contradictions of the position into which Dick Spring has manoeuvred himself. Whatever the voters of the nation had in mind in voting for Labour in such numbers (it is not necessary to suppose that they had anything very positive in mind, but they certainly had various negative purposes), it was certainly not to retain Mr Reynolds and his Soldiers in power, and that is what Mr Spring and his Bright Young Things have decided to do. They will certainly live to regret this, but it is reasonable to ask, what was the poor man to do? The Labour Party has been afflicted by the perils and problems of success – what to do with one's windfall of thirty-three seats? It seemed that one could not just sit on them. One had to hawk them around somewhere, and secure the best bargain one could in terms of Mercs and perks.

But not so. The only thing both principled and truly profitable for Labour to have done was to have sat firmly on their hands, resisted all blandishments from the capitalist parties (and moralistic jawings and abuse from the Meedja), and left it to FF and FG to form the Grand Alliance that both of them so abhor. It would have been quite easy, really. All one does is to let each of the two of them propose their own candidate for Taoiseach, and vote against both of them. One could propose one's own candidate for form's sake, but even that is hardly necessary. Then one sits back and lets the dust settle for a while. There would, of course, be hell to pay from the political pundits and editorial writers – a great deal about Labour's duty to help form a Government, and the dire state of the country bereft of leadership, and so on – but one simply replies that one was not necessarily elected to form a Government at all costs, and that in fact one is helping to form a Government, by putting the squeeze on the two ideologically compatible parties who could form one.

Meanwhile, the Soldiers of Destiny and the Tribes of the Irish will be explaining desperately to all who will listen how utterly incompatible they are, and how they could not possibly come together for this purpose, but the fact is that one of them has a debt of about £3 million and the other of about £1 million, and neither of them has the stomach for another, equally inconclusive election, so that, groaning and complaining, they would indeed form a government, and probably not a bad one either.

However, even if it turned out to be quite a good one, Labour would still be sitting pretty. No Mercs in the short run, but just wait till the next election! Instead, we will now have 33 tarnished angels trying to defend their decision to prop up Albert the Unspeakable until he and his Merry Men can get their hands on the £8 billion. When they achieve that, they will turn on their hapless socialist pals and dump them. They'll go back to their traditional 15 seats, if they're lucky, and serve them right.

It is a pity, for another reason, that Labour has not seen fit to take the path of principle. If FF and FG were forced back together into a single party of mildly conservative hue, one would no longer have to spend so much time explaining to bewildered friends from the rest of Europe what on earth is the distinction between our two main parties, the Soldiers of Destiny and the Tribes of the Irish.

Pushing a 'vow of poverty' a bit rich
January 17, 1993

Suddenly we, or more particularly our new rulers, are being snowed under with well-meaning advice, not unmixed with moral exhortation. The fledgling Government has responded to these voices with alacrity by appointing not only a Minister for Equality, but also a Minister for Poverty. Is it an unworthy thought to suggest that somebody, somewhere, is working towards the old-fashioned socialist idea that we should all be equal, or at least equally poor? Among those giving voice are that formidable body of men (and women), the Conference of Major Religious Superiors, the Irish Hierarchy (with their Pastoral Letter *Work is the Key*), the Combat Poverty Agency (presenting a catchy, well-produced little number called *Building a Fairer Future*), and a Dublin parish priest on *The Pat Kenny Show* during the week. All these winter warblers are usually to be heard in the run-up to Budget Time, but they are a little early this year, because of the unusual political climate.

I choose the Religious Superiors for special attention, since they were first in the field, and the others are really all singing the same tune. As usual, their proposals as to how the public finances are to be disposed are most stimulating and imaginative. Taking a vow of poverty, it seems to me, is in many ways a wonderfully liberating thing. It enables one to take a much broader approach to economic and social affairs. The fact that all the money of which one is prescribing the disposition belongs to somebody else frees one from any selfish cheese-paring or small-minded considerations when it comes to sharing it around. And this, once again, is a characteristic of the CMRS's proposals.

They start off on a distinctly combative note, with a call for the punitive taxing of speculators who profit from manipulating the currency markets. Now one would certainly like to nail and punish those sleazy, weasel-like parasites who prey upon the currencies, and thus undermine the economies, of any nation that shows any sign of weakness, but even here the CMRS might run into unexpected problems.

143

For many of these evil persons are none other than our eminently respectable building societies and pension funds, who are simply engaged in trying to safeguard the investments of their clients - who will certainly include, along with the rest of us, not a few Major Religious Superiors! So even that might turn out to be a little awkward. But this is not really the main thrust of their submission. We next get the usual call uttered by good-hearted but muddle-headed persons everywhere both for the immediate reduction of the burden of taxation to the PAYE taxpayer, and for a substantial increase in a wide range of social welfare and other services.

Taxes are to be slashed (except, of course, those on 'the rich' and 'big business', who are to be soaked). Unemployment is to be progressively eliminated, and at the same time life is to be made so enjoyable for those who are currently unemployed that they will never have the desire to work again. A noble plan! The CMRS (reinforced now by the Bishops and the Poverty Czars) calls upon the incoming Government to 'make the elimination of poverty the driving force of its policy'. It also, however, counsels against 'forcing the unemployed on to 'workfare programmes' (presumably as constituting a demeaning and stressful imposition upon those who have become accustomed to a life of ease), and urges instead that 'some of the massive overtime enjoyed by some people in the workforce be converted into jobs'.

Now certainly it would be most desirable to reduce the amount of overtime being worked, but this proposal blithely ignores the basic reason why overtime (and increasing mechanisation) is so much more attractive to employers than the hiring of more workers, and that is the crushing burden of PRSI payments. As for unemployment, one of the basic contradictions with which any plan for job creation in this country has to deal is that there is simply no marginal advantage for those on the dole to get off it into any of the sorts of occupation for which they are liable to be eligible.

Indeed, the situation is much worse than that. A study published recently (by the Economic and Social Research Institute, as I recall) showed that in order to equal the benefits derived from an income on welfare of approximately £5,000 a year (together with the various perks that go with that, such as very low rent and so on), a married man would need to be earning in the region of £13,000. This may seem quite incredible, but it is meticulously worked out, and it constitutes a devastating statement of the dimensions of the problem.

Work is indeed the Key, but what we need in this country is a Key to Work, and this is not it.

Sex and scandal diet is inedible to foreigners

April 11, 1993

There is nothing like a few months abroad for reminding one that Ireland is not after all the centre of the universe – indeed for bringing home the realisation that our actions and passions, joys and tribulations, are of almost no interest to the rest of the world, and are generally consigned to complete oblivion by our fellow earthlings. In fact, in three months in the US, the only news about Ireland that I can recall seeing – never mind in the *Seattle Post-Intelligencer*, but even in *The New York Times* – was, first, the awful incest case from Kilkenny (and the remarkable verdict handed down in it), the latest heroic exploit of the Armed Strugglers in Warrington along with, I am glad to say, the impressive peace demonstration in Dublin that followed it. Nothing else can I recall, from the whole first quarter of the year.

Not that I am complaining, mind you. It is actually rather pleasant to put Ireland entirely behind one for a space, and then check in after a decent interval to see how it has been getting on. My point is merely how easy that is to do. One does not have to go to the far side of the US to achieve this result. A spell in France or Germany or across the Irish Sea in Britain would do just as well. The fact is, our doings are just not very important to the rest of the world – as we were reminded, to the chagrin of many. When one departs these shores, in fact, Ireland sinks beneath the threshold of consciousness very quickly indeed.

Admittedly, even as I write these words, news comes in that both the President of the United States and the Prime Minister of the United Kingdom have jointly expressed an interest in finding a solution to the Northern Ireland problem, but I suggest that that is just the exception that proves the rule. If Bill Clinton ever turns his thoughts to Ireland (which he would do only very occasionally – John Major, to his grief, thinks about us somewhat more frequently), the first and perhaps only thing that would come to his mind is that problem with Catholics and

Protestants up in the North which he had been persuaded to make some noises about during the campaign. And now, since he has decided that this is to be a year for tidying up trouble spots, Ireland naturally comes to his mind (though considerably below the Middle East and Bosnia in urgency – on a par with Abkhazia or Liberia).

But enough of that. What I really wanted to talk about is what's new, and what's not so new, since I went away.

First of all, what hasn't changed? (Apart, of course, from the dismal morass of Ulster, over which I will draw a veil.) Well, first of all, there's the Beef Tribunal. This is proceeding just as many of us had foreseen, fulfilling the fondest aspirations of the legal profession, and boring just about everyone else witless. I am most interested to observe, just as we approach the feast of Easter, incipient signs of the resurrection of Larry Goodman, heralded by the prophecies and fulminations of the redoubtable Dermot Gleeson.

My original unworthy conjecture of well over a year ago was that this tribunal was originally set up by CJ, not to *incriminate* Mr Goodman, as might be supposed (and as Mr Gleeson is pleased to suggest), but rather, ultimately to free him from any danger of prosecution. This would be achieved by both boring the public rigid, dulling its wrath and, more importantly, by so confusing the legal position that a real trial will become impossible, since the whole issue will have been prejudged in this forum without anyone actually being accused of anything. So this enormously expensive charade is set to run for some while yet, with Mr Goodman slowly emerging from beneath the smoke and rubble with his reputation more or less restored. Mr Gleeson has certainly set the ball rolling in that direction.

And while we're on the subject of boondoggles, I gather that Mr Glackin's investigation into the purchase of the Johnson Mooney and O'Brien site is not yet completed. There should be a glorious bill for that when it comes in, fully comparable to the profits made by any of the amusing little offshore companies concerned.

It is good also to see some other old faces in the news still. I returned just in time to read of Ben Dunne being given the push by his big sister, and to see Annie Murphy confronting Gay Byrne on *The Late Late Show*. We have plainly not heard the last of either of these performers. Both of them would do quite well as TV mini-series, which could earn much-needed foreign currency for RTE, if it moves fast.

And then there are some new stars in the firmament. I am particularly attracted by Dr Edmund Farrell of the Irish Permanent Building Society. He certainly deserves a place in the Hall of Fame of Irish entrepreneurs. Perhaps he will go down in legend and song as the man who put "permanent" into Building Society. Certainly the concern of the Society for the building and rebuilding of his house (or was it *their* house?) seems to have been more or less unremitting. Such an inspiration for the less fortunate members of the IPBS who are suffering repossession in these hard times! Perhaps they too could persuade the Society to do up their houses a bit while they are entrusted to their charge, and then let them have them back again when times get better, at the original price. Anyhow, it shows that the spirit of Irish enterprise is not yet dead, despite all the bad publicity it has had to face over the last few years.

Last but not least, the adventures of the Labour Party in the embrace of Fianna Fail should continue to provide entertainment. I returned just in time for their first convention since Dick Spring's imaginative move, and noted the defiant mood with which they are facing those such as myself, who were spiteful or cynical enough to criticise this bold new departure in Irish politics. It is heart-warming, certainly, to see such unlikely candidates as Emmet Stagg and Michael D. Higgins as Government Ministers, solemnly propounding and defending policy, presiding at Church fetes, and opening old people's homes. Very good for their souls, I would imagine. It is only a pity that Mr de Rossa could not have joined in as well. He will have his chance before long, though, I do not doubt.

A raw deal for our young
May 9, 1993

Mr Bill Attley, the joint head of SIPTU, struck terror into us all the other day by uttering the dire threat that unless the Government rescinded its one per cent levy on incomes, and certain limitations on social welfare payments, both introduced in the last Budget, then the trade union movement would feel itself quite unable to enter into any further wage agreements on the lines of the present PESP. Meanwhile, other distinguished members of the trade union movement representing public employees have been making ominous noises, to the effect that their desires for more money and less work should be properly catered for the next time around, or they too would make no deals.

Now I know that what is termed 'industrial peace' and 'a national understanding with the social partners' is deemed almost universally to be a Very Good Thing, but I wonder if this is not being purchased at too high a price, and specifically at the expense of our younger generation, and of generations yet to come. After all, let us not cod ourselves. In an ideal world, perhaps, where the best Christian principles held undisputed sway, the so-called 'social partners' that is, workers and employers – would be as one, and lie down together like the lion and the lamb. As of now, I fear that that blessed state has not been reached. So if one of the partners, the trade union movement, is actually happy to enter into a national agreement on wages and conditions, then one must entertain the nasty suspicion that something is awry somewhere.

And that I think is what has been happening over the last two national agreements. The employers have never been particularly happy about these agreements, but have had their arms twisted very effectively by governments who needed success, or at least the appearance of it, in industrial relations. It all started with CJ, I think, back in 1987. Indeed it is one of his major contributions to the nature of modern Irish society. He always prided himself on his ability to relate to the trade unions, in a way which Garret, for instance, was never capable of. He could get them together in a smoke-filled room and hammer out a deal - talking man to man, like - no nonsense, language as blue as the smoke-rings, off-colour jokes flying back and forth. Actually it is quite easy to cut a deal with trade union leaders, if you concede to them virtually all they ask for. They are not unreasonable men. All they want is the full implementation of their initial demands. The only problem arises in the larger world, the world of the struggling small business, the world of the unemployed, the world of next year's school leavers.

And that is what is bothering me. What one seems to see arising from the last two national wage agreements is a situation where the 'haves' – that is, those that have a job, especially one in the public service - remain in a cocoon of relative comfort, no matter how dire the overall financial situation becomes, while those who have been excluded from this cosy consensus slip ever deeper into hopelessness, as any prospect of employment for them recedes further over the horizon. The only fly in the ointment for those of us who are fortunate enough to have jobs, is the preposterously high taxes we have to pay (including the incredible one per cent employment levy of which Mr Attley is complaining – I am at one with him there), to support the ever-growing army of those whom the present economic policies, including this PESP, have put out of work.

It should after all be obvious to everybody that the 20% unemployment level is very largely a result of the overpayment of those who are at work. What saddens me particularly, as one involved in the education of youth, is to see the desolation facing our best and brightest as they emerge from school and university. There is really nothing for them to do but emigrate.

Our only hope for a real reduction of the unemployment level, I'm afraid, is to allow a situation to develop in this country more like that in the United States, or even Hong Kong, where both welfare payments and taxes are drastically slashed, and a wide range of admittedly poorly-paid and uninsured jobs become available, which no one need stay in for very long, but which provide a start in life for the young and mobile. Those are the sort of jobs which our young people are glad to pick up illegally in the US. Why may they not pick them up on their own doorsteps, and help their own country to recover in the process? It is sad, therefore, that there is absolutely no prospect of the present Government embarking on any such experiment.

What is a poor old university to do?

May 23, 1993

So the nasty old universities are at it again, shoving up the fees in preparation for the new school year, a rise of over twice the rate of inflation, to impose further misery on students and parents alike. What, you might ask, makes them go and do a thing like that, when they know that times are hard, and that even as it is the proportion of lower-income students in higher education is far smaller than it ought to be? Well, obviously I think that there is some reasonable explanation of this behaviour, or I would not get involved in trying to defend it. Let us see what that might be.

To mount a defence of this fee hike, it is necessary to put it in proper perspective, and to do that I am afraid that we will need to indulge in some statistical data. I will try to make this as painless as possible. The present problem stems from a policy embarked on by successive governments from the early 1980s of progressively reducing the proportion of the universities' income which is paid by the exchequer. In 1981-82, for instance, 81 per cent of the income of Trinity College derived from the government, whereas in 1992-93 this was reduced to 54.7 per cent, and in 1993-94 it bids fair to go below 50 per cent. You get the picture?

So what is a poor university to do? The Department of Finance, acting through the Higher Education Authority, does not dictate how the universities shall make up the shortfall in funding. Oh no, that would be dictatorial – prescribing to the university how it shall run its affairs, what courses it shall cut, what facilities it shall curtail, what posts if shall leave unfilled, whom it shall fire. The Department of Finance would never do a thing like that. All the mandarins of the department do is to cut back the grant. They leave it entirely up to the university how it shall manage its affairs in the light of this reduction.

Now universities, you will appreciate, are not money-making institutions. Oh yes, we earn a bit of money from doing little jobs for industry, and then there are campus companies who invent things and provide services which are sometimes profitable. And then again, there are all those tourists who come to look at the Book of Kells. But all that, I'm afraid, is very much a drop in the bucket when it comes to putting a budget together. Basically, although we certainly add to the nation's intellectual wealth, and may even be said to add to the earning capacity of its youth (though, alas, that earning capacity, by reason of the enlightened economic policies of the government, must generally be exercised elsewhere in the world), we are not organisations that can be expected to turn a profit on day to day operations.

And that brings me to the second problem we have had to face in recent years: a substantial increase in the number of students in higher education, together with only a slight increase in the number of faculty to teach them, resulting in a steadily worsening student-teacher ratio. For example, in 1986-87 there were 7,815 students, both undergraduate and postgraduate, in Trinity College (the place is actually built to hold about 6,000), in 1992-93 there were 10,334; and next October there will be 400 to 500 more. It is heart-warming, of course, to see more young people every year enjoying the benefits of higher education, but the hard fact is that every student who enters the system costs us more money. Students may think they pay an arm and a leg in fees, but even at next year's proposed rate of £1,695 in Arts, or £2,153 in Sciences, an Irish national is paying only about 30 per cent or so of the economic cost of his or her education. So more students cost us more money, despite the increase in fee income – as does the increase in faculty, such as it is.

The inevitable result of these developments, then, has been the much-to-be-deplored eight per cent rise in fees. In view of the facts set out here, I must say I regard it as unmitigated nerve on the part of our new Minister for Education, Ms Breathnach, to 'deplore' this proposed rise, and to recommend a ceiling of five per cent (as for Mr Jim Higgins, opposition spokesman for Education, and his call for the minister to block the proposed increases, I forgive him, since this sort of mental farting is only to be expected from opposition spokesmen in such circumstances). I realise that Ms Breathnach has simply inherited this situation from her predecessor, as she has so many others, but she cannot properly evade ministerial responsibility for the progressive squeeze on the universities that has been going on for the last five years, which is the inevitable and obvious result of shifting more of the burden onto the already hard-pressed parents and students of the country.

I note that university administrators have been rather muted on this subject in the last week, meekly taking the scolding for their rapacity and improvidence that Ms Breathnach and the Higher Education Authority have been handing out to them. Presumably they feel that if they answer back they will be punished with even less money and more students next year. Well, I do not have to be polite, and I do not propose to be. Somebody has to place the blame for these regrettable developments squarely where it belongs – that is, with the government in general, and the Department of Finance in particular.

This country actually gets damned good value for its investment in higher education – much better value than it gets from the Department of Finance. There has never been any degree of 'fat' in this system, such as undoubtedly accumulated in the British system in the 1960s and 1970s, and if squeezed any more, by either incompetent politicians or short-sighted administrators with slide rules and pocket calculators, it will begin to fold up altogether.

Alms and the man
July 11, 1993

I knew it! I knew it! But sure didn't we all know it really, all along? It was never there at all. The money, I mean. It was all just an unfortunate misunderstanding. We jumped to certain conclusions, and wily old Jacques, cute hoor of a Frog that he is, did not bother to disabuse us of it a minute before he had to, having need as he did of our loyalty and enthusiasm in the interval. I realise that we are being exhorted on all sides to do all that we can to support the Government in its titanic struggle to secure our *rightful* share of the alms that are being distributed, and of course one is anxious to do one's bit. I feel that I can best contribute to the national effort by analysing the cause of the misunderstanding as I see it. It wasn't really Albert's fault at all. He had it on the very best authority – practically from the horse's mouth, as it were (or at least from some part of the animal's anatomy).

What actually happened, I believe, was this. At the meeting in Edinburgh, back in December, things were beginning to drag towards the latter part of the afternoon. Documents of very much more than a page in length, many of them in incomprehensible foreign languages, were being bandied about, and some Dutch fellow was being exceedingly pedantic about something or other. The room was getting stuffy, and Albert and the boys (the 'advisers' – Ó'hUiginn and so on) were developing distinctly dry mouths and beginning to doze off. And then someone, reading the delegation's mind, passed a note to the Taoiseach suggesting they all step out for a pint – just across the road to the Crown and Thistle, wouldn't be out more than a few minutes, just to get a second wind, like.

The Taoiseach approved this suggestion, and the Irish delegation excused themselves for a 'brief consultation.' Well now, they were barely settled in to the first pint and Albert his Ballygowan or Highland Spring, when didn't one of the lads strike up a conversation with this fella who was propping up the bar, and didn't he turn out to be none other than a security guard of Jacques Delors himself. Well, that was a stroke of

154

luck! So they offered him a drink, and they had another themselves, and he responded by giving them some extremely important and sensitive information. This fella said he was a very good friend – a very good friend, you understand – of Jacques Delors' personal secretary, and she had told him, the previous night, *in the strictest confidence*, that the boss had a really soft spot for the Irish, and that he had decided, in the new share-out of structural funds, which was to be twice as big as the present one, that he was going to let the Irish keep the same percentage as they had at present: 13.5 per cent.

Well, this was great news indeed! (It shows the value, which is something I have always maintained, of spending a lot of time, at academic conferences, in the bar. You really learn things that way, which one generally does not by listening to the papers). One of the economic advisers got out his pocket calculator, and they worked out the sums, and the total came to more than eight billion quid. So in view of that they all had another drink (the guard graciously accepted one as well – he really was a very decent class of a chap), and then it seemed hardly worth going back for the tail-end of the session, since after all they had the inside information right there. It was in the bag! After further consideration of the situation, they decided that champagne was called for, and after a bottle or two of that, nothing would do Albert only to call a press conference that very night, to announce the good news to the nation. The rest, as they say, is history.

It is such a pity, then, that it turned out to be all a mirage. It was, after all, the archetypal Fianna Fail wet dream. Loot beyond one's wildest imaginings, to be distributed for the sustenance of one's friends and the frustration of one's enemies. The prospect of a new golf course and an Olympic-size swimming pool in the constituency of each member of the cabinet. A new hospital, a regional technical college, or at least an interpretative centre, in every marginal constituency in the country. Grand new roads stretching off in every direction, harbours dredged and upgraded, wetlands drained, civic offices refurbished. A great National Development Plan was being drawn up. The Soldiers were safe into the next century. It was a political orgasm. To hell with the Spaniards, the Portuguese, the Greeks – feckless foreigners. And to hell, too, with the East Germans. They'll just have to wait. Albert has the inside track. Delors loves us. Everybody loves us – because we're loveable. We're quaint, and impish, and we have a great sense of humour. And everyone knows we'll put the money to very good use, as we always have in the past.

But alas, even the most delightful and plausible dreams come to an end, and there is the awakening. The bedclothes have fallen off, and the old head is pounding, but Monday morning must be faced somehow. The National Plan must be drastically revised, and a new strategy developed – one which involves unattractive options, such as working for a living, paying one's way, and standing on one's own two feet. It is a hard life, undoubtedly, and grossly unfair to leprechauns, but even from such debacles something useful may be learned. In this case, it is this: next time, Albert, *get it in writing*.

Consigned to the dustbin of history
July 18, 1993

It is, I must say, with a rather heavy heart that I have been observing over the last few months the progressive disintegration of the Fine Gael Party, culminating in the poll in this paper last week, which showed a *halving* of support for the party over the last ten years, from fully 39 per cent of the electorate in 1982, at the height of Garret FitzGerald's success, to a mere 18 per cent today, fully two percentage points lower than the Labour Party – despite the latter's current participation in a relatively unpopular government. I can't expect most of the readership, I suppose, to share my feeling of sadness, since the great majority of you, if we may judge by the recent poll result, have plainly already consigned the poor old party to the dustbin of history, but I would ask for a moment or two's silence while we consider the implications of this.

I must confess an interest. I have been a member of this party, in a loose sort of way, for over thirty years now, paying my (derisory) dues whenever anyone asks for them, and occasionally serving it in minor capacities. An uncle of mine was one of the founders of it, and was for some years its leader. And whether you like it or net, it (and its previous incarnation, Cumann na nGael) has been a prominent part of this state since its foundation. So it is a little sad now, you will perhaps agree, to see it in what may be a state of terminal decline.

That this decline may indeed be terminal is suggested to me by two factors; (1) that the fall in popularity has not been sudden, but fairly steady over the decade, (though particularly marked since 1987) and largely unaffected by periodic dips in the fortunes of Fianna Fail, which should normally have produced some corresponding rises in those of Fine Gael; and (2) that, as many commentators have unkindly, but accurately, observed, there is really now no longer any logical constituency left for a party of the perceived make-up and philosophy of Fine Gael – that is, other than that already cornered by Fianna Fail and the Labour Party. This would suggest to me that the national consciousness has evolved from a state where it was prepared to tolerate the mild absurdity of two quarrelling halves of a bourgeois nationalist party, divided by a civil war on which nobody wished to dwell any longer, but by no other significant ideological principle.

Therefore, I fear, one of them has to go, and it looks as if that one is Fine Gael. It is regrettable, perhaps, but political parties do die from time to time, even quite substantial ones. Look at the once-great Liberal Party in Great Britain, the party of Charles James Fox, of Gladstone, of Lloyd George! In the period between the two world wars it was simply crushed between the opposing Tory and Labour election machines, until it was left as an insignificant rump, now absorbed into the Social Democrats. The problem was, I suppose, that almost everybody in a way became vaguely liberal (with a small 'l'), and thus the party didn't seem to stand for anything distinctive any more. May it not be somewhat the same with Fine Gael?

If Fine Gael stood for anything, at least in more recent years, it was for a broader, more tolerant vision of an Ireland of various traditions, not just that of Gaelic nationalism, a progressive attitude to social questions (divorce and so on, but also a decent level of social services), but still a commitment to free enterprise. The question is, though, is there any group in public life now to which that description might not apply? Even the Democratic Left, after all, is sounding a good deal more democratic than left these days. As for the Labour Party, it may be officially committed to state participation in industry, but, as we see in the matter of Aer Lingus, if a public company is shown to be no longer viable in its present state, it is prepared to consider alternatives (though it did, admittedly, manage to wreck the Greencore deal with ADM).

Is there any longer, then, a market for what FG is offering? I very much doubt it, and I feel that if the party survives much longer, it will be due only to the power of inertia. This is to say that it is not just John Bruton's fault, though he doubtless hasn't helped. He was in an impossible position. The problem is far deeper than the competence or otherwise of a particular leader. Is there anything at *all* to be done, though, or do we just, with tear-dampened handkerchiefs, wave a great tradition goodbye? I have no idea what marvelous solution the party commission that is currently sitting on this question will come up with, but I would venture to suggest the following.

It seems to me that one might approach the Progressive Democrats with a view to a merger, and call the new party that would result something completely different. Such a party would be a fairly hard-nosed free enterprise party, but otherwise progressive, and it would be in a strong position to pick up the pieces when the present government subsides under the weight of its own contradictions. Of course there would be strains at the local level, but we must bear in mind that the party managed to renew itself in a similar manner once before, in September 1933, when it was also at a low ebb. Then Cumann na nGael, as it then was, proposed a merger with the recently formed Centre Party, led by Frank MacDermot and James Dillon (who both became Vice-Presidents of the new party), and, reinforced by the ten or so Centre Party members, lived to fight again, as Fine Gael, for another sixty years at least, contributing a great deal to Irish society.

This is all very well, one might say, but would the PD's have us? Well, I think one should approach them with due humility (not in the way that John Bruton summoned Dick Spring to his presence in the wake of the last election), but if the terms were right, I think that they would be very foolish not to. As things are, I don't see that either party is going anywhere much. The PD's still appear to be on the up and up, but they are not exactly taking the political scene by storm, as was originally hoped. At the present rate of growth, they should be in a position to form a government by about 2050, and they may not care to wait that long. Such a merger seems to me to have a lot of logic to it. But it is not really my business to suggest possible solutions. I started out to lament the demise of what I know to be a decent, honourable and on the whole pretty competent group of people, and perhaps I should leave it at that. If an institution's time has come to die, there is not much that anyone can do to revive it. I will miss it, though.

We need to put Saint Patrick to work!
March 20, 1994

Once again we are in the happy season of shamrocks, leprechauns, dreadful postcards from An Post and, above all, of migrating politicians. Around the world, from Moscow to Melbourne, they have celebrated St Patrick's Day. Some reflections are provoked by these migrations, and they are not entirely positive. I mean, one does not want to be too mercenary or hard-nosed about this, but one must ask: how much do we get out of all this outpouring of sentimentality and celebration at the end of the day?

One might very well riposte, of course: why on earth should we get anything out of it, over and above the pleasures of the event itself? Is it not enough just to celebrate our national saint, and the solidarity of the Irish race around the world? Why should we get any more out of the whole thing than a damn good hangover?

While that is, of course, an admirable attitude, and well suited to an island of saints and scholars, we must recognise that we are in a tough and ruthless world of triumphant capitalism and commercialism, and it is arguable that we need to mine occasions such as this for all they can yield. Consider the Irish component in the American body politic. The latest figure, I believe, is that 42,000,000 Americans are prepared to lay claim to some degree of Irish ancestry, and this not just on St Patrick's Day! We can muster a remarkable total, many of them now very distinguished, and – dare we say it? – very rich and powerful. Are we really making the most of them? One should not ignore or belittle the substantial efforts made by successive Irish leaders and administrations, over the last 20 years at least, to focus the loyalty of Irish-Americans into more profitable channels, both political and financial. One may cite as examples, on the political front, the well-organised and influential group of Friends of Ireland in the Congress, and – on the financial front – the Ireland Fund, currently chaired by none other than Dr AJF O'Reilly.

Nevertheless, ungracious though it may seem to say it, we still could do more. Let's compare ourselves with two other nations that have strong US links – though of rather different sorts – Japan and Israel. Neither of these nations can lay claim to anything like the numerical share of the population of the US that we can, but it is arguable that they wield much greater influence. There are a considerable number of Japanese-Americans, many of whom have attained distinction in many different fields – intellectual, commercial and even political. But no one, I think, could claim that, as a nation, they are widely loved. Not only did they fight a savage war against the US, during which they humiliated them at Pearl Harbor, but they have in recent years – by a mixture of superior skill and efficiency, and thoroughly ruthless trading practices – built up a dominant balance of payments surplus, and a dangerous degree of financial control, with respect to the US.

But Japan does not require to be loved, simply respected. It has built up its position not by plucking at people's heart-strings, but by dominating their purse-strings. As such, their example is hardly relevant to us, except insofar as we can persuade those who love us to buy Irish at every possible opportunity. I still remember being shocked long ago, in 1967, at my first St Patrick's Day party in America (run by the Irish Universities' Club in San Francisco, no less!), to observe that, even on that sacred day, there was neither Irish whiskey nor beer on offer - only bourbon, Scotch, and a selection of American beers (albeit dyed green). Unfortunately, we do not produce a great deal that is of vital importance to anyone (except perhaps high-class food products), but we should strive to ensure that no red-blooded Irish-American will drink Scotch when he could be drinking Irish – or indeed Perrier when he could be drinking Ballygowan – as well as eating, and wearing the right things, as far as possible, and taking his holidays in the right place.

A closer analogy, however, is Israel. In this case, of course, we must recognise both a degree of communal guilt about what the Jewish race has suffered, and a realisation of the danger in which the State of Israel has always stood since its inception, which have sharpened the attention and loosened the purse-strings of the American nation over the past 50 years. But we must recognise also that the Jewish lobby in the US has been a formidable force, after which we are still only hopping and jumping. It was actually quite a brave act by George Bush some years ago to take the Israelis in hand and force them into some kind of peace negotiations by threatening to cut down the enormous subsidies which they had been claiming for so long as of right.

We do have some influence, but have never been able to crack the whip at the Americans in the way that Israel consistently has up to now, despite our much greater numbers. I do not really want to suggest that we should try to outdo either the Japanese or the Israelis in the exercise of their particular talents. I would simply propose that, in the nicest possible way, and without shedding the old-world charm and droll inconsequentiality for which we are justly famous, we should continue to make the very best of what we have going for us.

Parallels of an Easter's mad decline
April 3, 1994

I imagine that most of you have given at least a passing glance to a rather amusing billboard ad by Smirnoff currently beautifying our highways. It features a number of large stone statue-heads arranged on a hillside, with one, decked out in forage-cap and sunglasses, reflected in a bottle of Smirnoff vodka. What the specific message embodied in this image may be quite escapes me, I must confess, but I find it entertaining nonetheless. It even provoked me to thought (though not yet to buying any Smirnoff vodka).

The thoughts it provoked me to were these: The statues, as you may or may not be aware, constituted for centuries – indeed, ever since the island of Rapanui was 'discovered' by Europeans on Easter Day, 1722 (and therefore called Easter Island) – one of the great unsolved mysteries of the world. The problem was that when the Europeans arrived, the population of the island was less than 3,000, consisting of rather bewildered and depressed Polynesians of minimal material culture, but there were hundreds and hundreds of these statues all over the island, some of them up to 36 feet in height, and weighing upwards of 50 tons, along with some 260 massive platforms of finely wrought stone to support them, and no one could give a coherent explanation of how or why they had been erected. Speculation ranged from lost Atlantis-like civilisations which had sunk into the Pacific to the intervention of visitors from outer space, and every nut and visionary in the business had a chance to put his or her oar in. But a convincing explanation remained elusive.

Until, that is, about 10 or 15 years ago. Then a team of American anthropologists, after exhaustive investigation, finally cracked the Mystery. They have revealed a truth that is stranger than most fictions, and one, it seems to me, that has a powerful lesson to impart to our own civilisation, It seems that what happened was somewhat as follows. Rapanui was first colonised by Polynesian settlers from the East sometime in the 14th century. The settlement prospered for a number of generations, but then things began to go strangely wrong. The island became divided into a set of rival clans and villages, and these units began to compete with each other. This competition took a remarkable form. There had already, it seems, been a cult of ancestors, involving the erection of stone platforms and statues (always taking the form of stylised busts), but progressively an element of competitiveness began to enter into the erection of these by the various villages. It became a point of honour to erect ever more and larger stone busts, with increasing disregard for any rational justification, solely for the purpose of one-upmanship over one's neighbours. All productive activities, agriculture, fishing and handicrafts, were increasingly allowed to decline, while more and more energy went into the insensate competitive carving and erection of statues. These vast objects had to be hauled from the quarries in which they were carved to the hillsides on which they were erected by primitive means that even now baffle us – and for what? To attain some sort of spiritual ascendancy over the next parish.

There could be only one end to this: economic and social collapse. And indeed this seems to have ensued after something less than 100 years. Rational, productive activities fell into terminal decline. The population, which is estimated to have been more than 6,000 in the island's prime, declined to less than half of that by the time the Europeans arrived, and a kind of communal nervous breakdown ensued, from which the remaining inhabitants have never really recovered. It took a great deal of careful questioning to get this much of the story out of them.

But why do I inflict on you this curious tale? What relevance can it possibly have to us? Well, I wish I thought it had none, but I'm not so sure. You all remember the Cold War, and the Arms Race? Most of us, I imagine, can remember nothing else throughout the extent of our conscious lives. I know we are all trying to forget it, but let us just call it to mind one more time before we consign it to oblivion.

Have you ever thought how we are all going to explain to our grandchildren why the greatest nations of the earth gradually began to stockpile weapons against each other, weapons of such destructive power as had never been dreamed of before, until after about a generation they had collectively accumulated enough weaponry to destroy each other about 16 times over, and to render the whole planet Earth uninhabitable as well? And not only had they stockpiled enough bombs to blow each other up this many times, but, in case that that somehow failed to do the trick, they had also developed extraordinary, unheard-of plagues and nerve gases, even a drop of any of which on the skin would reduce a human being to a writhing helpless heap. This enormous build-up of destructive power progressively drained resources from every kind of productive activity, as well as causing worldwide environmental pollution. It would certainly have ended in mutually assured destruction, but for the fact that the economy of one of the partners in this crazy game proved unequal to the strain, and they folded.

I hope we all live to tell our grandchildren this remarkable tale, for by then it will be suitably ancient history, but I am sorry to say that as I pen this it is all very much still with us. We tend to forget that at least 75 per cent of this hardware is still in existence, and some of it in the hands of characters like the Ukrainians, who are getting very desperate indeed these days. Only last week *The Sunday Times* started a scare that scientists in Russia are still working on a doomsday plague to which there is no known antidote, which would make the Black Death seem like a vicarage tea party. The rumour may very well be correct. And the real danger, of course, is not that the Russians themselves will make use of such a weapon (though I wouldn't he too sure about Mr Zhirinovsky), but that in their desperation they (or the Ukrainians) will sell what they have to some Third World dictator with more money than sense who will be only too glad to do so.

So the saga is very far from over yet, I'm afraid. Let us cross our fingers, and remember the poor old Easter Islanders on this Easter morn – and maybe have a shot of Smirnoff!

Health Police handcuffed our national fun
April 17, 1994

I was alarmed earlier in the week, as I dare say were many of you, by the announcement of the findings of what was billed as "the first survey of health behaviour in Ireland", the Happy Heart National Survey, conducted by the Irish Heart Foundation. The Foundation found, to its surprise and sorrow, as a result of a survey of 1,798 men and women between the ages of 30 and 69, that we are a thoroughly slothful, sedentary and overweight nation, devoted to drinking, smoking and watching television, and that most of us will die of heart disease. More than half of those surveyed, it seems, were overweight (of whom fully 10 per cent were obese). One-third of them smoked, 20 per cent drank more than the weekly recommended limit of alcohol, and 20 per cent watched more than four hours of TV a day.

Of course, one always wonders with these surveys how they can provide for the element of boasting and playfulness that might enter into a certain proportion of replies. Surveys of sexual prowess must be particularly prone to such mischief, but might one not also be tempted to claim that one was five feet tall, 17 stone in weight, smoked two packs of cigarettes a day, and liked to put away at least six pints after work, before coming home to slump down in front of the television for the rest of the night? But let us suppose that these statistics are broadly correct, what are we to say about them? Are they a slashing indictment of our behaviour as a nation? Do they amount to a clarion call to pull ourselves together?

I must say that what I find worrying about the figures is the large proportion of people who are not eating and drinking too much, who have recently given up smoking (a 25 per cent drop in smokers, they tell us, since the last survey), and who are paying very little attention at all to the television. What is the country coming to at all? I ask. We are in danger of ending up like the rest of Europe. The Irish have long been notorious, after all, for being what used to be regarded as the best-fed nation in the world. Now, of course, we are in the doghouse for consuming far too many saturated fats – butter, cream, large fries (sausages, rashers, black and white puddings, and so on) – and thick slices of bread, washed down by far too much good strong tea (very noxious) or pints of creamy stout (unspeakable). And we sit around far too long doing it.

What does the Irish Heart Foundation want from us, really? Give up the cigarettes, first of all. Then cut down on the booze. Then attack the saturated fats – turn to lots of fruit, raw vegetables, salads. Then get up off our arses and out round the neighbourhood in the shorts and sweatshirt for a nice brisk jog, preferably every day before breakfast, but, if you insist that you can't manage that, then at least three times a week.

Will that do? Well, there are many serious thinkers who propose that we should eliminate tea and coffee, and also most minerals (full of noxious additives), and of course sweets, chocolate and desserts. And, I almost forgot, red meat. There are really appalling things in a charcoal-broiled steak, for instance – and how about a nice stuffed loin of pork, with the crackling intact!

But let us not give in to impure thoughts. Let us instead suppose that the Irish nation, by some miracle, reconstitutes itself, and emerges bursting with health and purpose, ready to live forever. What then? The first consequence, I think, would be that the economy would finally collapse, large sections of it having been effectively eviscerated by our new philosophy of life – the tobacco and drink industries first, but the dairy and meat industries not far behind. And I'm very much afraid that our personalities would change for the worse as well. We might become more industrious and businesslike, with days off "sick" – (particularly Mondays) – dramatically reduced, and productivity seriously increased. The problem, though, would be that whatever it is that makes Ireland Ireland would go out the window in the process, and that, I should say, would be bad for tourism. I mean, Germans, for instance, do not want to make the journey to the fabled Grüne Insel in the West only to find themselves confronted, in effect, by more Germans!

No, I'm afraid that a considerable part of our distinctive charm resides in our staying very much the way we are - carefree and inconsequential slobs, who are not concerned with getting up too early, and who devote considerable parts of the day to gossiping over pints - and if we have to drop dead of a heart attack at the end of the day, then that is part of our destiny.

Democracy could make history Yet

May 1, 1994

Well, this has been quite a week, has it not? One of those weeks, in fact, for which one had waited a long time (especially if one had taken more than a passing interest in the dismantling of apartheid), and after which one can feel that one has lived through a significant piece of history. The South Africans have at last got themselves to the polls together (even if not without some hiccups), to elect a national government. And, as if stimulated by this remarkable achievement, old enemies like the Israelis and the PLO, and notable eccentrics like the inhabitants of Bosnia, have edged a little further forward towards some rational solution of their problems.

At such a time I find it stimulating to turn back to a remarkable book that appeared some two years ago, *The End of History and The Last Man*, by Francis Fukuyama. Fukuyama's thesis is that, with the collapse of Communism and what he sees as the triumph of the concepts of liberal democracy and the free market economy, History (with a capital H) is on the verge of coming to an end. By 'History', I should specify, he means the cyclical, or dialectical, process of the rise and fall of nation-states and political systems, with the conflicts attendant on this – not the succession of banal, everyday happenings such as budgets, floods, plane crashes, World Cup soccer tournaments, and Eurovision song contests, which will doubtless continue as before.

Fukuyama, a Japanese-American political scientist and public policy adviser, argues that the imperatives of modern technology are inexorably driving all regimes, East and West, North and South, towards an acceptance that they need an educated and free citizenry to run the sort of technologically advanced society that is being forced upon them if they are to survive at all. Admittedly, one gets mavericks such as the clique of generals who rule Burma, or neurotic reactionaries like the Islamic fundamentalists of Iran and (perhaps) Algeria, and a few crooked or mad dictators popping up in odd corners of the Third World, but they ultimately don't matter a great deal. The trend is set firmly against them, and they can only delay the inevitable temporarily and partially.

Now I wish I thought that Fukuyama was right (though an endless expanse of liberal capitalist democracy stretching out in all directions might, after all, seem mildly boring), but I fear that his thesis comes across as rather fatuously optimistic and complacent. It was a product of the first flush of enthusiasm produced by the collapse of the Soviet Union and its satellite regimes, before the fearful economic and social problems arising from the change-over to a market economy became obvious. And yet perhaps Fukuyama may be onto something after all.

It certainly seems to be the case that, if a nation wants to prosper in the long run (as distinct from such short-term gains as a command economy may be able to achieve by forced labour and ruthless concentration of resources), it must allow market forces to work and its citizens to educate themselves and exercise freedom of choice. And when citizens do that, they tend not to establish theocratic monarchies or oligarchies or military dictatorships, but rather liberal, pluralistic democracies. In an impressive table on pp 49-50. Fukuyama shows that, whereas back in 1790 there were just three states that one could describe as democracies (France, Switzerland, and the United States), and even in 1975 there were only 30, in 1990 there were 61 – many of whose inhabitants in 1790 were still powerless serfs in feudal monarchies . . .

So there may be a trend here, after all, and developments in South Africa this week may be a step in the right direction. There will still, however, be lots of little post-historical problems to niggle us. One that is much on my mind at the moment is the matter of excessive and reckless insurance claims and awards. This is a major plague in the United States, but within Europe, this country continues to be the most foolish and improvident. One consequence, as we all know, is that it is becoming increasingly difficult to stage amateur sports and cultural events, because of the vast accident insurance that must be taken out, in case some litigious idiot sprains their ankle while entering your marquee, or whatever.

The instance that disturbs me most at the moment is the threatened demise of the Trinity Ball, for just this sort of reason. The organisers just cannot afford the insurance rates involved in holding it on the College grounds, because lunatics will try to gate-crash by climbing over the College railings, with the consequent risk of castration or disembowelling – for which, of course, they would sue the College. Now I can't expect to arouse much sympathy on this question. I suppose, "Good riddance!", you may say, "Damned elitist romp. Let them go to a disco – or better still, a céili – down the road." Yes, no doubt, but that is not the point. The point is that yet another relatively innocent recreational activity – attended, I may say, by a wide cross-section of our sons and daughters – is in danger of biting the dust because our natural litigiousness and greed is being fostered by a self-serving and cynical legal system, which has rendered itself more or less impervious to reform on this matter.

But let me dismount from this hobby-horse. All I really meant to say was that, even if the End of History is truly at hand, we will be left with lots of little problems to occupy us for the foreseeable future.

Paradise Island, of Corse
August 7, 1994

It is true what they say in the travel brochures. Corsica is indeed an aromatic isle. Fortunately my sense of smell was in good form as we stepped off the plane at the little airport of Calvi, because, apart from the blessed heat, what hits you first is the intoxicating smell of the *masochia*, the carpet of aromatic bushes which covers most of the island – rosemary, thyme, sage, garlic and God knows what else. We had picked a little hotel just south of the delightful port of Calvi, on the north-west coast of the island, for a restful, vegetative holiday in the last half of June, and that is what we got, but Corsica is also a place for the adventurous. Basically, the island is jagged green mountains, slashed by valleys, running down to the blue sea, there are fine beaches on the northwest coast, stretching north from Calvi to just beyond Ile Rousse, but I must say I preferred the smooth rocks in a little cove just south of our hotel, where one could snorkel spectacularly over huge boulders that some primeval disturbance had hurled into the sea, and commune with the many varieties of fish that swam around them.

Another basic aspect of any lazy holiday, apart from sun and sea, is food and drink. Here Corsica is interesting, though not exceptional. A typical Corse menu might comprise a hearty bean soup (excellent, but the victim of sundry ribald remarks), a fish soup, wild boar paté, a warm goat's cheese salad, or what came to be termed in our circle 'coarse crudities' (in effect slices of well-smoked ham and sausage with raw vegetables); then an equally hearty lamb or veal stew, with olives, peppers and so forth (lovely grilled fish, too, is available, but expensive); and a pleasant cheese-cake, served warm, or various cheeses, of sheep and goat. The wines are not going to take the world by storm, but a top red wine from the Patrimonio region near St Florent (to the north of us) is not at all bad, and the sweet Muscat or Cap Corse fortified wines make a pleasant aperitif, over ice. There are also various liqueurs, concocted from various elements of the *masochia*, which are of different degrees of vileness.

As I say, this was a lazy holiday, but if one wishes (which we did not, especially as the thermometer crept towards 100 degrees), one can head up from just above Calvi, either from the little mountain village of Calenzana, or from the Forét de Bonifato, and back-pack clear across the island, on well-marked trails. It will take you about 15 days, I understand, and is best done in late spring – when the snow is gone from the lower elevations, and before it gets uncomfortably hot. The wild flowers are luxuriant, and the views breath-taking. We visited the Forét one morning, and viewed various knobby-kneed enthusiasts setting off up the trail, but we were not tempted. Just too strenuous.

Corsica is an odd place in many ways, if one considers its history. Various distinguished visitors can be found who have praised it over the centuries, including Boswell and Balzac, but in general, from Greek and Roman times on, it was regarded as the back of beyond, and a suitable place to which troublesome persons might be exiled. The Corsicans themselves have always been extremely troublesome, both to each other and to whatever outside power - Greeks, Romans, Arabs, Pisans, Genoese and finally (from the late 18th century) French – tried to take them over. They have had brief moments of independence, but generally they have been engaged in guerilla warfare against some oppressor or other. And they are still at it. But they do not, it seems, shoot tourists. If one wishes to travel outside Calvi, one amusing thing to do is to take the little railway to Ile Rousse, just 20km up the coast, which it reaches in the best part of an hour, chugging along rather shakily, and stopping at all the little resorts on the way. It is very much the West Corsica Railway (*Es-tu prêt là, Michel, es-tu prêt?*). One does not actually have to get out and push, and no cows got onto the line, but if one had, it would not have been at all surprising.

The road system is still fairly primitive, by all, except Irish, standards. I was burdened with ladies who do not like precipitous drops and hairpin bends, so there was a limit to what one could do in the way of visiting charming little mountain villages, but we did take a car to drive across the island to the east coast, on the one reasonably good road, to visit the site of the Roman town of Aleria, which was of some interest to me. Actually, the most spectacular antiquities of Corsica are not Roman, but prehistoric – possibly erected by the same fellows as gave us passage graves and dolmens. Most remarkable are stone statues of warriors, rather like the Easter Island ones, and rows of standing stones, chiefly in the south of the island, going back to about 3000 BC.

Well, taken all in all, is Corsica an island paradise? I should say it is a pretty good candidate for the title, but ideally in the late spring or early summer. The place fills up unbearably in July and August, I understand, and it just gets too hot – though relieved, I believe, by the occasional thunderstorm.

It's criminal to neglect our own
August 28, 1994

It may well seem by now that everything profitable has been said about the life and death of Mr Martin Cahill, and that the attention of the Great Irish Public may better he moved back to the contemplation of topics of greater weight and permanence, such as the Peace Process or the death struggles of TEAM Aer Lingus. I feel, however, that a few more moments might he spent on the topic of the late Mr Cahill. Let me start with what seems to me a significant detail. Did anyone take note of the fact that the General, when he was sent so unceremoniously to his reward, was wearing his seat belt?

So? What is to be made of that? Simply, I should say, that here we have an essentially orderly man. Either he was concerned about road safety, or, at the very least, he was concerned to give the police no trivial reason to harass him. We know that this man of very little education planned his operations in meticulous detail, and this action of his is therefore quite in line with what else we have learned of him. What we learned in the wake of his death, I must say, put me in mind of something that Malcolm X remarks in his autobiography, that it struck him, during his career as a small-time criminal in Boston and New York, that there were many of his acquaintance, engaged in the same wretched and largely unprofitable activities as himself, who were possessed of remarkable talents – one man could keep long strings of names and numbers in his head, another was a genius at fixing mechanical objects, and so on – but that the inequities of society ensured that these talents would never be put to any good purpose.

So it surely was with Martin Cahill. The man plainly had organisational skills which would have been welcomed in any industry, and of which the country in general is in sore need, but the structure of society ensured that these skills would never be put to any constructive use. Rather they would be employed to cause mayhem and misery, and all because their master was born into a stratum of society which gave him very little hope of a satisfying career by any honest means.

The other significant aspect of his demise, and one that was quite widely adverted to in the media, with some bewilderment, was the spontaneous outpouring of emotion on the part of many people, young and not so young, from his own community. This emotion involved what seemed to be genuine sorrow at his death, and anger and hostility directed both at the police, as symbols of the law and order imposed by the state, and at the media, seen also as agents of the state. We have been urged, repeatedly and correctly, over the last ten days, not to romanticise or glamourise the General, but it must be admitted that in certain circles - those who gathered round his corpse at the scene of the assassination, for instance, and those who attended his funeral - the General was a distinctly and disturbingly popular figure.

But why? I mean, the man wasn't exactly Robin Hood, after all. He was, no doubt, good to his family (or families), but it is not attested that he distributed much largesse round the neighbourhood, out of all that he undoubtedly got his hands on over the years. No, his popularity rests on something else, and it is that, I think, that we should brood on, as it constitutes a profound danger signal. Let us think back a moment to Malcolm X's memoirs, and the situation in African American and Latino neighbourhoods in America. In many of these, the alienation from the dominant (white) society is so complete that role models are not those who are trying to struggle up through the system (apart, admittedly, from successful athletes), but rather pimps, gamblers and minor hoods, in sharp threads and gleaming white Oldsmobiles, who have done time in prison and survived.

The attraction of such people for the young has always been considerable. This is well-illustrated by that genius of social commentary Roddy Doyle, in his recent masterpiece, by young Paddy Clarke's admiration for the 'cool', tough Charles Leavy. But when this sort of admiration becomes endemic in a whole adult population as well, then society needs to take note. We have not yet reached the level of alienation of 'submerged' ethnic populations in America and many parts of Europe, but we are getting there. We agonise over the fact of 80 per cent unemployment in Ballymun or Darndale, or many parts of Finglas or Tallaght, but we seem quite helpless to do anything about it.

Well, do I have a solution? No, of course I don't. There probably isn't one. But I have a naive suggestion - derived, strangely enough, from one of Fidel Castro's nicer ideas in the early days of his regime in Cuba. He decreed that everyone who knew how to read and write should take on someone who didn't, and teach them: "Each one teach one." Could we not work towards the idea that everyone who felt themselves to be reasonably comfortably settled and employed in this country - not rich, mind you; just comfortable - would 'adopt' one family or individual from one of these areas of greatest social blight, and give them what help, advice, companionship and even material assistance one could? God knows we are ready enough to pour millions of money into distant continents. Could we not do something at our own back door – and ultimately for ourselves?

Of course such action would not absolve the Government from its normal obligations, but I believe there is comparatively little that governmental agencies can do about such concentrations of misery – except perhaps greatly improving the school system, but even that is of limited use. New levels of local enterprise and concepts of self-help have to be developed, and a sense of solidarity needs to pervade the whole people of this nation. That can only come, I think, from getting to know each other better, and as a consequence, one hopes, coming to sympathise a little more with the problems of our own less fortunate communities. It is all too easy to make ourselves feel virtuous by saving children in remote parts of the world. Let us try a little of the same generosity on the children that need it right on our own doorstep - before they grow up, and come and get us!

Labour takes a leap from Albert's book
December 4, 1994

Well, Well, it hardly seems fair, does it? Less than two years after Dick's daring and imaginative salmon-leap into the arms of Albert Reynolds, propelling Albert from being just a footnote in the history books to the status of one of the Great Statesmen of the Twentieth Century, and in the process creating what proved to be really quite a good government (though many of its promises are yet to be delivered upon), the whole thing collapsed like a pack of cards – and all because of one clerical paedophile too many.

These things always seem to happen when I am out of action for some reason or another either in some remote part of the world, where the affairs of Ireland are a subject of massive indifference, or in the air going in that direction. So it was when GUBU broke; so it was when CJ finally packed it in, and so it was, too, on this occasion. Even as the final (?) revelations were emerging from the Attorney General's office, I was on a plane bound for Chicago, on business of a thoroughly metaphysical and unworldly nature.

This time, however, our affairs did not escape the notice of the American public. Ireland has been relatively in the news in the US ever since the "peace process" got under way, and the possible fall of the Irish government, with its presumed consequences for that process, therefore attracted more attention than it might otherwise have. As it was, Irish news made *The New York Times* for fully five days in a row, which constitutes some kind of a record, I think. We even attracted the notice of such an organ as the Notre Dame student newspaper.

My friends were thoroughly intrigued by developments. "What in hell is happening in Ireland?" was the repeated query. "What's this about a *paedophile priest* in the Attorney General's office?" and so on. Americans do like other nations to behave absurdly, within reason (it makes foreign news entertaining, which is how it should be), but they also expect them to act relatively true to form – especially Ireland. A leprechaun in the Attorney General's office would be quite acceptable, but a paedophile priest? I must say I was at something of a loss to explain how the Government could have fallen on such an issue – especially when I made it clear that the priest in question was not in the Attorney General's office, but had actually been in jail in Northern Ireland for some time previously. The best I could do was to present it as a case of gross hubris on the part of Albert.

Becoming one of the World's Great Statesmen (especially from very humble beginnings) plainly has its dangers. Mainly, one develops the notion that one is invincible, that one's judgment is faultless, that one can do no wrong. There was also, surely, the desire to put one's foot on the neck of the despised Dick Spring and his Labour Party, especially in the wake of a set of by-elections where one's own vote had held up reasonably well, while theirs had slumped. The wretched worms would not dare to turn, and after that one would have them where one wanted them. It would hardly be a coalition at all! And so poor old Harry Whelehan became the shortest-lived President of the High Court in the history of this (or any other?) state (we must await the verdict of the *Guinness Book of Records* on that), and Albert himself can get back to the development of a better dog food.

Even as I write this, it does seem as though the wily Bertie will once again ensnare Spring and his party in the embrace of the Soldiers of Destiny. John Bruton, despite his desperation, could not, after all, offer Dick the one thing that might have tempted him away into new liaisons, and the Labour Party certainly do not want an election. In any case, they can look on the whole thing as a kind of victory. The worms did turn, and they caused an earthquake. That must after all be a source of deep satisfaction, whatever other humiliations and anxieties they may have to endure.

So let us assume that the Coalition will after all be patched up, and Bertie and Dick will go forward together into a glorious (short-term) future. What interests me now is the probable long-term effects on Irish public life, and the Irish psyche. The Irish electorate is a funny beast, as one has had repeated occasion to observe. It says now, by a large majority (one must believe these awful polls, I suppose), that it wants nothing so much as for the Coalition to continue, but I think that this whole business has left it deeply disillusioned.

My friends, who for their sins were condemned to campaign

in the recent by-elections in Cork, reported that it was a particularly disheartening process – despite the relatively heartening result (for them). Never had they found people so utterly fed up with all parties, and this despite the relative degree of upturn in the economy. The Labour Party seem blessedly oblivious to how deeply they have hurt and disappointed the Irish electorate. They have plainly forfeited all the hope and confidence that was reposed in them in the last election by choosing to prop up Albert and Fianna Fail, when the electorate had tried to make its views clear on that question. So Labour is in the doghouse, but no one else has come along to attract the electorate's loyalty. The citizens trudged out to vote, in greatly reduced numbers, and inevitably produced a result, but they would have been just as happy, I gather, if the whole lot had been carried off by a mysterious disease.

Compounding this disillusion with the secular authorities, there is now plainly a growing disgust with the Church. Fr Liam Cosgrave of Baldoyle, dying in the arms of two fellow priests in a gay massage parlour, certainly did not help the cause of a Church rocked by a succession of paedophile scandals. While it may not sadden many of us to see the clergy taken down a peg or two. I fear the time may come when we may feel the lack of that source of authority, in the awful moral and political vacuum that I can see coming upon us. We do desperately, after all, need someone to look up to.

Performing without a safety-net
June 25, 1995

There are some signs at the moment that we as a people are in a self-reflective mood. If so, that is a good thing. Something constructive might come of it, if such reflection is channeled in the right directions. Such an event as the death of a national newspaper, however ineptly managed, does tend to concentrate the national mind somewhat, though it cannot be said that most of the reflections that have emerged have been to much purpose. One of the most insidious notions that has floated to the surface in the last few weeks is the usual one in such situations: "The Government should step in".

This has taken the form of calls for a government-sponsored "Commission on the Press in Ireland", which would be expected to do remarkable things – not by governmental fiat, mind you, but by some sort of dialectical osmosis – like decide how many 'titles' would be appropriate for the Irish market. Would this be three, like the Blessed Trinity? Or four, like the Four Evangelists? Or perhaps five, on the model of the Aristotelian elements? It would also decide who should own them – must such a person be Irish, and, *if so*, how Irish? Irish enough to play on the Irish football team, or more Irish than that? And finally, how should they be funded – by people actually *buying* them, or by some more exotic method?

Now one shouldn't be too satirical, of course. There *is* a problem, and one can't blame people for worrying about it. Newspapers are special. They are not like boxes of cornflakes. The soul of the nation is somehow involved. I do not personally, I must confess, much miss the *Irish Press*, but I recognise that there are many (even if a shrinking band) who do, and who feel spiritually impoverished, and threatened, by its demise. It is certainly a great temptation, in such a case, to raise the cry that *somebody should do something*. And indeed I feel that something should be done, but on a much broader scale than just stepping in and saving moribund newspapers. The field of battle is much larger than that. It is no less than the struggle in which we have been engaged

181

since at least the end of the Seventies in the western world (and now in the eastern world as well) between Big Government and Minimal Government.

Now Mrs T and Ronald Reagan have come and gone, the pendulum might appear to be swinging back from them somewhat, but it is not as simple as that, I think. Instead, a sort of Hegelian dialectical process has evolved, in which the 'left' has actually moved closer to the 'centre' than has the 'right', to the extent that these terms are beginning to lose their meaning. A consensus seems to be emerging, beneath the party rhetoric, in countries such as the US, Britain, France, Germany, and even Italy and Spain, that, on the one hand, large-scale government intervention and the throwing of money at problems is not going to produce, in the long term, either jobs or happiness; and on the other, that it is not even in the national interest (setting aside all humanitarian considerations) that there should be no social 'safety net' at all.

People do get stuck at the bottom end of society through no real fault of their own, and certain emergency services must be provided for them, together with a series of well-directed incentives for getting themselves out of that situation. Without that, a dangerous and desperate underclass is created, whose only relief is drugs, and only enterprise is crime – the results of which ultimately cost a great deal more than measures of relief and the encouragement of enterprise.

So, as I say, a broad consensus does seem to have arisen on this great question that has dominated western thought ever since the Enlightenment of the late 18th century, the age of Voltaire and Rousseau, of Goethe and Schiller, of Tom Paine and Adam Smith, of Charles James Fox and Edmund Burke – the question whether or not *somebody should do something*, and if so, what. If the Labour Party in Britain, for instance, took over tomorrow, there would be a certain change of emphasis, perhaps, but not, I think, any radical change of direction. And conversely, in France, Chirac and the conservatives are having to address the problems of unemployment and welfare in more or less the same way that the socialists were doing. All that people argue about, really, is the best way to achieve common objectives.

So there is a sort of consensus around Europe. The question is, though, has the penny dropped in this country yet? One would have thought it might have, but the intoxication of coming into power with a budget surplus that plainly so stimulated Mr Quinn that he decided to make a splash with the country's first (and perhaps the western world's last) Socialist Budget.

Now one would not want to criticise every aspect of that budget – any tax adjustments that get people back to work, for instance, are surely to be welcomed – but it does seem to have revived in many breasts the vision of a government gravy-train (with a cultural restaurant car presided over by the ebullient Michael D) that can ultimately do no good to the national psyche. It is this that sends the remarkable team of Richard Bruton and Pat Rabbitte riding off again and again to save lame ducks, and it may even lead (though this is, admittedly, unlikely) to the raising-up of a kind of zombie *Irish Press* Group, to give the unfortunate employees of that organisation something to do.

The problem is that such moves as this gather to themselves an aura of high-mindedness that is hard to argue against, and very hard for full-time politicians, totally dependent as they are on the pleasure of the electorate, to resist. That makes the role of a truly independent press (and, one might add, television service) doubly important. Questions that are not immediately popular must be raised, and the public must be induced to think about them, even if that process makes it initially very angry. That is a process to which this newspaper has been making notable contributions over the last decade or so, which I hope it will long continue to do.

High IQs and the cow's tail
August 27, 1995

Good God, the points are up again! And with the points there rises, inevitably, the annual tide of discussion as to what is to be done about them - a discussion to which I am now proposing, if I may, to add my pennyworth. The problem does concern me, though not with any great immediacy. Nothing that I have the honour to profess, I'm afraid, gets into the Top Ten, or even the Top 20, on the Points Table. Top of the pops this year, I observe, is something called "Actuarial/Financial" in UCD, which sounds immensely boring, but also seriously profitable. For that you need 585 points, which I calculate (my actuarial skills are not great) to come out as just a little under six A1s. That is 10 points up on last year, and would probably have given Einstein himself a bit of trouble. How was his Irish, by the way?

On the other hand, the news for aspiring scholars is not all bad. If you want to settle for Classical Civilisation in TCD, I observe with some anxiety that the points are down this year from 415 to 380. This is now very attractive. I would plunge heavily into this. Latin, on the other hand, I note with interest, has gone up, from 330 to 355, but is still within the range of most people, and a bargain at this level. (Don't mind the Greek, by the way – at 380, down from 410. You wanna do Greek, you come and see me. I'll give you a glass or two of sherry, and we'll see what we can work out.)

But enough of self-advertisement. Let us try to focus now for a moment on the Larger Issues. What, people are asking, is the Points System doing to our educational fabric? What is doing to our young people? What does it measure? Do we need it at all?

Well now, to take these questions in order: first of all, despite all blather about egalitarianism, it is plain that this system is all about creating, and richly rewarding, intellectual elites. I'm not actually sure, as I say it, what is wrong with that, though it is undeniably a bit hard on the mentally challenged – or, to put it otherwise, on any feckless, lazy layabouts that there may still be in the system. The odd thing about it, though, is that it is creating a sort of hierarchy of subjects, at the top of which one finds things like veterinary medicine, physiotherapy and pharmacy, which are thus consecrated as subjects to the study of which only the absolute cream of intellectual youth should aspire. Now one doesn't want to be snobbish about this, but, really, putting one's arm up a cow's bottom in the middle of the night, for example, does not require an IQ of 155 or more (and 575 points). On the other hand, it could be argued that the complexities of the Middle Irish verbal system require greater scholastic aptitude than is represented by a score of 320, which is what is currently demanded for that particular field of learning.

But the operators and protagonists of the points system will freely admit that the hierarchy of subjects is purely a reflection of supply and demand, not an estimate of intellectual content or worth. They will also grant that the system is not an aptitude test, but simply an indication of basic intelligence and, normally, ability to concentrate one's energies for a period of time. These are things that will stand to you in most circumstances, but do not guarantee that you will make a great doctor, or even a reliable actuary. Their pertinent riposte is, however, 'What do you propose instead?' There is no point, I think, in rambling on about interviews. There are some subjects, I know, such as Drama Studies or Music, for which interviews are mandatory, for fairly obvious reasons, but the strain that imposes on staff is appalling. I know that my friends in Drama are mental and physical wrecks at the end of conducting 200 or so interviews, of reasonably plausible candidates, for 15 places in Drama Studies, and they can never be sure that they really made the right choice. And then there is, in a country like this, the problem of the personal factor. No, no, forget interviews. On the other hand, something like the Scholastic Aptitude Tests (SAT) practised in the American system could well be useful. They do measure natural aptitudes – though they don't tell you what people actually know. That suits the US reasonably well, since one graduates from high school there knowing virtually nothing, but it might not serve us so well at present as a substitute for exams.

So I think that we are stuck with the points system for some time to come. The only real alternative that occurs to me is the rather utopian one (but one that is practised to some extent, for instance, in the New York City school system) of no restrictions on entry to subjects at all, apart from certain basic qualifications, but stringent testing when one is enrolled, which weeds out, after a year or so, all but the best motivated and suited to the subject. That, of course, has its traumas too, but it at least ensures (more or less) that the right people are in the right course. I recognise that our problem in this country is one of resources – both financial and spatial – so I regretfully declare the NYC solution utopian. This, however, I think, is what one should be working towards (something that was, after all, on a much smaller scale, largely the case when I went to College at the end of the fifties) – that one should be welcome, once one has achieved some basic standard of competence (equal, perhaps, to about 320 points), to have a go at whatever line of study might attract one. We may, indeed, get back to that situation, somewhere in the next century, but for the moment, I'm afraid, we are stuck with a bit of a bulge, and this is no fun for anybody.

A slow case of liberal burnout

November 26, 1995

Perhaps I am just getting old (I am getting old, let's face it, though that may not be the significant point), but there does seem to me these days to be something troublesome in the air, at least from the perspective of the liberal agenda. What I sense is a sort of war-weariness, or exhaustion with doing good. We trendy liberals having been fighting the good fight now for almost as long as we can remember, and we have won a fair few victories along the way – from the unbanning of *Ulysses* to the unbanning of Trinity College to the unbanning of *Playboy*, from the provision of contraceptives to decent women in danger of death from excessive child-bearing, to the availability of condoms in every pub jakes in the country, and the right at least to travel abroad for an abortion. But are we now at last beginning to feel, just a little – how should I put it? – shell-shocked?

What I have been sensing over the past few weeks, if not longer, is what one might term a "liberal burnout". You know how the Poverty Czars go on anxiously about exhaustion or resistance on the giving front, when they present us with one too many famine or massacre? Well, I wonder if something of that sort may not be happening in the minds of many (like myself) who would like to think of themselves as liberal? After all, as I say, we have come a rather long way in the past 30 years or so, divorce or no divorce.

I am old enough to remember the heady days of the early 1960s when we, in such organisations as Tuairim (led by lively young chaps such as David Thornley and Declan Costello), or the Irish Association of Civil Liberty (with such figures as Seán O'Faoláin, Frank O'Connor, Owen Sheehy Skeffington and Christo Gore-Grimes at the helm), delighted in tweaking the tail of the establishment or in striking blows for a more pluralist society. Not to mention winning small victories on the censorship front (with the help of that bright young Minister of Justice, Brian Lenihan).

It seemed obvious then that any decent, educated person should be striving to advance the cause of pluralism, secularism and free access to serious works of literature, art and cinema, even if they exhibited some acknowledgement of the facts of life. It also seemed plain that some degree of socialist planning was necessary to redress the inequities endemic in the exercise of untrammelled capitalism. Now, in the mid-1990s, I'm afraid it doesn't any longer seem so simple. One is, of course, 30 years older, but I don't think it's just that. I mean, I was sitting last Sunday in front of the telly watching, just after nine o'clock on BBC 1, that very amusing and clever, though very cynical, mini-series, *The Final Cut*, and noting that, at prime family viewing time, we had a great deal of quite unnecessary adulterous bonking going on. My wife was a trifle depressed, in addition, having just been speaking on the phone to an old friend of ours in California whose husband of 30 years had recently deserted her for a graduate student. We looked at each other, and decided that, on mature consideration, we wouldn't mind putting the liberal agenda on ice for a little while, just to let ourselves and the rest of society assess the situation.

After all, where do you stop? For instance, my friends in the present Irish Council of Civil Liberties have taken a stand against the operation of any censorship at all, even of so-called "video nasties". They would also, I think, be against any constitutional time restrictions on the granting of divorce. I am unwilling to give up my liberal credentials, but I am forced to say that I do not agree with them. It seems to me that the State has a right, and a duty, to suppress exploitative and depraved materials. whether on film, in pop songs, or in magazines, even as it has a right and duty to restrict access to guns or explosives, and that the constitutional provision for a delay for four years fixed on by the Government in this present divorce referendum was well-balanced and wise, as against the simple dropping of the relevant article, as advocated by the PDs.

Maybe I'm just running out of steam, but I rather think I am not alone in this. I propose to go out and vote in favour of this referendum, and I hope that it passes, but after that I must say that I also hope, and I think that this hope is shared by many, that the country will award itself a breathing space – of perhaps 10, or even 20, years – and give us all the time to assess the pros and cons of the new society which we have created. The communist dream, after all, has gone up in smoke. Faith in a socialist solution to the ills of society has been gravely dented. And now I fear that the phenomenon of liberal burn-out may be upon us. But we shouldn't worry too much. This may after all just be a case of society, like a living organism, taking steps towards self-preservation.

Time to look into our hearts
July 7, 1996

I returned to Ireland on the boat to Rosslare on the morning of June 27, after an absence of six months, during which I had had virtually no news of the dear old country. A little along the way to Dublin we stopped to buy a paper. "Hey, look at this," said my wife. "Veronica Guerin's been shot."

"I know," I said, "but that was last year. A fellow shot her in the leg. That's not news. Unless they caught him or something."

"No, no," said my wife, reading on, "this was yesterday afternoon. And they shot her dead."

I pulled over the car, and we studied the paper together. A cold wave of depression flooded over me. I was inclined for a moment to drive back to Rosslare and take the next boat out. A bit over the top, perhaps? I don't know. I can't claim even a basic acquaintance with Veronica Guerin, though we sometimes appeared in the same issue of the paper, and I greatly admired what she was doing. It was rather the wider implications of the act that depressed me.

What the present juncture is a golden opportunity for, I should say, is a comprehensive National Forum on Justice, Law Enforcement and Crime, on the model of the Forum on Education which did a lot of useful work a couple of years ago. I would strongly urge Nora Owen to organise such a Forum for the autumn, and to invite submissions from as wide a spectrum of organisations and interests as possible - not just lawyers, prison officers, and policemen, but social workers, prisoners' rights organisations, even drug addicts - anyone at all who has experience of the problems and a point of view.

We need to discuss the legal system, the structure of the police, the organisation of the prisons, bail, the right to silence, community service, rehabilitation, detoxification, a host of other details. The whole country needs to think about the problems, and in particular the intimate connection between unemployment and crime, and what, if anything, it is prepared to do about that (e.g. in accepting the need for more work-sharing). Only a well-publicised national debate will succeed in bringing all the dimensions of the problem into the open.

There are serious difficulties in the way of this, unfortunately. The fact is that powerful forces intimately concerned with these problems do not at all want any general discussion of the issues, as any such discussion would inevitably focus on their inadequacies. I refer, of course, to the Department of Justice, the senior echelons of the Garda Siochana, and the legal profession. That is quite a lot for a Minister of Justice to take on, but I think that this one is going to have to take them on, if she wants to go down in history as a great reforming minister, rather than just another harmless cipher, triumphantly neutralised by her department. Certainly any such Forum as I propose would generate a great deal of vacuous waffle, but the waffle could be subjected to firm and rational criticism, so that purely silly proposals would be winnowed out, leaving a solid core of useful ones, which could then be embodied in a report. The appointment of a good chairman (or woman) and panel of assessors would of course be of great importance, but there are a number of excellent candidates. To propose names would be invidious. I leave that to the Minister.

Of course, a Forum in itself is not going to solve the problem of crime, organised or otherwise. What it will do, however, if properly managed and, publicised, will be to make this society look at itself, and ask itself what features of it in particular are those which would tend to induce unemployment, the despair and lack of self-respect consequent on that, and the dependence on alcohol and drugs that is in turn the consequence of that. In the unlikely event that such a Forum is convened (I very much fear that the Dept. of Justice would move effectively to squash any such proposal), and in the even more improbable event that I were called to make a submission before it, I would have a few things to say.

They would concern such matters as:

(1) the conditional provision of drugs - as well as every provision for detoxification if desired, of course - to registered addicts;

(2) an agency to establish a sort of "after-sales service" to released prisoners, in the way of assisting them to find jobs and reintegrate into the community;

(3) encouragement of a system of paid "tutors" for teenage youths in deprived areas, taken from among student volunteers from somewhat more privileged backgrounds, who could give them a notion of what life should be about; and

(4) the establishment of some sort of non-military "national service" system, to take young people off the streets for some period during the vital years of 17–19 and help to put some order into their lives.

But all that is material for another occasion, perhaps. To conclude, let me return for a moment to Veronica herself, and a disquieting thought that has occurred to me. How many and what sort of people had occasion to know that she would be in Naas on June 26, to answer a speeding charge? Could it possibly be that someone tipped someone the wink that this troublesome female was going to be in Naas on that particular forenoon? But no, that's a terrible thought! Let's drop the subject.

Ulster has great potential as a theme park

January 11, 1998

There seemed for some little time last year, especially in the wake of the triumph of the eminently flexible Mr Blair, to be a grave danger of peace and reasonableness breaking out in that fascinating corner of the planet termed 'Northern Ireland'. Over the Yuletide, however - that season which the rest of the civilised world fatuously associates with benevolence and good cheer – this danger has considerably receded. We are now set, it would seem, for a restoration, on the part of all parties concerned, of business as usual.

In the days of the promulgation of 'framework documents', I recall that the Taoiseach of the day went on record as welcoming all the other framework documents which had been emerging over the period, and even as exhorting all groups and individuals concerned to produce their own framework documents, so that full and frank discussion could take place on the widest possible front. An excellent sentiment! If anyone at all in the coming weeks feels a framework document coming on, then I think it is a splendid idea that he or she should get it off his or her chest. In that spirit, I thought I would modestly contribute my own tentative framework, since it differs in some respects from any of the other frameworks so far published, or likely to be in the future.

These ideas, let me say first of all, are not new. In fact. I proposed them to the Editor a number of years ago, when framework documents were all the rage, and he put them straight into the wastepaper basket. Now, however, it seems to me that a propitious occasion has arisen for reviving them. Two considerations in particular have prompted me to these proposals: first, the current problems that the Office of Public Works are having in finding anywhere to situate their interpretative centres; and secondly, an ingenious concept devised recently by an entrepreneur in the former East Germany, which came to my notice a little while ago.

This gentleman, stimulated by the growing wave of nostalgia for the appurtenances of the old German Democratic Republic, has decided to create a sort of theme park somewhere outside Berlin, preserving all the characteristics of the former state (even including, I believe, the possibility of being interrogated by the beloved Stasi), and he expects it to do very well. Just the thing for a Sunday afternoon excursion for all the family! I think we could learn from this. In short, and not to beat about the bush, I think that this whole idea of introducing rationality and consensus into the area conventionally termed 'Northern Ireland' is quite misguided, and should be abandoned. It is plain from the frenzied reaction of the majority group in that preposterous place, the so-called 'Unionists', that no hope can be entertained of any agreed solution to the problems of the area – or rather, of the contradictions inherent in it.

Instead, I propose that the place should be preserved just as it was up to August 1994 – when the first of these spurious 'ceasefires' was declared – and turned into a theme park. Plainly, nostalgia is growing, especially in the 'Unionist' community, for the 'good old days' of indiscriminate violence – the jolly sound of gunfire, soldiers roaring around in armoured cars, bombs going off in all directions, the crackling of fires, buildings collapsing, and then the soothing background noises of funeral processions, and of women and children weeping for the dead.

It may seem to an outsider that such phenomena were malign and much to be deplored, but that would be a superficial view. The canny Ulster mind can see beneath the surface, and discern, behind every burning or collapsed building, glorious claims for compensation, lots of work for the building industry, and ever-increasing employment in the security sector. As for the regular deaths, they certainly kept the funeral homes busy. And, above and beyond all these advantages, there was the profound comfort of knowing where one stood. There was an obvious enemy, who could be relied upon to commit periodic atrocities. There was the Union to be defended, a whole way of life to be preserved, ancient grievances to be clutched to the breast.

Is all of this to be surrendered for the uncertain joys of sweet reasonableness? No, let us not continue to torment our Northern brethren in this way. We are trying to fit them into a scenario for which they are not in the least suited. That sort of thing may be all right for black and white South Africans, or for Arabs and Jews, but it is simply not appropriate for Ulster. Much better to turn the clock back, and let them have at it.

Only this time, I suggest, we should try and make some money out of them. Let the Americans and the Europeans take their largesse away. It was kind of them, but it really wouldn't have worked. Instead, we should take matters into our own hands. Just declare the whole place a theme park, set up a ring of interpretative centres all round the border, and charge tourists to come and view them at their favourite activities. We can offer Orange marches, Lambeg drums, ould Orange flutes and all, along with Nationalist stone-throwing and baton charges from the RUC, pub massacres, ambushes, funerals (Protestant and Catholic), and perhaps a rousing sermon or two (recorded) from a giant inflatable Ian Paisley. All these attractions to be viewed, at one's own risk, for a modest fee.

As other areas of conflict round the world progressively fade away – Palestine, Bosnia, Chechnya, Cambodia, Rwanda, Algeria - Ulster will be left alone on the world stage as the Greatest Show on Earth. That should please them. It is certainly the role to which they are best suited.

Getting off this merry-go-round
March 8, 1998

Just two months ago, on the eve of the present round of constitutional deliberations in the North, I wrote a piece in this paper which was in fact intended as humorous, though it was not so taken in certain quarters. I ventured to propose that the efforts to arrive at any peaceful, rational solution in that part of the world were quite misguided, and the whole place should be simply turned into a theme park, where the rest of the world could come (and pay good money) to study the effects of prejudice, superstition, violence and irrationalism. Now I did not really intend this proposal seriously – I emphasise this just to reassure readers in remote parts of the country, such as Dublin 4. Indeed, if anything, I had some naive hope that this sort of squib might provoke the parties concerned into taking their task a little more seriously, and arrive at the reasonable solution that is staring them in the face. However, two months further on into this dismal farce, I am beginning to wonder if I was not onto something after all.

The latest charade surrounding the expulsion of Sinn Fein seems to me to reveal with grim clarity something most important, not so much about Sinn Fein and its degree of commitment to the Mitchell Principles, as about the degree of sincerity and commitment of the Ulster Unionists. After all, 'informed sources' and mere common sense both indicate that the recent bomb attacks in Moira and Portadown are not the work of the Sinn Fein leadership, nor even the work of the IRA leadership, but of disaffected elements within the latter organisation.

No doubt Gerry Adams has a pretty good idea who these persons are, and he could condemn, or even shop, them, if he wanted, but to ask him to do either of those things is to ask him to cut his own throat politically (if not literally), and thus make him quite useless in the negotiating process. There is simply no sense in Adams and McGuinness undercutting their own efforts in this way. In face of that, then, the posturings of Mr Trimble and his men would reveal them either as total idiots, which they certainly are not, or as cynical exploiters of the difficulties of their opponents.

This latter is, I'm afraid, what they are. They had a glorious time down in Dublin last week. And they didn't have to budge an inch on anything as unpleasant as cross-border institutions. They were able to frustrate the process of the whole session by focusing on the mechanics of expelling Sinn Fein from the talks, all the time hammering away at their mantra of the two-facedness and treachery of 'Sinn Fein/IRA', with the clear implication that Mr Adams was ordering car bombs to go off in quiet market towns while he sat at the negotiating table talking about peace. Now, if we agree that no sensible person could believe that scenario, we are driven, I fear, to the conclusion that this shows with dreadful clarity what Mr Trimble's agenda is. He has no interest whatever in any settlement other than a return to Stormont in its pristine form, and an agreement by the Croppies that they lie down again, and accept their lot.

In fact, Paisley and Robinson, loathsome as they are, are more honest about the whole business. His Reverence's fixed view is that, in his words, "God does not negotiate with the Devil," and he has nothing to say to the other side. Mr Trimble has acquired the skill to appear plausible and reasonable – something that Jim Molyneaux scorned to do, preferring just to squat there like an old tortoise until things blew over – but he has no intention of giving anything away.

A perfectly sensible and workable solution is now staring everyone in the face, after all. This involves (1) a power-sharing assembly, on the South African model, complemented by (2) a set of north-south committees, whose work should be constructive and unobtrusive, concentrating on practicalities such as agriculture, fisheries and tourism; the monitoring of the whole arrangement should be the hands of (3) a committee or Council of the Isles, formed from the parliaments of England, Scotland, Wales and Ireland. It's a bit messy, a bit unwieldy, but it's not bad, in the circumstances.

That, as I say, is staring these gobdaws in the face. If the DUP and Sinn Fein don't like it, then that is too bad, but it is foolish to suppose that it is fatal to the process. If Sinn Fein reject such a solution (as they probably will), and return to violence, I think that they will find that they are out in the cold. Without the fuel of a sense of exclusion and injustice, they, and others similarly minded, will find that their support dries up, leaving them a fairly easy prey for a reconstituted and community-based police force.

There it is, then, in a nutshell. But to get any further, somebody has to be prepared to bang heads together. Mo Mowlam may be just the lady to do that.

Insurance war needs a 'plan of campaign'

August 10, 2003

Can it be that a grass-roots revolt against the great post-September 11 insurance scam, fuelled by desperation and the conviction that the Government will ultimately do nothing, is finally getting underway? In the *Irish Independent* of Saturday, June 21 came the heartening news that a number of major enterprises, such as Supermac, Avis and a number of major hotel chains, had decided to suspend payment of grossly inflated premiums to the insurance companies, and "go it alone", simply setting aside a sum of money themselves to cover possible claims against them. Now this is all very well, but, as Gerry McGaughey, of the Alliance for Insurance Reform (himself the owner of the building firm Century Homes), has warned, no "self-insurance" scheme is likely to survive the shock of a major injury or damage claim, certainly at the present preposterous rates of compensation awards, and there is a grave danger of bankruptcies resulting from such a course of action. And yet somehow a stand must be made.

Is there any better, safer way of proceeding than this? I think that there is, and it is a proposal that I have already made to the heads of the Irish universities, in response to the recent round of cutbacks that we have all had to face in higher education. In our own case, in Trinity College, one can make a direct connection between increases in insurance premiums and the necessity for stripping the modern language departments of the native-speaking assistants that are an essential part of their elementary language programmes, and likewise, science departments of lab assistants. In other words, our young people shall be hamstrung in their education in order that the insurance barons may grow even fatter, and buy even larger yachts.

My proposal, which would apply equally well to the world of business, both large and small, is as follows. It is actually borrowed from the techniques practised, with considerable success, by leaders of the Irish Land League of the late 1880s, such as Michael Davitt and my grandfather, John Dillon, against the rapacious landlords of those times. It was called the "Plan of Campaign", and it worked like this: the tenants did not simply withhold their rent; they offered the landlord a fair rent, based on the rates prevailing before the latest round of unjustified increases. If that was refused (as, initially, it normally was), the money was paid into a common bank account, administered by the Land League (often under the auspices of the local parish priest), and used to defend and compensate any tenant who was evicted. The process of eviction was troublesome and expensive, and most landlords settled fairly quickly – though there were some conspicuous holdouts. The campaign ran from 1886 to 1891, and, despite some setbacks (including a conspicuous lack of support from Charles Stewart Parnell himself), it very largely achieved its objectives. So, how can that be transferred to the situation we face at the present day?

Well, what I would propose is that whole segments of industry, such as building firms, car-hire firms, or the hotel and restaurant sector, having offered their respective insurers a fair premium (and this having been rejected), form themselves into consortia, pooling sums of money equivalent to their pre-September 11 premiums, and holding them in common bank accounts – preferably of an interest-bearing nature – and sit tight. ISME could do the same for small and medium businesses, which are often the hardest hit. Despite the enormous reserves built up by the insurance industry over the last few years, such determined and coordinated action would inevitably begin to bite within a relatively short time. And the publicity generated by such a move should stimulate the Government to some kind of decisive action. And meanwhile, every claim against anybody will be contested to the death.

Of course there will be squeals of protest from the insurance industry, and prophecies of doom. They will, with much justification, blame the rapacity of the legal profession, and our crazy compo-culture. We will grant them that, while reminding them that they so often foster this themselves by going along with unreasonable claims through an unwillingness to meet them in court, simply passing on the consequent increased premiums, without consultation, to the customer.

But the fact is that a start has to be made somewhere, and we would propose to start with them. From their discomfiture the collapse of the rest of this evil empire will surely follow.

Charged a whopping €25 for a single transaction

September 28, 2003

I would regard myself as a normally satisfied bank customer. I have enjoyed good relations with my local branch of the Bank of Ireland in Raheny, in fact, for very nearly half a century (back to 1957, to be specific). If I have been ripped off in the past, it has been in so genteel a fashion that I quite failed to notice it. It is with all the more annoyance, therefore, that I recount the following tale. A month or so ago, I had the need to send a subscription of €100 to a learned society that I belong to which is based in Germany, and to that end I went down to my local branch to draft the money across to the society's bank account. That I had to do this is, of course, a gross outrage for a start, arising from the fact that, despite allegedly being a single uniform monetary zone, one cannot just write a cheque to another section of this zone. I know the excuse: there is no European central clearing house. But such an excuse is quite absurd; they had fully 10 years to think about that, if they had wanted to – or if the European Union had had the wit, or the will, to force them to.

Anyhow, I asked the girl behind the counter to do this thing for me. She did mention that there would be a charge, but I grandly waved that aside. How much could it be, I thought – €2, maybe even €5? What the hell! So off I went about my business, and a week or so later there arrived a notice, reporting the transaction, and specifying the charge. It came to €24.78 – €17.78 from the Bank of Ireland itself, and another €7.00 thrown in by the German bank; that is to say, pretty nearly a 25 per cent charge for this simple electronic transaction. I stormed back to the bank at the earliest available moment – which actually took a few weeks, since I was rather busy – and demanded to know the rationale behind this. All they could tell me at the bank, blandly and smugly, was that that was the regular charge for such a transaction, and they showed me the brochure.

Indeed it was so: Interpayplus, which takes three working days, costs this amount (just as well I didn't choose Interpayexpress: that would have run me a further €12.70!) And that's the minimum charge. So if I had to pay a subscription of, let us say, €25 – as I very well might – that would amount to a 100 per cent mark-up. And all that for an electronic transaction that shouldn't take much more than a few seconds – and in relation to a country with which we are meant to be locked together in fiscal unity. Not Swaziland. Not Paraguay. Not North Korea. Just Germany!

This is not, of course, just a difficulty with Irish banks. It is a euro-wide problem. I have lived long enough in the United States to appreciate that, despite the existence of 50 distinct states of the union, and a vast proliferation of banks, there is not the least problem about sending a cheque from California to Maine, or North Dakota, or indeed Alaska, without any special charges. I find it quite incomprehensible, in this electronic age, that such a feat should be beyond the capabilities of the European banking system. The truth is that this is *not* beyond their capabilities; it is simply a scam, dreamed up to compensate for the loss of their profits on the exchange rate, and it is being connived at by the national governments concerned, for reasons not clear to me. Perhaps some economist will explain?

We need to encourage dropping-out
August 22, 2004

The latest crop of school-leavers have come through their strenuous academic rite of passage, and we in the university sector are left wondering what we will be faced with in the coming year. The pundits have performed their annual chewing-over of the results. Various interested parties, from the business community, parents' organisations, and teachers' unions, have lamented the failure rates in certain key subjects, such as Maths, Physics and Chemistry, and Biology, while the Minister, predictably, looked on the bright side. And he had a few good points to make. One was that the failure rates in these subjects were actually a little lower than last year, which appears to be true. Another, which is certainly true, is that we have attained an almost 60 per cent rate of progression to third-level education - more or less the highest in Europe.

Now it may well be that a fair proportion of that 60 per cent would be better employed, in the words of the immortal Myles na Gopaleen, out there snagging turnips; but since this valuable economic function is now much more efficiently performed by large machines, it is arguable that they may these days suitably turn their hands to such higher studies as Baking Technology and Management, Hospitality Information Technology, Aquaculture, or Multimedia Applications Development. The serious problem remains, however, in the eyes of the authorities, the relatively high failure rate in Maths, and the relatively low take-up of courses in Science. But is this, after all, such a great disaster? Speaking as one who gave up Maths, very happily, at the age of 15 (after getting through O Levels), and who never did any Science at all, I am moved to wonder whether this might not be all for the best, and a sign that the youth of the country are beginning to assert themselves, albeit dimly, against the neatly wrapped futures that are being planned for them.

What is it that leads me to have some hope of this? Well, there are certain straws in the wind. One considerable authority, the Chief Examiner in Maths, has delivered himself of the view that the youth are too frivolous and fun-loving to give Maths the concentration it requires. The youth, it seems, are out there boozing and fornicating when they should be in doing their sums, and when they are not engaged in that activity, they are working at part-time jobs to finance their lifestyles. That may very well be so, but the Chief Examiner should bear in mind that Maths, for the great majority of us, is a very tedious subject, the very thought of which can bring on a strong desire for spiritous refreshment. Only a select few, in my experience, have been gifted with really mathematical minds, and they should be left to come to grips with the higher reaches of the subject. The rest of us can be left to add, subtract, divide and multiply, and even to calculate fractions and percentages, with the help of a pocket calculator.

But what, IBEC and the Government wonder, is going to happen to the Celtic Tiger, if insufficient young people turn to such sciences as Biology and Chemistry? I really don't see that they have to worry too much about that. The fact is that 6,207 took the Higher Level Chemistry paper this year, up from 5,731 last year, and 16,015 took the Biology paper, up from 13,783, and this in a period of falling numbers overall. What more do they want? At the higher level, Biology is the third most popular subject in the curriculum, after English (32,471) and – surprisingly to me, at least – Geography (21,746). This year, it pushed Business (15, 034) into fourth place.

It seems to me, therefore, that quite enough of the youth are doing the bidding of their elders; I am only relieved to observe that some few are resisting them. This Government and its agents, in fact, remind me a little of the rulers of earlier days, who were accustomed to call upon the mothers of the nation to produce more and more stalwart sons, so that they could send them into battle to die gloriously in pursuit of whatever imperialist adventure had caught their fancy that particular year.

Now, admittedly, filling a slot in some biotech, IT, or financial services enterprise is considerably less unpleasant than going over the top at the Battle of the Somme, but it is arguably far more boring, and I have a certain sympathy with those who would prefer to head off for a beach in Thailand rather than do their duty in that area. In fact, what I would hope for from this generation is a little more dropping-out. What we need, I would suggest, is a return to the spirit of the Sixties.

A generational revolt, after all, is long overdue. I rather hoped for something like that back in the Nineties, but no such luck. There was far too much money to be made, and that was a pleasant new sensation for most people in this country. Now we have done that, though, and it might be time for a rethink.

The sixties, for those too young to remember, were preposterous in many ways, but actually quite fun. There was Peace, and there was Love, and there was lots of pot, but above all there was a profound revulsion against the idea of going out and earning one's living in any sort of a nine-to-five way. What was life for, we asked ourselves? Was it not important to get fully in touch with ourselves? Now, I don't want to instil too much terror into the authorities, but I just wonder if another generational wave of revulsion against the ideals set by the establishment might not be on the cards.

Meanwhile, let me leave the statistics buffs amongst you with one upbeat snippet: numbers taking Greek in this year's Leaving Certificate were up by almost 8 per cent – from 14 to 15! I hope to see many of these gallant souls in my Greek class in October, but I rather fear than many will be bullied or seduced by their elders into heading for Law, Medicine, or even (God help us) Actuarial and Financial Studies. Any free spirits, though, who decide to stick with Greek will be richly rewarded.

Apocalypse now, or at least soon
September 5, 2004

Sadly, as we all know, the last blow for Ireland at the recent Olympic Games was struck, not by Cian O'Connor in the equestrian arena, but in the marathon, by Fr Neil Horan, late of Scartaglen, Co Kerry, who was not himself in pursuit of a medal, gold or otherwise, but something far higher. In fact, Fr Horan has been commissioned by the Lord Himself to inform us all that the end of the world is at hand. Naturally in view of the enormity and urgency of his message, Fr Horan cannot hide his light under a bushel. He must proclaim his news where he is most likely to be heard. That means, ideally, at large gatherings of the witless and ungodly, when they are gathered in pursuit of some vain or illusory goal – the Olympics being one good example of this, the Silverstone Grand Prix being another.

It is a little harsh to condemn him for this. What would St Paul have done, after all? St Paul in his day, as we are told in Acts, ch. 17, turned up in Athens and attempted to bring the business of the state to a standstill by preaching in the marketplace. And why? "His spirit was provoked within him," we are told, "as he saw that the city was full of idols." In the event, he was seized and brought before the Council of the Areopagus, the Supreme Court of the Athenians, where he informed the state elders that they were worshipping entirely the wrong gods, and that they should turn to the worship of the One True God without delay. He actually made a few converts, including a certain Dionysius, but he did not much impress the Council as a whole. They decided he was pretty harmless, though, so they decided not to imprison him, but (reading between the lines) to run him out of town instead. At any rate, he left for Corinth shortly afterwards.

Fr Horan is similarly moved to convey to us the urgency of our situation, and his warnings are falling generally on deaf ears – though I believe that he has had some success in Northern Ireland. His is a lonely and thankless task, but he is not entirely alone. I am credibly informed, by an Israeli friend, that there are fully 40 Messiahs incarcerated at any one time in various looney-bins in and around Jerusalem (which is a place that they would naturally head for) and there are probably a few more wandering around loose as well. Now at least 39 of these gentlemen are plainly imposters, but what about the fortieth? How can we be sure?

The world, after all, has to come to an end some time, and this time is as good as any. The millennium attracted a good deal of attention from the prophetic fraternity (there was a noticeable increase in Messiahs, for example), but it was naive to suppose that God would do anything so obvious – they should have learned that from the fiasco of the last millennium. He will much more likely come like a thief in the night – if, as I suspect, He has not simply given up on us, and turned His attention to something more promising in another galaxy.

However, we are assured that, before the end comes, there will be Signs and Wonders of various descriptions. In fundamentalist circles in the US, there is a widespread belief that, before the Second Coming of Christ, the Temple in Jerusalem will have to be rebuilt, and that is why they are so active in egging on extremist elements in Israel. The catch here, however, from the Jewish point of view, is that, soon after the Temple is rebuilt, the Jews are all to be either converted to Christianity or destroyed.

I am actually inclined to give more significance to a far more sinister sign that has manifested itself in recent years, and that is the alarming indications that the White House has been taken over by aliens. It has long been an article of faith among the American survivalist fraternity, holed up in cabins in the mountains of the western United States, that the Federal Government has been thus taken over. Just of late, though, it is beginning to look a good deal more plausible. Now of course the beings presenting themselves as Bush, Cheney, Rumsfeld, and Condoleezza Rice look like perfectly normal human beings – regular straight-up guys (and gal), in fact – but of course they would, wouldn't they? Admittedly, there is a shadowy layer of figures behind them, not often seen in public, persons with names like Perle, Wolfowitz and Rove, who are really masterminding the whole operation, but even they look passably human.

We must not be deceived by that, however. What, after all, would you expect? Little green blobs with waving antennae would simply not be acceptable to the public. So these entities are not going to be identified by the way they look The key thing is to observe what they are doing. In that connection, I have just been reading a most intriguing book called *The New Pearl Harbor* – I recommend it warmly – proving beyond any doubt that the destruction of the Twin Towers and the attack on the Pentagon were in fact engineered by the US Administration itself (the details are too complex to go into here). The purpose was, of course, to acquire an excuse to invade Iraq – but not, as vulgarly supposed, to gain control of oil supplies. No, these people knew that they could never succeed in bringing peace and democracy to Iraq. They are simply attempting to bring on an apocalyptic Third World War, after which they will retire to wherever they came from.

Now why, you might ask, are they doing this, and who is behind them? I'm afraid I can't answer that, though it has to be admitted we are a pretty sinful lot. If the Lord has anything to do with it, one can only reflect that His ways are infinitely mysterious. But that something of this sort is afoot I have no doubt, and it seems a plausible preamble to the end of the world.

So, after all, Fr Neil may have the last laugh on us, though it may be but a brief one. Meanwhile, I expect we will be seeing and hearing more of him. A pity he didn't make the recent Madonna Concert in Slane, but then one can't get to everything. Perhaps a streaking diversion at the next Fianna Fail Árd Fheis?

Europeans are wimps, long live America

September 19, 2004

It was surely a shrewd move by the EU establishment to appoint our own John Bruton as the Union's Ambassador to the US. He is Anglophone, he is an Irishman, and he is personally amiable and highly intelligent. It is good to think that before long his well-known belly-laugh will be echoing through the drawing-rooms of Washington. However, his job will not be an easy one. Apart from the problem of establishing an identity distinct from that of the ambassadors of, say, Britain, France, Germany, or Italy, he is facing into quite a new era in European-American relations – especially if George W. Bush triumphs in November, as now seems probable.

US-European relations are generally agreed to be at an all-time low, and not likely to improve under the present American regime, especially after being returned to power. I have just come upon a little book, however, which might prove to be of some help to our John in his new environment. It is not reassuring reading, but it does, I think, help considerably to explain why things are the way they are. The book is *Of Paradise and Power* (Knopf, New York, 2003) by Robert Kagan. Its 103 pages will not take him more than a day to read, and it will be well worth it. Its significance is that the author is one of the ideological gurus of an entity called the Project for a New American Century, a group that includes such luminaries as Dick Cheney, Donald Rumsfeld, Paul Wolfowitz, Francis Fukuyama (of *End of History* fame), Dan Quayle (remember him?), and Jeb Bush.

I was not disposed to like this book, knowing whence it emanated, but I must admit that it is well written, and shows evidence of wide research and considerable philosophical reflection. I am not entirely surprised by this, as the author is the son of a distinguished ancient historian, Donald Kagan, a major authority on the origins of the Peloponnesian War, but it is actually all the more spine-chilling for that. The thrust of this extended essay is, in bald terms, that Europe is clapped out, Europeans are wimps, America has to carry the can in defence of the world order, and, in consequence, diplomatic niceties apart, there is no longer any real community of interest between Europe and the US. Of course, Kagan does not spell things out thus baldly, since this is written in a scholarly rather than journalistic mode, but he makes his views clear enough, and he argues for them very shrewdly. His title establishes the polarity which he wants to develop. 'Paradise' is the state of post-modern bliss at which he feels Europe has arrived – a fool's paradise, though he is too tactful to say so – while 'power' is what the US is left wielding, all by itself. Europe is able to enjoy its happy state only by virtue of the maintenance of American power – which Europeans are so ungrateful and inept as to incessantly carp at.

Kagan begins his essay as follows:

"It is time to stop pretending that Europeans and Americans share a common view of the world, or even that they occupy the same world. On the all-important question of power – the efficacy of power, the morality of power – American and European perspectives are diverging."

America, in fact, is still in the 'real' world, a Hobbesian universe where dog eats dog, and power comes out of the barrel of a gun; Europeans aspire to a Kantian world, where reason prevails, and consensus is reached by negotiation and compromise. Kagan's (not unreasonable) position is that this beautiful arrangement is not going to work as long there are boyos like Saddam and Osama and Kim Jong-Il and Robert Mugabe on the loose, even as it did not work with Hitler and Mussolini. In fact, the nub of his argument is that Europe simply exhausted itself in the last century in a succession of disastrous wars, and it has elevated that exhaustion into an ideology.

His chapter titles give a good impression of the tone of the treatise: 'The Power Gap'; 'Psychologies of Power and Weakness'; 'Hyperpuissance' (this a begrudging French epithet for the American position); 'The Postmodern Paradise; Is it still "the West"?'; 'Adjusting to Hegemony' (this last is a call to America to shoulder its responsibilities). And Kagan is no voice crying in the wilderness – the book is warmly praised on the back cover by such notables as Henry Kissinger, Sen. John McCain, and George P. Schulz. He is speaking from within the charmed circle, and he is being listened to. For ideologues like Kagan, 9/11 was a providential development, and he does not mind saying so. "America did not change on September 11," he proclaims, "it only became more itself. For younger generations of Americans who do not remember Munich or Pearl Harbor, there is now September 11."

There is indeed. It is most interesting that Kagan should dwell as he does on Pearl Harbor. Even as revisionist historians are now inclined to postulate that FDR had advance warning of Pearl Harbor or something very like it, and let it happen, so suspicious minds these days are increasingly driven to speculate as to whether Kagan and his friends in the White House did not at least know about the imminence of 9/11, and did nothing to stop it.

At any rate, John Bruton would do well to read and digest this little book. It will not exactly brighten his day, but it will at least give him a good idea of what he is up against.

Sinn Fein would have made us into a Burma
October 9, 2004

The old chestnut of 1916 has raised its hoary head in recent weeks, sparked by the most interesting speech of John Bruton on September 18 in the Mansion House, Dublin, to an outfit called the Reform Movement. John Bruton's "coming out" as a supporter of the Irish Parliamentary Party is indeed a notable development, and it naturally greatly delights me. But it has also roused the ire of moss-backed old republicans everywhere.

I should say, first of all, that the proposal to rejoin the British Commonwealth, at this stage of our history, seems to me to have little to commend it. If we had never left the Commonwealth, admittedly, I should certainly feel no need to do so now (think, after all: of all the nations formerly colonised by the British, who else has left – apart from those who were thrown out? Burma! Is that the company we wish to keep?). But there seems little sense in rejoining now, in the context of the EU – and it is hardly going to impress the Ulster Unionists too much, after all, if that is part of the point. However, a rather different kind of association of the island nations – Scotland, Wales, England and ourselves – might have something to commend it, now that Scotland and Wales have attained a measure of independence, and the Reform Movement might turn its attention to exploring that.

But to the present. A number of basic claims have surfaced in the last two weeks that need to be confronted. The first is what I would term the Sinn Fein tradition's "Big Lie": that the Home Rule Act of 1914 did not confer a sufficient measure of independence to satisfy the historic aspirations of the Irish nation. Well, they have to say that, of course, don't they? Otherwise the much-vaunted Blood Sacrifice of Easter Week, and all the dismal consequences of that, up through the Civil War of 1922-3, would be revealed as superfluous. Of course the Home Rule Act was a pretty limited instrument, but I don't think that any respectable historian would now deny that it provided just as effective a "freedom to achieve freedom" as did the Treaty of 1921.

Once the Brits had pulled the troops out, one had only to proceed with a reasonable degree of deviousness and circumspection in order to achieve whatever measure of independence has been now achieved by such nations as Canada, Australia or India.

It would be optimistic, perhaps, to claim that Home Rule would have avoided Partition, as the Unionists were already in an extreme frame of mind long before 1914, but the fact remains that my grandfather and Sir James Craig knew and respected each other, and would have been in a position, after 1918, to work out a much more satisfactory system of relationships than in fact developed.

One could argue that we would almost certainly have been involved in the Second World War, but, first of all, I would regard that as a far more honest position to have been in than what we were stuck with, and secondly, such involvement would certainly have resulted in much more rapid social and economic development in the post-war years, instead of leaving us in a time-warp until well into the Sixties (cf. Tom Garvin's recent excellent book, *Preventing the Future: why was Ireland so poor for so long?*). So, if the conditions of autonomy and nationhood had been substantially achieved by 1914 (and the fact is that the Irish Party had been largely running the country, at the local level, for a decade or more before that), where does leave the Easter Rising?

The best that can be said for it is that it was a very shrewdly-planned terrorist act – let us call a spade a spade! – and, like many terrorist acts, unfortunately, it largely achieved its objective. To give Pearse his due, unlike many modern terrorists, he was not concerned to kill large numbers of innocent people – though he had no compunction about seriously disrupting their lives. And he was quite content to die himself. But he shared with modern terrorists the desire to bring down the established order by delivering a violent shock to it, and he certainly achieved that. The British, of course, in the middle of a war, could be relied upon to do their part by responding with violent repression (my grandfather, in the immediate aftermath, urged Asquith, instead, to introduce Home Rule forthwith, but that naturally fell on deaf ears), and events proceeded to their natural conclusion in the election of 1918.

At that election, I would contend, this country was in effect hijacked by a relatively small group of enthusiasts, whose agenda included reimposing an idealised Gaelic language and culture on a largely multi-cultural nation, and taking that nation effectively out of the modern world, to become a kind of Burma. That this did not happen, in the long run, is a tribute to the basic good sense of the Irish nation, and of the leaders who emerged from the Civil War. But the fact remains that the agenda of the original Sinn Fein leaders was very different.

All that is left of this now, for most of us, is a sort of dull pain in the back of the head, a small cranky voice telling us that we are never quite Irish enough, that we are eternal backsliders and traitors to the cause. And that, I think, is something that we could all do without as we move on into the 21st Century.

Organised religion has truly wrong-footed Him

January 16, 2005

Poor old God! What with the tsunami in South-East Asia, and then the abduction and murder of young Robert Holohan in Middleton, He has had a pretty grim few weeks, both on the larger world stage and in our own little corner of the planet. Prominent churchmen of all denominations, and other assorted thinkers – even the unfortunate Tony Blair, last Sunday, got at by Sir David Frost, who should know better – have had to face the media to explain how a good God can either do these things Himself, or at least allow them to happen.

We all do assume, of course, that God is good – that He/She is not just out to get us, or is taking pleasure in tormenting us – and also that God is all-powerful, and that is why the problem arises. We all do also know, I presume, with one corner of our brains – though this may not hold true in parts of Ulster, Afghanistan, or Alabama – that the tsunami was a natural disaster, caused by the violent shifting of tectonic plates deep in the earth's crust. It is not even a function of global warming, so we can't even blame George Bush and the American gas-guzzlers for it. It is just something that happens from time to time, and it was programmed to happen in just that place from a very long time back.

Similarly, sooner or later, some twisted misbegotten individual will be hauled into the light somewhere in or around Middleton, sniveling and whinging, and saying that he didn't mean this to happen, and he's very sorry for what he's done. We can then set ourselves to investigate the totality of the genetic or societal failures that went into making him what he is today. We may or may not be able to find someone else to blame in the process, but what we are faced with here is, inescapably, a human sequence of events.

But for persons of religious temperament, this does not dispose of the problem. God made the world, after all, they argue, and He continues to watch over it, so He is substantially responsible for the appalling element of snakes-and-ladders which seems to have been built into its composition. And so the cry has been rising up from all sides, how can a good God allow these things to happen?

Now I am not a theologian; I am only a philosopher, of the Platonist persuasion. But as such, I am actually much concerned with divinity and its workings in the world, so I venture to offer here some thoughts on the problem from a Platonist perspective. To me it seems that God has been placed in a most invidious position by generation after generation of His (largely self-appointed) spokespersons, in the Jewish, Christian and Muslim traditions particularly, from the prophets of the Old Testament, through a host of Christian functionaries of all denominations, to the latest fulminating Iranian mullah. They would all claim that God takes a detailed, personal interest in every aspect of our lives, and indeed micro-manages all of His creation. One should therefore pray to Him unceasingly for benefits, and ask His forgiveness most humbly for all our transgressions.

The problem with that is, if He is then allowed to claim credit for finding your lost wallet, or granting you success in your examination or job application, or arranging for Liverpool to beat Manchester United, He then also becomes liable for dreadful cock-ups like this tsunami. From the Platonist point of view, or indeed from that of such a religion as Buddhism, this is all sadly misguided. The Platonist God is a benevolent, but quite impersonal entity, known as the One or the Good, who (or which) has indeed generated the universe (though eternally, not at a point in time), and exercises a general providence over it, but does not intervene in its historical development, nor does He step in to save us from ourselves or from our fellows. If we wish to seek Him, He is there to be found. But apart from exercising a generally positive influence in favour of order and rationality, He will not intervene to assist us. The One, in fact, unlike Yahweh, *does not fuss*, one way or the other.

That said, can one attempt some sort of Platonist theodicy, or justification of God's working in the world? I think one can, and it goes something like this: God, as a creator, must create something worse (in the sense of less perfect) than Himself, since He is, after all, the most perfect being possible. He cannot create something better than Himself, and to create something exactly like Himself would be to achieve nothing, so His creation must be an imperfect thing, though He wishes it to be as good as possible. Nonetheless, in the course of the full development of all the possibilities of the world, some things will get in the way of other things, and suffer in the process – there have to be zebras and lions, for example, and lions are going to eat zebras, not vice versa. And so, in the course of the unfolding of all cosmic possibilities, both natural and human disasters will inevitably occur. This is an austere message, but at least it does not put God in a false position, nor encourage us to unreasonable expectations.

Left Google-eyed by my alter ego as a raunchy guitarist

June 19, 2005

Poor Mike Soden! To be put out in the street thus ruthlessly by his (rather seedy) organisation just because he took a peek (or two?) at a naughty website while on duty – this, of course, to divert attention from their many other reprehensible activities, and reclaim the moral high ground in the banking industry. For after all, how great a crime is this of Mike's, at the heel of the hunt? Let us bear in mind what a very boring activity top-level banking is – stressful, certainly, in some aspects, but, taken all in all, asphyxiatingly boring! In such circumstances, the mind needs diversion.

Bill Clinton, in a similarly stressful situation, sought diversion in more interactive ways. Soden chose a solitary, electronic one. It didn't do anyone else any discernible harm, and it rhymes with banking. And for this he has been cast forth upon the world with a mere €2.3m in his pocket. That may sound quite a lot to you, but I assure you that in the circles in which Mike is wont to move it does not go very far. I mean, have you any idea how much it costs to keep a yacht in Majorca these days? Or a racehorse in training at any respectable stables? And as for membership of the K Club!

I have actually been provoked to some serious thought by this predicament of Mike Soden's. There but for the grace of God, and that sort of thing… University teaching is, of course, an infinitely more interesting and fulfilling activity than that practised by Mike, but still … there are certain times of year, such as the present, in the depths of exam marking, when both boredom and stress can become positively overwhelming, and it is then that one begins to fiddle about aimlessly on the Internet.

One of the things I like to do occasionally, I must confess, is to check out 'John Dillon' on that excellent search-engine Google, just to see how I'm getting on. In the process I discover many fascinating things. After I get through my publications (many of which are available at cut price!), and curriculum vitae, I discover many other curious details. I am a used-car salesman, for instance, offering many attractive deals. I am quite a successful racing driver. There is also a John Dillon Fellowship available. I don't suppose that I am eligible for that myself, but some of you might be, so check it out!

Among my many and varied occupations, though, there is one of rather *avant-garde* and raunchy rock guitarist. But if you check that website, you will be in for something of a shock. Suddenly one is surrounded by a proliferation of jolly bare-breasted chicks offering all sorts of interesting consolations, and inviting you to call them. What this has to do with my guitar-playing is not clear to me. I think, in fact, that my website has simply been colonised by some awful parasite – just as happened to Bertie some time ago, I believe.

Actually, this is not my first encounter of this sort. I have an old school friend, Victor O'Reilly, who resurfaced recently, after being out of touch for about half a century, and he now turns out to be a writer of thrillers – this after a number of years in the Special Forces, and then as a mercenary in various distressed parts of the world. He gave me a number of his works, and they read very well, though I would not recommend them to your granny, unless she is a very boozy and fun-loving old lady. Indeed he complained to me that, although they are available in drugstores and airports in many parts of the world, Easons will not distribute them – which is, I suppose an accolade of a sort.

Anyhow, Victor, as befits a successful thriller writer, has a web-site, which I have looked at in the past. But when I checked it out recently, lo and behold, it was filled with bare-breasted chicks offering interesting consolations! So where is one to turn? I think, on mature reflection, I will just arrange to be discovered by the cleaning lady grooving on one of the web-sites, and then the Provost, with great regret, will have to dispense with my services. A golden handshake of, say, half a million or so would be perfectly satisfactory, I think, as my needs, and those of my dear wife, are fairly modest. And one would never have to correct exams ever again!

Nation's favourite Hobbs
is skating on extremely thick ice
September 4, 2005

It has been most entertaining, over the last few weeks, to observe the gyrations of the government parties in face of the onslaught of Eddie Hobbs and his *Rip-off Republic*. Now, after an initial barrage of dire threats and efforts at intimidation of RTE and the redoubtable Mr Hobbs himself, an effort which has backfired dismally, they have resolved, it seems, to hold their fire until the series concludes. Then, we are instructed to believe, they will weigh in powerfully with countervailing facts with which to demolish Mr Hobbs and his tendentious factoids. In fact, though, by the end of the series, they may decide to leave things lie, bad and all as they might seem. Because the truth is that Eddie, despite his undeniable entertainment value, has really only been scratching the surface of the problem. One must recognise, of course, that not everything is amenable to being presented in a TV show that has chosen the stand-up comedy format, even with some background visual aids, but the truth is that to get to one of the root causes of many of this country's immoderate costs, one has to probe more deeply than perhaps makes for good box office.

Let us start with two of the major sources of expense in this country, one that impacts primarily on the young and upwardly mobile amongst us, the other on every taxpayer: housing and road-building. To acquire a grasp of the causes of the problem one has to go back more or less to first principles. In both cases, in fact, one must start with basic provisions of the blessed Irish Constitution. It was that great conversationalist and constitutional lawyer, the late John Kelly, who first alerted me to the fact that it is the absolute assertion of the rights of private property enshrined in our Constitution that renders it so very difficult to control the immoderate profits resulting from the sale of land. In most other countries, there exists the countervailing principle of the national interest, which can be employed to override the rights of the individual property owner.

Even in Great Britain, that paragon of individual freedom, there persists the basic principle that all land belongs to the monarch. The highest interest that an individual subject can acquire in it is 'freehold', and that is always subject to the higher claim of the national interest – though with, of course, due provision for equitable compensation. We do have a rudimentary form of this here, but it has not been allowed to interfere seriously with the absolute right of a landowner to maximise the profit accruing from being in the right place at a certain moment in history – either in the path of a projected motorway, or in that of an expanding metropolis. It also, of course, helps to have paid one's dues in brown envelopes to the right people, but the fact remains that the chief engine of immoderate profit-making is the Constitution itself. So for Eddie simply to rail at house prices or overruns in the cost of motorways is only to scratch the surface of our malaise.

Of course, costs are not solely due to greedy landowners or speculators. We must not forget the contribution of the lunatic fringe of environmentalists. How long was the Kildare bypass held up by the Friends of the Snail? Or the last segment of the M50 by the Friends of that dismal heap of rubble known as "Carrickmines Castle"? And wait till the Friends of Tara get to grips with the M3! All these flights of self-indulgence cost many millions on top of all the other causes of overruns, but they are still only subsidiary to the main problem.

As for house prices, they are largely conditioned by the fact that there is no mechanism for either the government or a municipality to acquire building land in the periphery of a growing urban centre at prices that are moderate and fair – they must always pay the market price, a very flexible, and ultimately absurd, concept. And so often it is not the original honest farmer that is the recipient of this largesse, but a shrewd speculator such as the redoubtable John Byrne, or the Bailey Brothers – or shadowy companies such as Jackson Way, with Liam Lawlor on the board.

This is no way to run a country, certainly, if one has the interests of the ordinary citizen at heart. But the ordinary citizen is really only there as cannon fodder, to be bamboozled at election time. The country is run by, and for the benefit of, the Fianna Fail Party (most of the time) and a combination of well-heeled interest groups, notably big builders, publicans, doctors and lawyers. This complex of interests Eddie has taken a few digs at – the publicans did come in for something of roasting a few weeks ago – but really has hardly laid a hand on. Are we going to hear anything, for instance, about lawyers' fees, whether at tribunals or in the general run of business?

Are we going to look at the deals that consultants make with hospitals, or the fees charged by either GPs or specialists – or the really extraordinary charges indulged in by our dentists? No, it seems that we are not. And if we were, I suspect that the attack would be on a very superficial level, with a focus on the stupendous daily charges of a Senior Counsel at a major tribunal, or the routine €120 for a ten-minute chat with one's cardiologist, or the €5,000 charged for some piece of cosmetic dentistry, without enquiring into the deep structures that have led to these extraordinary excesses – such as, for instance, the hidden insurance costs for doctors, themselves generated by the demented compo culture that has grown up here, which is fostered in turn by the legal profession.

But to delve seriously into the causes of our enslavement to this complex concatenation of parasites would be something that would land RTE in a cauldron of hot water that it probably could not survive, so I fear that we will have to be content with Eddie's most entertaining but ultimately superficial caperings. The Government may grumble a bit about that, but in their hearts they must know that they are getting off pretty lightly.

For true happiness, philosophers advise that less is more

January 8, 2006

I suppose it is something to do with seasonal surfeit, or perhaps it is just the onset of a cranky old age, but suddenly I notice that the process of being incessantly wished a Happy New Year is beginning to get to me. The problem, I suppose, is this: Do any of us, I wonder, any longer have much of an idea what happiness is? Would we recognise it if it rose up and bit us in the bum? I realise that this is laying quite a lot of philosophical baggage on what is after all a rather vacuous, but essentially decent, seasonal greeting, which only amounts, after all, to hoping that we may attain our lawful desires and avoid life's banana skins during the coming twelvemonth, but still, once a train of thought is begun, there is nothing to be done but pursue it.

I am put in mind, in this connection, of the memorable formulation – handed down now for many years in the family – of an aged retainer in my father-in-law's law firm, who would appear at the door of the various partners' offices in the week before the Feast, tipping his forelock (they still had them, in those days, and *tipped* them), and utter the delightful line, "A Happy Christmas to ye, sir, if it's *convanient!*". One knew, of course, exactly what he meant, but yet this pregnant utterance can serve as a stimulus to philosophical speculation. How convenient it would be, indeed, if we knew what it was in which happiness truly consists!

Is there, I wonder, any consensus at all out there on this question? The evidence of one's eyes and ears tells one that levels of stress and anxiety, among those who have done well out of the Celtic Tiger and those who have not, are increasing all the time – and the frantic borrowing, spending and boozing goes on apace. And yet bothersome statistics keep popping up on the radar, disseminated by such respectable sources as The Economist Intelligence Unit, The European Commission's Eurostat survey, *The Social Situation in Europe,* and our own Amarach Consulting's report, *Quality of Life in Ireland*, to the effect that we are, by our own account, the happiest nation in Europe, if not the world. Fully 86 per cent of us apparently say that we are either quite happy or very happy – this presumably excluding the ever-increasing percentage of us who are bent on committing suicide. This beats such nations as Germany, France or Britain into a cocked hat (the most miserable nation in Europe is, it seems, Bulgaria - despite the copious infusion of Sinn Fein funds to develop leisure centres there).

It is a funny sort of question to ask, of course: "Are you happy?" Can one hope to get a straight answer to it? I have heard a wise saying propounded to the effect that, if you have to ask yourself whether you are happy or not, you're not happy – but that may be an excessively cynical line to take. It seems to me that, though one can be happy without knowing it, it is perfectly possible, while feeling happy, to reflect on what that state might consist of.

The Greek philosophers are not, I fear, going to give much consolation to the contemporary Hibernian hedonist. The overall concern, after all, of such men as Socrates, Plato or Aristotle was the moderation of one's desires, and the effort to free oneself as far as possible from attachment to 'external' things. Aristotle, it is true, was not averse to the possession of a modicum of external goods, and indeed felt that the exercise of certain virtues, such as generosity, would be gravely hampered by their lack (you can't give the stuff away in gobs, after all, if you don't have it in the first place), but the overall feeling was that the desire for wealth and possessions in general can only lead to grief, as it is by its very nature infinite.

And certainly we do observe that the very rich are usually obsessed with becoming even richer – apart from those blessed few, such as Chuck Feeney or Bill Gates, who are now devoted to giving the loot away for the benefit of mankind. What gets Dermot Desmond, or JP McManus, or Michael Smurfit, up in the morning – as it does a host of lesser mortals – is the prospect of turning another buck, or rather million bucks, preferably at the expense of each other.

Now to a certain extent this money-making may have taken on the nature of an absorbing game, but in my observation of various rather wealthy friends, there is also the nagging conviction that, however rich you are yourself, there is always someone else richer down the road, with a more palatial mansion, a more monstrous SUV, a larger yacht, and this makes sleep difficult at night. It is towards combatting this nagging feeling in the gut that much Greek philosophy is directed.

What the philosophers recommend, from the most extreme, such as Diogenes the Cynic, to the most moderate and worldly, such as Aristotle, is that we each think out carefully how little we can actually survive on, in order to enable us maximally to develop our spirit. which they regard as our true self. and so attain true happiness. Anything over and above that comes in the nature of a bonus, which we can take or leave alone. Such a recommendation may indeed not seem "convanient" in the present climate, but it is, of course. The Christian message as well, and that of all the great religions which we have been systematically ignoring over Christmas.

So think on that, as the surest recipe for a truly happy New Year.

Come back Fr. Mathew, we need help to drink sensibly

June 11, 2006

The recent announcement that Ireland tops the EU league in binge drinking – and presumably in projectile vomiting (not yet, unfortunately, an Olympic sport) – bestows special significance on a celebration that is taking place this week, while most serious drinkers will be focusing on the World Cup. This year is the 150th anniversary of the death of my collateral ancestor, Fr Theobald Mathew, the revered "Apostle of Temperance". To be specific, he was the great-uncle of my grandmother, Elizabeth Mathew. This weekend, there will be a gathering of his descendants in Tipperary, organised by my cousin Veronica Mathew, in co-operation with the Tipperary Historical Society, centred on the ancestral home of the Mathews, Thomastown Castle, where Theobald was born in 1790.

Fr Theobald was certainly a phenomenon. As a humble Capuchin friar – he had always wanted to be a priest, but had got himself expelled from Maynooth for holding a party in his rooms – he devoted himself to the welfare of the poor in Ireland. After doing heroic work during the great cholera epidemic of 1832, he turned his attention to what he regarded as one of the root causes of the misery in Ireland, and that was the demon drink

On April 10, 1838, at a public meeting in Cork (where he was based), he founded the Pioneer Total Abstinence Society, with the ringing exhortation: "Here goes, in the name of God." At the time, total abstinence had been very much a Protestant concern, and Fr Theobald acknowledged he was following in the footsteps of the worthy Quaker William Martin, who had recently founded an (only moderately successful) temperance society in Cork. In taking over from Martin, he was courting the opposition of every publican in the country, and of the brewing and distilling interests (of which his own brother and brother-in-law were part, as directors of the distillery in Midleton).

Fr Mathew did not, I think, give much thought as to why the Irish peasantry drank so much – that would have led him into politics. He saw drunkenness as a moral failing which dissipated men's energies, prevented them doing an honest day's work, and destroyed family life. His campaign, even in the midst of the Famine, was, for a while, phenomenally successful. Hundreds of thousands took the 'pledge', often at monster meetings, and his fame spread to Britain and America, where he was even invited, in November 1849, to address the US Congress – after which he dined with President Zachary Taylor.

All this wild enthusiasm, sadly, ebbed away over the next few years or so, and by the time Father Theobald died, the temperance movement was pretty much a spent force, though it acquired a new lease of the life from 1874, under Fr James Cullen, supported by much of the hierarchy, and continued as a feature of Irish life up to the present.

So could my revered ancestor have anything to offer the youth of today's prosperous Ireland, who are drinking themselves into a stupor for reasons more or less antithetical to those of the peasantry of the 1840s? Frankly, I doubt it, but there might be no harm in having a go.

One proposal might have some chance – though Fr Mathew would not have approved, since he saw total abstinence as the only solution – and that is moderation. All that is required, except in the case of alcoholics, is a resolve to take no more than, say, two units of alcohol per day – or save some of that for the weekend. Such a pledge would represent such good sense that it just might catch on. There need be nothing wrong with moderate indulgence in what is arguably a gift from God.

In pursuance of this line of thought, indeed, the Fr Mathew celebrations this weekend will begin with a wine reception.

How Charlie cast his spell
June 25, 2006

The (long-anticipated) passing of Charles J Haughey certainly provoked an outpouring of both emotion and judgement, in either case very mixed, but for all that we are still very far from a balanced assessment of the man. This, I hasten to specify, is not it. Nonetheless, I hope that these reflections and reminiscences may contribute something to that.

As I watched the funeral and read the weekend papers, I was moved to think back with some nostalgia to the early Sixties. There was not that much to the period, I suppose, if compared with the recent Celtic Tiger years, but following on the dismal Fifties it was quite something – and politically it marked the arrival, under the benevolent supervision of Sean Lemass, of a bevy of young Celtic tiger cubs, notably Donogh O'Malley, Brian Lenihan, and Charles J Haughey.

I arrived home from a few years in Africa in the summer of 1963, and found the new spirit abroad in the country quite exhilarating. It happened that Haughey was our neighbour in Raheny at the time, we in Kilbarrack House, he up the road in Grangemore (both now, through his agency, housing estates), and we had a nodding acquaintance with him. I had also written some months previously a rather laudatory article about him in the magazine *Hibernia*, and he appreciated that. As part of my research for the article I had submitted a series of questions to him, which he duly answered.

He was by this time Minister of Justice, already developing a reputation for effectiveness – though already too there was a mystery about the source of his apparent wealth. Rumour had it, as I recall, that he was profitably involved in a chicken farm! At any rate, that autumn our paths crossed, rather unexpectedly, and that led to my becoming quite a fan of his. How it came about was this: my sister Elizabeth was at this time involved in a little school, under the aegis of the worthy philanthropist Victor Bewley, teaching Travellers. It happened also at this time that a fellow called Grattan Puxon (a sort of upper-class hippie) had come over from England and was organising the Travellers to campaign for their rights. My sister had made his acquaintance, and introduced me to him as well.

One day, however, Puxon was rounded up by the Gardaí and expelled from the country. There was indignation in the little circle of those who knew him, and somehow I was roped in to go as a one-man delegation to the Minister of Justice and intercede on Puxon's behalf. I can't remember whether I wrote or phoned the Minister's office, but, remarkably, he agreed to see me, and in fact invited me to come and talk with him at home.

So up the road I went one evening to Grangemore, and the Minister received me in his study. It is then that I fell under Charlie Haughey's spell, in a way that quite a number of my friends and acquaintances have done since. I was only 24 at the time, and no one in particular, but Haughey decided, for whatever reason, to give me the full treatment. He sat me down, and looked me in the eye.

"You've come to me to intercede for Mr Grattan Puxon," he said. "How well do you know this fellow?"

I had to admit that I hardly knew him at all.

"Well, let me tell you something about Puxon. He is actually damn lucky to be expelled from the country. He could be in jail, but it didn't suit us to put him there. Acting on a tip-off, the guards found an arms cache buried in his back garden. I don't think you'll be seeing much of Mr Puxon around here in the near future."

I was of course totally disarmed – gobsmacked, certainly, but also enormously flattered that I was being entrusted with this classified information. It did not occur to me from that day to this to doubt its veracity. Only now, on mature reflection, do I realise that there was probably not a word of truth in it. Puxon was certainly making something of a nuisance of himself, and that might have been enough to provoke the authorities to get rid of him, arms cache or no arms cache, but CJ preferred to present me with a palpably unanswerable case against the fellow, and he did it in a way calculated to charm me to bits.

He also delighted me, in the course of the subsequent conversation, by referring casually to "that old bastard the Bishop of Galway", who must have been sounding off at the time about Travellers' Rights. This was splendidly unparliamentary language from a Minister of Justice about a prince of the church, directed at a young cub of 24, whom he had agreed to receive in his home rather than in his office – or indeed, rather than refusing to meet him at all.

The article in *Hibernia* that I had written before all this was indeed enthusiastic, but also to some extent prophetic. It ended as follows:

> *"Mr Haughey has now been exercising his talents at the Department of Justice for more than two years. It is not to be supposed that he will remain there for ever, and we may expect soon to see him promoted to some Ministry nearer the seat of power. I think this interview shows that wherever he goes from here he will bring with him great powers of organisation and concentration, and, though he modestly denies it, an admirably progressive political philosophy as well."*

This is plainly the work of someone who has fallen under a spell. So when in later years I have heard such people as Brendan Kennelly or Anthony Cronin or Professor Gerry Wrixon, or quite a few others I could mention, testifying to the enormous charm of the man, I know just what they mean. I never had another interview with him of that sort, but I had occasion to correspond with him in later years on various topics, and always found his replies frank and incisive and to the point. CJ was without doubt an enormously talented man, and an enormously charming one when he wanted to be, but one has to feel also deeply grateful for the wisdom of the Irish electorate in never granting him an absolute majority at the polls, because the consequences of that for the health of democracy in this country could have been very troublesome indeed.

Just coincidences, or beginning to look a lot like Armageddon?

August 6, 2006

As one's ears are assailed hourly by ever-worsening news from the Middle East, the gloomy reflection has been recurring to me that the summers of 1914 and 1939 were, so far as I can recall, unusually hot as well. But now we have yet another thing to worry about, on top of that. This darned psalter that was found the week before last in an Irish bog, and duly acquired by the National Museum, happened to be open at Psalm 83.

Now what is the problem with that, you might ask. Well, just get down your Bible and have a look at Psalm 83. It is pretty strong stuff. Let me give you the first four verses:

> *O God, do not keep silence;*
> *Do not hold thy peace or be still, O God!*
> *For lo, thy enemies are in tumult;*
> *Those who hate thee have raised their heads.*
> *They lay crafty plans against thy people;*
> *they consult together against thy protected ones.*
> *They say, "Come, let us wipe them out as a nation;*
> *Let the name of Israel be remembered no more!"*

You get the picture? Does that sound just a bit like President Ahmadinejad of Iran after a few pints of the oul' orange juice, or what? But of course this psalm is composed by a Hebrew prophet (Asaph, to be exact), so it can't end on that note. In fact, Asaph hits back strongly in the second half:

> *O my God, make them whirling dust,*
> *Like chaff before the wind.*
> *As fire consumes the forest,*
> *As the flame sets the mountains ablaze,*
> *so do thou pursue them with thy tempest*
> *and terrify them with thy hurricane!*

231

This is more like it, is it not? Very reminiscent, indeed, of current Israeli operations in southern Lebanon – no tempest or hurricane as such, but lots of F-16s and Apache helicopter gunships, which are really just as effective.

Now, all this could not be happening to a nicer bunch of guys than Hezbollah, who have been asking for it, in fact, for quite some time, and who even seem to be quite enjoying it, in their own peculiar way. But in fact, as we know, the chief victims have been local Lebanese women, children and old men. Hardly a feather seems to have been knocked out of Hezbollah itself, which is far better dug in and prepared than the Israelis imagined – used as they are to easy victories over blustering and disorganised Arabs.

No more Six Day War scenarios, then. But the trouble is that, every day that this goes on without a solution, we all get nearer to a larger conflict. Syria and Iran are waiting in the wings. Al-Qaeda helpfully calls for an all-out rising of Muslims everywhere against the "crusader" forces. And that is where Armageddon begins to loom on the horizon. Because, sadly, we have to keep reminding ourselves that not all the loonies are on the one side. The West has its loonies too, and, in the United States at least, they have never been so powerful and well-organised. Over 40 per cent of the American people now, it seems, believe in Armageddon: that is to say, the final showdown between the forces of God and those of the Antichrist (whom many of them believe to be already upon the earth), which will be followed by the Rapture, in which the Just will be invited to ascend into heaven – and to hell (pretty literally) with the rest of us!

There are firm indications that this scenario is informing the thinking of at least a segment of those who are keeping George W. Bush and his associates in the White House – whether or not it is one which has actually occupied the mind of that great statesman himself. An American friend of mine, the distinguished journalist Chris Hedges (long-time war correspondent of *The New York Times* and author of the superb book *War is a Force that Gives Us Meaning*), has been devoting himself for the last two years to an in-depth study of the American Religious Right. He has written a book, to be published next January (if the world lasts that long!), whose conclusions are deeply alarming.

These people are just as impervious to reason as the mullahs of fundamentalist Islam, and they are actually far more capable of doing something about their convictions. They are now supported with all the facilities of a modern technological structure, and they know how to use the media to their advantage. It is their view that Armageddon will arise out of events in the Middle East, and that the rebuilding of the temple on Temple Mount in Jerusalem (which would involve some significant redevelopment of that site – currently occupied by the Dome of the Rock) will be a prelude to this happening. For this reason, they are doing everything they can to encourage and bankroll Jewish extremists, who also aspire to rebuild the temple, to drive the Arabs from the site.

The question is whether they can be stopped. As we sit here helplessly, in the midst of this unusually fine summer, it begins to seem as if all things are conspiring to bring about their dearest wishes. As is so often the case in these situations, good and decent people can only sit on the sidelines and lament, while the mad and dangerous have at each other with every weapon at their disposal. Blair flies to Washington, and flies back with egg on his face, having failed to persuade George W of anything. Condi flies to Jerusalem, and is met by the biggest Israeli atrocity yet – and at Cana, where once water was turned into wine! The United Nations has to sit by and wring its hands, since the US will veto any resolution that inconveniences Israel in any way. It is all rather like a slow-motion movie of a multiple car crash.

Now, let me make myself clear. I don't believe for a moment that our bog-psalter is an omen – the evidence is in fact, that it was actually open at Psalm 84, a much more harmless piece of work – but the worldwide reaction to it is at least a reflection of the state of mind that many of us are in; and, all things considered, who can blame us?

It's just dandy, I feel I can be a yankee doodle again

November 12, 2006

This week, for the first time in many years, I can feel reasonably comfortable being an American – and the same is true, I think, for many friends of mine back in the home country. I have friends who have been so ashamed of themselves, especially for electing this clown and his cronies a second time (the first time didn't really count, being a palpable fraud) that when they have come to Europe recently they have pretended to be Canadians.

No more of that, then! When I heard Allen finally conceding the Senate seat in Virginia, I felt at last a wave of pure satisfaction. American democracy has not been permanently hijacked after all. It is still possible for common sense and common decency to prevail over the deluge of fabricated hysteria, negative propaganda and bogus jingoism that the big bucks of highly organised right-wing Republicanism has been able to orchestrate over the past few years since 9/11 – whoever really arranged that!

But let us not get too optimistic. A great deal of damage has been done to the fabric of civilised discourse, and, registered Democrat though I am, I am far from convinced that the Democratic majority in Congress is either able or willing to redress it in all respects. Let us take some of the chief evils perpetrated over the last few years in turn.

First, we must rank the so-called War on Terror. George W, one is glad to observe, does at last look somewhat chastened (less swagger, less smirking), but he is still very strong on the War on Terror, and he is just daring the Democrats to appear to let up on that. What people must, however, come to accept is that the War on Terror is a concept straight out of 1984. It is the ultimate unending and unwinnable conflict, since it steadily generates its own enemy even as it grinds out various small successes to keep the gullible public both encouraged and on their guard. George W needs Osama (let's hope the bugger isn't dead, as

French intelligence has been maintaining for some time now!), even as Osama needs George W. I was only grateful that between them they didn't manage to fabricate a nice little atrocity in the last few weeks, to save the Republicans' bacon on November 7.

But can the Democrats row back on this preposterous crusade without exposing themselves to hysterical accusations of going soft on terrorism, putting America at risk, and undermining the morale of our boys in the combat zone Probably not, but they could resolve to face the barrage head on, by arguing forcefully that it is precisely Bush's actions over the last four years or so that have systematically created terrorists, and will continue to do so, unless radically modified. But this may be just too much to expect.

Above all, are the Democrats prepared to take on Israel, and the Zionist lobby in the US? Frankly, on the record, I very much doubt it. Support of Israel, in whatever it may decide to do, has been pretty much a bipartisan position in mainstream American politics for a very long time, and that is unlikely to change now. Not a squeak of protest, one may note, from either side of the US political divide, at the latest gross atrocity in the Gaza strip – "an unfortunate technical error" on the part of IDF artillery.

So I am not very sanguine on that issue. How about the world environmental crisis, then, to which the US is the major contributor – along with China? Here again, in spite of the excellent publicity done by Al Gore, I have no great hopes that the Democrats will be prepared to take on the industrial lobby and the myriad owners of SUVs, and pledge themselves to responsible behaviour. Indeed, it is dear old Arnie Schwarzenegger in California, if anyone, who is leading the way here, but how many outside of California are prepared to follow?

And lastly, what about the economic crisis generated by Bush's encouragement of Americans to go out and spend, spend, spend after 9/11, just to show those bad folks out there that we aren't downhearted? This has now created a situation in which the country is largely in hock to such creditors as the Saudis, the Chinese and the South Koreans. Admittedly, all these players need to prop up the dollar for their own advantage, but supposing they began to call in their chips? The US balance of payments deficit is in a state which completely eclipses the excesses of the Reagan years, and any untoward movement in the financial world may bring down the whole house of cards at any time. The Democratic majority in Congress will have to move very firmly, but also discreetly, to begin to arrest this, and that may well prove to be beyond them.

All that said, though, it was a good week for American democracy, and I am set to enjoy my feeling of euphoria just a little while longer.

Supreme beings must work in the real world
January 7, 2007

I used to know Seán O'Leary back in the Sixties, when we were both involved in that notorious outfit, the Fine Gael Youth Group. I remember him as lively, humorous and incisive – a canny, irreverent Corkman, who did not stand for nonsense from any quarter. Since then, I must confess, I have had no direct contact with him, but I hear from friends in the legal profession that he did not change that much. The extraordinary testament, therefore, which he bequeathed to the nation on his recent lamentable demise is something that I have read with extreme interest. Plainly, certain recent developments had been preying on his mind for some time.

Apart from his criticism of the Supreme Court's fancy footwork in the matter of the freeing of Mr A, to which I will return, he takes a trenchant crack at the practices of our burgeoning and proliferating tribunals, and at the Personal Injuries Assessment Board, which was put in place to impose some degree of moderation on our notorious "compo culture" – fostered as it was by so many of his colleagues in the legal profession. To take the last first, I find his position somewhat disingenuous.

If we cast our minds back a little, we may recall that, when, in an effort to prevent the reckless distribution of what was regarded as some sort of "free money" from insurance companies, juries were removed by the Government from personal injury cases, judges (all of whom had once been barristers) continued, with obstinate malice, to be guided in their awards by the previous grossly inflated standards established by juries, just to show the Government that this inconveniencing of the legal profession would do them no good. It was in response to this persistent gerrymandering on the part of the judiciary that the PIAB was set up, and it is a bit rich of O'Leary, in view of that, to condemn it for "going too far". This wretched country was becoming virtually uninsurable, and the lawyers were sitting back rubbing their hands; a firm rebalancing was long overdue, and I don't hear anyone but lawyers complaining too much about that.

As regards the tribunals, however, and the inadequate protection they accord to those they are investigating, I should say that he is on stronger ground. A tribunal, after all, is a curious beast. It is not a court of law, and therefore those who come before it are not officially on trial. But of course, *de facto*, they are on trial, and their careers and lives can consequently be ruined, without their actually being convicted of anything. Therefore, they need proper legal representation, even though this adds materially to the already exorbitant cost of these circuses.

And now for the Supreme Court. It is here, I should say, that Legality comes nose to nose with Reality – in the form of mere common sense, and a very reasonably outraged public. Grim legal logic, it must be said, is on the side of O'Leary. The concept of "unlawful carnal knowledge" was a legal fudge designed, benignly enough, to free an under-aged person who had been involved in a sexual incident, regardless of the circumstances, from the trauma of having to testify in open court. The perpetrator got a lesser sentence than he might otherwise have got (in Mr A's case, a trifling three years), but at least there was no cross-examination. All fine and dandy, but, alas, it disregards the constitutional right of every accused person to plead lack of knowledge of the facts, or, technically, of *mens rea*, "guilty intent". One cannot play fast and loose with this right, even for the worthy purpose of sparing young people the rigours of cross-examination. Ms Justice Laffoy was right. If one fires a shotgun at what one thinks is a rabbit or a fox, and one kills an unfortunate tramp who is sleeping in the grass instead, one may be convicted of something, but it will not be of murder. And so it has to be in all cases.

But then reality kicks in. Was Mr A, who had taken advantage of a 12-year-old girl, whom he cannot possibly have imagined to be over the age of consent, to walk free? Faced with this appalling vista, I do not think that their Honours of the Supreme Court need be accused of cravenly bending before the howlings of an insensate mob (still less the blandishments of an overwrought Bertie) if they sought for some way out. And they found a reasonable way out, through a somewhat elastic interpretation of the principle of non-retrospection in legislation.

Even if the law under which Mr A was convicted was no law, the understanding of the law under which he was convicted should be respected. The alternative raised truly horrendous prospects. It could reasonably be argued that O'Leary's recklessly purist interpretation of the law, if pursued, would have brought the whole legal system into disrepute – rightly or wrongly, it is no matter – and our political leaders were surely right to plead for a little reality to seep into the august chambers of the Supreme Court. What sort of a legal mess they have left us with now, on the other hand, is matter for another treatise. And Sean O'Leary has, in death, done the State some service, after all, in raising these questions for discussion.

Opposition parties need to think outside their own box
January 14, 2007

The recent flurry in the media concerning a leadership problem in Fine Gael may well owe much to the post-holiday silly season, but, in view of the looming election, it may serve as a lead-in to broader reflections on the future of the party, and in general on the desirability of an effective opposition to the present Fianna Fail-dominated Coalition. It is, after all, arguable that, even if the present Government were much better than it is, it is not good for democracy that any party should enjoy too lopsided an incumbency of office. If Mary Robinson had not exercised her powers creatively in the crisis following on Labour's withdrawal from government after the Harry Whelehan affair in December 1994, and called on John Bruton to see if he could form a government, instead of simply dissolving the Dail, we would have had a situation where Fianna Fail would seem to have presided exclusively over the whole growth and flourishing of the present Celtic Tiger boom. They would thus have appeared to be the sole architects of our prosperity, whereas, arguably, they have grossly mismanaged many aspects of the bonanza which more or less fell into their laps.

As things turned out, however, it was (rather fortuitously) demonstrated that a FG-Labour Coalition graced, indeed, by the first Labour Minister of Finance in the country's history, in the person of Ruairi Quinn – was well able to manage and promote the Celtic Tiger, and the myth that only Fianna Fail could deliver was effectively dispelled.

Now, however, the danger once more is that, for want of any very exciting alternative, a distinctly clapped-out, but nonetheless increasingly arrogant, Coalition will coast, or at least scramble, into power again, and that this could lead to distortions and irregularities reminiscent of the Haughey years, as well as more reckless over-spending. In face of this, there is one possible development that would make the coming contest a good deal more interesting and well-balanced. First, however, let me draw attention to one other possibility that looms on the horizon which should make us a little nervous.

Let us suppose that Sinn Fein, after wrestling long and agonisingly with their conscience, graciously consents to recognise the legitimacy of the police force of the Northern Irish State, and in consequence manage to form a government with the DUP. This development would doubtless be applauded by all persons of goodwill on this island, but we must not ignore the fact that this would give SF a considerable electoral boost in any southern election. We must also recognise that any inhibitions that Bertie might have against going into Coalition with them would rapidly melt away, if no other winning formula presented itself – and SF would have a perfectly good argument (which they have used already): if we are good enough as Coalition partners in a Northern Ireland government, how come we are so untouchable in the South? A counterweight to such a scenario is urgently needed. Sinn Fein has gained considerable kudos from being the only 32-county party in the island, and they are now poised (fortified by the proceeds of successful bank robberies, and judicious investments in Bulgaria and elsewhere) to cash in on that.

The answer to that threat, I would propose, is to create another 32-county party, embodying a set of moderate left-of-centre political principles, and a tradition of decency and integrity. This may be done in the following way. First of all, building on the current degree of understanding between Fine Gael and Labour, the two parties should appoint a joint negotiating committee to see if there are in fact any insuperable ideological obstacles to their formally coalescing. I am quite well aware of the objections that would be raised – indeed, have been raised – to such a proposal, but I am not greatly impressed by them. 'Our traditions are quite different!' `Who would lead?' The grassroots would never stand for it.'

Let us address these briefly – particularly the first one. What traditions did you have in mind, I would ask: James Connolly? General Eoin O'Duffy? I doubt that that are too many unregenerate Blueshirts or old-style Marxist Socialists gracing the branches of either party nowadays. We are all moderate socialists now, after all, even as we are all moderate free-marketeers. We all want a society which encourages enterprise, while providing a tolerable safety net – and if we didn't, the boffins in Brussels, and the realities of world trade, would pretty soon straighten us out. We are mainly arguing, if at all, about details of implementation.

Furthermore, let either party recall that even as it stands, it is a coalition of previous entities: in the case of Fine Gael, an amalgamation of Cumann na nGael and the Centre Party of Frank MacDermott and James Dillon; in the case of Labour, the existing Labour Party and Democratic Left (who, in fact, fill most of the positions of power in the present Labour Party, from leader on down). So let's not go on too much about ideological purity. If we are to fix on a suitable name for the new amalgam, how about just the Social Democratic Party? But what about the grass roots? Well, talk to them. Take soundings at local branch level, and then poll the membership. If there is solid resistance, then of course the idea is a non-starter, but I think you might be surprised. As for the leadership question, toss for it. Taoiseach Kenny? Taoiseach Rabbitte? What runs most trippingly off the tongue? In any case, there might have to be something like a triumvirate, if the rest of the plan is brought to fruition.

For this would not be the whole solution; indeed, it might after all be the easy part. What the new Social Democratic Party would then need to do is to approach the SDLP of Northern Ireland, and propose a merger. Ideologically, the differences would be trivial to non-existent, but certain procedural matters would have to be hammered out. However, if Sinn Fein can do it, surely it should not be an insuperable problem for more decent, moderate forces?

The new 32-county party, while maintaining separate personae North and South, would nonetheless be able to draw on its combined strength for electoral contests in both jurisdictions, and as such constitute a formidable counter-weight both to Sinn Fein in the North and Fianna Fail in the South. Indeed, I would expect it to find itself in power very quickly in both places.

But will such a development take place? I doubt it. What would be required is vision and courage to an extent that I do not discern in the leadership of any of the three parties involved. What we are much more likely to be facing, in the second half of this year, is a Sinn Fein presence in Coalition governments both North and South. And at that point I might consider looking for somewhere warmer to live in my old age.

Would Enda put the Shinners in Cabinet?
June 3, 2007

As I write this, a week after the election, all is still to play for, and the outcome is, if anything, murkier than it was in the immediate aftermath. It is almost as if the electorate wanted to elect nobody. Bertie has a range of options, all of which carry certain drawbacks, and he is in no hurry to choose between them. On the other hand, the bedraggled double act of Enda and Pat is conscious that the numbers are still there, if they throw caution to the wind.

Just short of 60 years ago, in mid-January 1948, the de Valera-led Fianna Fail government – which had been in power for 16 years, but which had been facing a rising tide of dissatisfaction, due to a mixture of scandals and inefficiencies – called an election for February 4. FF lost eight seats to 68, in a Dail of 147, well short of a majority, while the combined opposition came to 79, a pretty comfortable majority. Fortunately for the opposition, single-party government was still a core value for the Soldiers of Destiny, so the most another party could be permitted to do would be to support them humbly from outside government, and there was no rush to do that. Indeed, the new Clann na Poblachta party, led by Sean MacBride, which came through with 10 seats, was pledged to dismiss FF.

But what else was to be done? The opposition was a motley lot. FG could only come up with 31 seats. There were two Labour parties, boasting 14 and five seats respectively. The Farmers' Party, Clann na Talmhan, had seven seats, and there were 12 independents, including the former FG deputy leader James Dillon, the remarkable Oliver Flanagan, Patrick Cogan (a tempestuous farmer from Wicklow who had on occasion threatened to murder Dillon), former Lord Mayor of Dublin Alfie Byrne, and a foxy gentleman known as the Fiddler Flynn, who enjoyed the distinction of having been expelled from FF for immorality. A successful alternative government would have to embrace all these components. Under the tactful leadership of John A. Costello, such a government was formed, and held together for three years. Whatever else it achieved, it had broken the mould by providing an alternative to indefinite FF dominance, and thus struck an important blow for democracy in this country.

What can this teach us today? It seems that it contains the following lesson: if one is serious about change, one cannot be too fastidious about how this is done. And that brings us to Sinn Fein. Sinn Fein, despite its blessedly poor showing, is the elephant in the drawing-room. All parties are blue in the face protesting that they want nothing to do with it. But as between Sinn Fein in 2007 and Clann na Poblachta in 1948 there is really not that much in it, from the perspective of either respectability or policies. Sean MacBride may have gone on to win the Nobel Peace Prize, but in 1948 he was still pretty much an unreconstructed terrorist, and one who knew quite a bit about the murder of Kevin O'Higgins in 1927. You might say he was Gerry Adams with a French accent. He had decided to try the parliamentary route, and was duly welcomed for that, with not too many questions asked.

So, Enda and Pat, come off your high horses and do a deal with Sinn Fein and the Greens – and rope in the Independents too – or you know what will happen. Bertie will make any deal that he has to make. Because, after all, there is the Mahon tribunal, and, let's face it, despite the elaborate explanations that we have been treated to over the past few weeks, there are still a number of unanswered questions which Bertie might well prefer to face as Taoiseach.

In that connection, a friend of mine, who shall be nameless, in the hope of getting a rise out of me, has been advancing the idea of a Blueshirt putsch. This would not take the form of a march on Leinster House led by some latter-day O'Duffy, but rather of the further leaking of confidential documents, with the purpose of discrediting our gallant leader at a very critical time. Certainly, documents were leaked, and in a very suspicious way. Bertie plainly believes that there are Blueshirts among the leakers who are out to get him, and he may well be right. The leaking of these documents is just as worthy of investigation as their contents. Could this be designed as the orchestrated counterpoint to the formation of the ultimate Rainbow coalition?

On the other hand, perhaps it is better, Enda and Pat, if you stay on your high horses and let Bertie back in for a bit. There is undoubtedly something of a bust-up coming in the economy, and it really would not be good for democracy if it could all be blamed on the foostherings of a ramshackle Coalition government, which would then collapse after about a year and a half, amid mutual recriminations, and allow FF to coast back in. Better to let Bertie clean up his own mess. Because he is not the Messiah; he is a very naughty boy. And he should not be allowed to wriggle out of the consequences of his cosying-up to the building industry, and the other profligacies of the last five years.

Bertie's chief sins are now cast in bricks and mortar

November 25, 2007

In a comment in this paper just before the election last summer, I ventured to say, paraphrasing *The Life of Brian*, something to the effect that 'Bertie is not the Messiah. He is a very naughty boy.' I think that I was right in that view, though the majority of voters, in their great wisdom, still preferred to take him as the Messiah after all. More light has been cast since then on some of his personal financial peccadillos, but I think that it would be misleading to focus on those when estimating the full extent of his naughtiness – and that of his close associates, such as Finance Ministers Charlie McCreevy and Brian Cowen. What I would regard as their chief sin, in fact, and the one that impacts on the lives of virtually the whole of the younger generation of this country, is their conniving at the ripping-off of the home-buying public (and in particular the first-time buyers, who will be mainly the young) by the builders and the banks – while also indulging in their own kind of rip-off by means of a creative manipulation of the originally rather marginal charge of stamp duty.

If I look back to the purchase of our first home in 1973 – this, admittedly, in California rather in Ireland, but the rules then obtaining there were pretty similar here – our bank, the Bank of America, had a set of clear guidelines covering the granting of a mortgage, which were fair and rational, and worked perfectly well. First of all, they would not grant a mortgage for more that 80 per cent of the purchase price; and secondly, the mortgage could not be for more than two-and-a-half times your gross annual income. So there you were. I don't know who had originally made these rules, whether the banks themselves or a federal regulatory body, but they had the admirable effect both of protecting the banks' investment, and of imposing some cap on the recklessness of purchasers, and the greed of builders and speculators. One simply cannot raise the price of housing beyond what the buying public can pay, at least if one wants to sell houses in any great numbers. If one can't actually produce a house for what the buyer can afford, then of course the whole process grinds to a halt, to no one's advantage.

That has not, however, been a problem in recent years. Rather, in Celtic Tiger Land, on Planet Bertie, the opposite has been the case. There came to be, over the last ten years or so, no price so fantastic and outrageous that one could ask for one's Luxury Home (always luxury, we may note, never just ordinary) that there would not be a stampede of frantic punters beating down your door, waving their cheque-books and begging to allowed to 'buy off the plans'.

Now, these people did not, in general, have the money to make these purchases. They only thought they did. They were cruelly deceived both by the seductions of a banking system exempted from all governmental control – handing out 100 per cent mortgages for as much as 10 times one's annual income – and a building industry, aided and abetted by the government, which was fostering a spirit of recklessness in the acquisition of property on the insane premise that it could only continue indefinitely to appreciate at an ever-increasing rate. The warnings of responsible economists, from such sources as the ESRI and the Central Bank, and, ultimately, even from the OECD, were brushed aside, not least by Bertie himself, as the moanings of nay-sayers and prophets of doom, who would be much better employed going out and hanging themselves – and for a few glorious years they were indeed proved wrong, and the boosters and promoters apparently vindicated. Now, however, the chickens have come home to roost, and it becomes, I fear, all too sadly clear what a scam it all was.

But what should a responsible government have done, you may ask? Well, firstly, they should have imposed strict limits on mortgage lending that would have controlled the supply of funny money. Secondly, they should, from the outset of this housing boom (as was done in such responsible societies as Sweden, for example, in the case of the post-war expansion of Stockholm), have imposed firm regulations on the profits to be made from building land on the periphery of Dublin, in particular. The city fathers of Stockholm simply took an option on all land on the periphery of Stockholm, compulsorily purchasing it as required, paying the owners a reasonable premium over its previous value as farming land, and prescribing to builders what services they should provide along with the houses or apartments that they erected.

But that is socialism, you protest. We can't have that here! And yet Bertie has declared himself to be the only true socialist in Irish public life. If that were so, this would have been an ideal area in which to practice his principles. But then the receipts in the tent at the Galway races, and at so many other venues, would have fallen away very drastically. And where would that leave the Great Cause?

Sinn Fein at the heart of the anti-Lisbon lunatic menagerie

June 8, 2008

Well, the referendum campaign has warmed up at last, and we may look forward, I think, to a fairly torrid few days up to the election. As one can observe, not for the first time, there is nothing like a good old referendum on Europe to bring out the loonies. The loonies are always with us, of course, but an issue like this causes them to sprout up like exotic blooms in the desert after a rare rain shower. What I thought might be useful to do at this late stage of the campaign is to provide a sort of bestiary to help those interested to sort out the wide variety of persons who are concerned to oppose this Treaty. The problem is that they are really very varied, so varied that the ordinary punter can become dizzy in trying to discern where they are all coming from. They arise, after all, at both the right and the left wings of the political spectrum, both high up and low down.

One has, for instance, conservative Catholics, concerned that liberal, secular influences from Europe will dilute what is left of our national ethos, pushing gay marriage, compulsory abortion for all, cloning of entities half-pig, half-human for the purpose of curing disease, and so on. Then one has hard-nosed US-style neo-conservatives worried about creeping socialism, higher rates of taxation, and the imposition of decent standards of healthcare and education for all – ideals anathema to the American Way of Life (Neo-con version). But one has, on the other hand, from the other end of the spectrum, concerned pacifists who fear the end of our much-vaunted stance of neutrality, and hard-line socialists, who deeply distrust the EU as a capitalist monster, despite the embarrassingly comprehensive welfare states that most of our fellow Europeans enjoy. And over all these there presides, like a sort of octopus, the figure of Sinn Fein, gathering all these particular No's into one comprehensive NO, adorned, in Dublin, at least, by the smiling countenance of Mary Lou McDonald (who I suspect is actually

249

enjoying her stint in Europe a good deal more than she is prepared to let on).

Let us, then, proceed to anatomise in a more scientific manner this odd collection of beasties, as our contribution to the enlightenment of the electorate:

First of all, then, we find *Tyrannosaurus Catholicus*, thundering in the Celtic twilight about such matters as the sanctity of human life, and of the institutions of marriage and of the family, all of which the godless hordes of Europe, who are being given carte blanche by this treaty (as by all previous treaties!) are hell-bent on destroying. This is not a dangerous beast, despite its mournful expression and heartrending groans, but best avoided, as, if it engages you in conversation, you may never get away.

Secondly, however, there is *Lupus Neoconnus*. This is another phenomenon entirely, with fiery blasts of breath and savage teeth, roaring about liberties about to be abridged by treacherous European socialists. When these liberties are looked at closely, though, they turn out to be primarily the liberty to make money untrammelled by taxation or environmental controls, as promoted by their American masters. Such facilities as health and education should be paid for to the full, with the devil take the hindmost, and all mention of the myth of global warming, put about by European socialist wimps and do-gooders, should be banned from the airwaves.

In quite another mode again, we find our third specimen, *Agnus Pacificus*, a harmless little creature, normally sporting a white woolly coat, and bleating of the danger that the ruthless and belligerent Europeans will force decent, peace-loving Irish lads to engage in military adventures around the world at the whim of a group of unelected functionaries in Brussels. There will be conscription, military service, and Irish lads who never previously harmed a fly, drunk or sober, may have to take aggressive action. Ireland, having never previously polluted itself with taking sides in any conflict, will now have to face up to defending itself, instead of letting others do it for us.

And lastly, we have a slippery creature right out of the Garden of Eden, *Anguis Pseudosocialisticus*, who hisses to all who will listen that this European Union is simply a gross capitalist plot, invented by the bosses to give themselves free rein to make money multi-nationally, and screw the workers. In the traditions of Connolly and Larkin, we should have nothing whatever to do with such an abomination.

So there we have it. To all these creatures, Europe is the irreducible and fearsome Other, the agency responsible for all that the creature in question most deeply fears or abhors, and this Treaty is just another nail in our coffin. The fact that the wretched document is quite incomprehensible simply confirms their worst fears. The pleas of its supporters that its incomprehensibility is simply the consequence of its being something of a tidying-up measure, and thus somewhat fiddling in its details, is brushed aside as simply part of the Dastardly Plot to slip something over on us that we can't understand.

Sinn Fein's role in orchestrating all this activity is quite interesting. Of course, there is a opportunism in this, since no other political party has come out against the Treaty (though the dear old Greens, as befits their nature, are dithering), and that leaves an opening for gathering up disaffected votes. But we must bear in mind as well that Sinn Fein, does, after all, mean Ourselves Alone, in the sturdy isolationist tradition of Arthur Griffith and Eamon De Valera, and therefore the Party does not favour foreign entanglements. Cooperation with the FARC guerrillas of Colombia, Libya's Colonel Gaddafi, or Czech arms dealers doesn't count; that's just business. But the whole European adventure Sinn Fein does not like the look of at all.

Americans feeling the chill wind
of anxiety as autumn approaches

July 6, 2008

I declare to God that I did not invent this. I found it in the Sky Mall magazine on my recent flight back from Atlanta, Georgia, after a two-week visit to the United States:

Don't Leave Your Cat Home and Bored –
Leave a 'Programmable Mouse' in the House!

Most of us work 40 hours a week, leaving our house cats alone in empty, quiet homes, leading to separation anxiety, laziness or behaviour problems (for the cat). Our new automatic programmable cat toy plays with your cat when you're away! Its programmable timer activates the toy at set intervals, arousing a cat's hunting instincts and encouraging activity. It can also be activated with the push of the red button, either by a human or by the cat.

Upon activation the toy emits small animal sounds to signal to the cat that the mouse is coming out. The cat will try to keep the mouse from getting away, but after a few tries the mouse goes away until the next sound signals his return.

This marvellous device is available for a mere $79.95, plus postage and packaging.

Admittedly, in the next few years, if current trends persist, there are likely to be rather fewer of us working 40 hours a week, but this will nonetheless prove a most welcome diversion for both man and beast. One could even take to playing with it oneself, with the cat pushing the buttons.

It is a well-known statistic that much more money is expended on pets in the US than on aid to the Third World. Now I personally don't have much of a problem with that. After all, what has the Third World ever done for us? But it does perhaps point up an order of priorities that Americans may have to think about over the next few years. Because the American way of life is plainly facing something of a crisis. Compared with any previous visit I have made to my erstwhile homeland in the last 25 years, I find the public mood, so far as one can judge it from the media and from personal contacts, noticeably downbeat, not to say badly rattled. Publicly, the emphasis is on energy saving and environmental protection – people are being urged to turn off electrical appliances, turn up their air conditioning, get onto bicycles; but so far few have abandoned their beloved SUVs, even if ads for models with lower fuel consumption abound.

There is much talk of the squeeze being put on the middle class – even of the death of the middle class. As in the last days of the Roman Empire, you are either very, very rich (and pay hardly any taxes), or you are scrabbling to make ends meet. The American Dream is becoming a mirage.

It is said that the approval rating of George W is running nationally at 23 per cent, while only 13 per cent feel that America is set on the right course. Well, I can tell you that in my little circle (admittedly, of the liberal, academic persuasion, but good Americans all, and lovers of their country) the figures are approximately, zero per cent and zero per cent. And that is not a comfortable state to be in. After all, if you think about it, many of us in this country might have had some reservations about Bertie, and there are many Italians who have little use for Berlusconi, or French for Sarkozy, but at least our countries do not embarrass us.

Again and again, over the few jars, among participants at the conference I was attending, the subject came back to the election, now only about five months away, and the prospects for mayhem in the autumn. There is a feeling that Bush might even face indictment for some of his more free-wheeling acts. Someone heard a rumour that the Bush family had been engaged in buying a large hacienda in Paraguay, but the deal fell through when Paraguay signed an extradition treaty with the US. Looks like it may have to be Albania after all for Dubya! They love him there.

These are relatively light-hearted speculations. But darker forebodings were being aired. There is a real fear among my acquaintances that, if things begin to look bad, the Bushies may actually stage a coup. This could involve a staged "atrocity", to be blamed on either Bin Laden or the Iranians, which might even include a pre-emptive strike on Iran, or the assassination of Obama, if the polls look too ominous. It does seem as if the President, by declaring a state of emergency, has the power to postpone or cancel an election, "in the national interest". All he needs is some kind of "event" suitable to the declaring of a "red alert" (the alert was actually orange as I left Atlanta, but nothing untoward occurred); and Middle America, as opposed to the liberal establishment of either east or west coasts, is almost infinitely gullible, nourished as it is on a diet of Fox News (and worse). All this may seem profoundly silly, if not hysterical, but it is sad to report these are the sort of speculations that are going the rounds when otherwise well-balanced liberal intellectuals get together these days. Let us hope that we can get through these few months without any of this coming to pass, and that we can all face into a very different future under the leadership of President Barack Obama!

Meanwhile, I might send off for that programmable mouse. I could do with a bit of diversion.

A sacrifice for the benefit of education
August 10, 2008

The call by the Minister of Education for all institutions of higher education to accept their part in the general belt-tightening by imposing cuts of 3 per cent in their payrolls has evoked the expected degree of indignation and despair from all academic quarters. And not without good reason, after all. Irish universities, over the last decade, have been under continual pressure from Government to excel. Much stress has been laid on the concept of the knowledge economy. Unprecedented resources – from a very minimal base, it must be said - have been pumped into special projects, all of which, on the science side at least, involve hiring teams of researchers, and fitting them out with places to work, and highly expensive instruments to work with. But only the usual bare minimum has been provided for the ordinary day-to-day activities of the universities concerned – that is to say, the education of the basic Irish undergraduate - and that little has, over the last few years, actually shown a net decline. It is from that little, in turn, that a cut of 3 percent has now to be made!

After such a preamble, the proposal that I am about to make will, I fear, sound very strange indeed. But let me start with a story. When I arrived in the University of California at Berkeley in 1966 it was still remembered with awe that at the height of the Great Depression, in 1932 or 1933, in face of serious budget cuts from the state legislature, President Robert Gordon Sproul put it to the faculty that either he would have to fire 10 pet cent of them, or he could keep them all, but they would have to take a 10 per cent cut in salary. The faculty deliberated long and hard, and ultimately decided to take the cut. And the University of California never looked back. What Sproul was doing was positioning them for growth, after first securing the goodwill of the legislature. It was a gamble, and it worked pretty well. What I am now proposing is that we should be prepared to do something of the same.

I would call upon the more senior ranks of university personnel – on the academic side, lecturer and above, along with the equivalent ranks on the administrative side – to offer to take, let us say, a 5 per cent cut in salary (or pension, as the case may be) for the coming academic year (Oct 2008 to Sept 2009), in order to keep in place the host of less fortunate temporary and part-time staff that will otherwise have to be let go, and whose tasks more senior colleagues will, in many cases, then have to perform if students are not to be seriously short-changed. But I would only make such an offer on the clear understanding that there would be proper reciprocation from the Government when things begin to look up again, as they should from 2010 onwards, if we all behave ourselves prudently now.

The university system in this jurisdiction is indeed seriously underfunded. We have the testimony of the recent OECD report for that – as if we didn't know! It has, for some time, been customary to take such universities as Edinburgh or Copenhagen as suitable benchmarks for what funding the Irish universities should expect, and we fall seriously short of them at the moment. Even Queen's, Belfast, looks pretty good by comparison! Let the Minister give a solemn undertaking, in response, to bring us up to the level of those target universities when the present economic clouds lift, and we should be prepared to make a short-term sacrifice in return now. Such an arrangement should establish the groundwork for a greatly enhanced educational environment for the young people of Ireland in the decades to come, and much more rewarding conditions for the dedicated and long-suffering personnel who teach and minister to them.

Athens at war: could Greek mob rule take root on streets of Ireland?

December 14, 2008

Let us imagine a certain scenario. A Garda vehicle noses its way into a narrow street in Temple Bar, Dublin. It comes under attack from a group of youths. Stones and bottles rattle on its roof and windows. Suddenly, there is a burst of fire from the car. A youth, who turns out to be only 15 years of age, falls dead, shot through the chest. Almost instantly, rioting breaks out throughout the quarter, fanned by the rhetoric of radical elements among students from nearby Trinity College. Soon, whole streets are aflame, cars torched, rubbish bins set alight, shop-fronts smashed, pubs looted. Roadblocks are erected, and students and others hurl paving stones and hastily created Molotov cocktails at the police, who respond with teargas and baton charges. A number of arrests are made.

At the end of the first day, the radicals and anarchists retire to Trinity College, where, by convention, the police cannot follow them, since the university is a place of 'asylum'. There they regroup, digging up cobble-stones, breaking pieces off the Georgian facade, and manufacturing Molotov cocktails, in preparation for future battles. For they do not propose to give up easily. Indeed, they want to carry this all the way, to force the fall of the government.

Why all this overheated scare-mongering? Well, as it happens, I am currently besieged in war-torn Athens, trying to preserve the Irish Institute of Hellenic Studies, of which I am Director, and which is situated in the quarter of Exarchia, the epicentre of the current unrest. Exarchia is a part of the city for which, despite its undoubted grottiness, I have considerable affection, but today it is not a nice place to be. The inhabitants, being a mixture of hippies, drug addicts and students from the nearby Polytechnic and University, normally go about their business peaceably enough, but currently they are in a state of revolution, and I am cut off from my favourite coffee bars and tavernas. Further, the uprising has spread to other parts of the city, notably to Syntagma Square and its environs, including parts of the Plaka.

Like so many other inhabitants of this town, both foreign and Greek, I am baffled by what has happened. Why should they want to do this to themselves, just coming up to Christmas? (Symbolically, perhaps, they burned the great Christmas tree in Syntagma last Sunday). It cannot all be about the shooting of one wretched youth, tragic though that may be. What, then, we ask ourselves, is the root of this great and destructive rage which consumes so many people – mostly but not exclusively young, and not by any means all radical anarchists? And further, I ask myself, could this happen in Dublin? And if not, why not?

Well, it has to be said that, in many ways, Greek standards of propriety in politics and public administration make us in Ireland look pretty good, despite our various shortcomings. It pains me to say it, this being the cradle of democracy, but in some ways Greece retains more than a whiff of the Middle East, or even of the Third World, in its public life.

It is a widespread perception that nepotism and corruption prevail in politics, not only among the ruling New Democracy Party (which has neo-conservative tendencies), but also in its predecessor, the socialist PASOK (despite its creditable record in ridding the country of the junta). The public services are pervaded with inefficient and self-serving functionaries (Athens garbage collection, for one thing, rivals that of Naples, despite recent outsourcing). And as for the police, they are poorly trained, boorish, and badly paid – and thus prone to corruption, as well as internal discontent. So we are not just talking about the shooting of one rather foolish lad – for the record, Alexis Grigoropoulos, 15, son of a bank manager – who should not have been doing whatever he was doing in the place that he was doing it.

The disaffection, however, goes a lot deeper than that, and it has now, coming up to Christmas, dealt a hammer blow to a Greek economy which was already reeling, as is ours, from foolish building and banking practices, inflation, and the over-extension of credit. The successful calling of a general strike on Wednesday indicates a more general undercurrent of sympathy with the rioters, appalling though their behaviour has been.

But let us not get too complacent. I am assuming that it won't happen here, and that my Temple Bar scenario is just a fantasy, but there are underlying tensions here too, which will be exacerbated in the coming months. The Gardaí may have to keep their cool in a series of difficult situations. But basically, I think that it is fair to say that we have a level of acceptance of the state and its institutions that many in Greece, regrettably, do not have, for reasons that I have sketched above.

It's 10% off everything in recession escape plan

December 28, 2008

It has been a sobering experience wandering about town on the couple of mornings I have done so recently, in the run-up to Christmas. Shoppers seemed distinctly thin on the ground, despite the remarkable bargains on offer. I can only sympathise with the traders of Ireland in this dire time. In my favourite cheese shop, where I went to collect the ration of Stilton, instead of the usual queue extending out into the street, I was the only customer, and they were very pleased to see me. The Stilton, I may say, was not on sale!

All this, though, has been provoking me to thought. The most respected national pundits have been grimly analysing the situation, and pouring scorn on any attempts of the Government to relieve it – but I must say I have not heard any positive suggestions emanating from those quarters, nor yet from the parliamentary opposition. If a professor of Greek may step in where economists and politicians fear to tread, I think I have a solution to at least one aspect of our present situation – the fact that we have priced ourselves out of the market internationally.

I mean, have you ever heard a really persuasive explanation for why prices in the shops here, even in the most economical chains, are vastly higher than those, not only in mainland Britain, but even in Northern Ireland, which should have all the same problems of transportation and of non-economies of scale that we have? In their attempts to deflect accusations of inexcusable mark-ups, traders down here bleat about high rents, energy costs, local authority charges, and high wages. Well, if that is the root of the problem, then let me propose at least the broad lines of a possible solution. I will call it the Ten Per Cent Solution.

There has been talk recently of a pay freeze in the public sector, even of pay reductions. I think that such talk is very much on the right lines, but it doesn't go far enough, since even if one could secure agreement on this, the consequent reduction in spending power on the part of a large segment of the population would only aggravate the recession. It would take money out of circulation, when it should be going to the purchase of goods and services. Yes indeed, so it would – unless one also provided at the same time that all the chief areas of expenditure were brought down as well, viz, mortgages, energy costs, transport costs, professional fees (medical, legal, etc), restaurant meals, and of course food.

Now let us imagine that all wage-earners were prevailed upon to take a 10 per cent cut in salary (on condition, of course, that workers were kept on in employment who would otherwise be let go). This would normally lead to a serious reduction in discretionary spending. But what if the other side of the deal was that the main components of their expenditure also came down 10 per cent? Then we have a situation where the wage-earner is very little worse off, at most, while prices of products that we need to export can be brought down accordingly, and the country becomes correspondingly more attractive to visitors.

But we have then to go to the banks, and direct that mortgage payments be reduced by 10 per cent, and even that 10 per cent be sliced off the value of the original mortgages (since in a well-regulated society they should never have been granted in the first place, being grossly out of line with incomes). And then we would have to turn to doctors and lawyers and make the same demand. If that works so far, then the pressure on all other sectors of the economy would, I think, become overwhelming, to the extent that one could simply refuse to engage with anyone who would not undertake a similar cut.

Of course, there would be difficulties in supervising all this, but, with a minimum of good will, it is by no means impossible to achieve. Indeed, it has a sort of precedent in the brilliant move that helped to get the Celtic Tiger moving in the first place, back in the early 1990s, orchestrated by the Great Fixer himself, Bertie. He proposed, if you recall, that, if the unions would accept a pay freeze, he would lower income taxes, and so they would actually have as much more money in their pockets as if they had insisted on a pay rise – and they would still have jobs, which they might very well not have had in the latter case. The unions went for that, and the rest is history.

Now history needs making again. What about it, boys? Let us all declare ourselves *On Sale*, from the Great and Good on down, and we may yet get back to being a competitive economy once again.

Can we survive our awful greedy binge?
March 1, 2009

Unbelievable as it may seem, in the current economic climate, two bronze heads, one of a rat, the other of a rabbit, were sold last week in Paris by Christies for over €31m. Now these were admittedly antique Chinese bronze artefacts – whose return, indeed, is actively sought by the Chinese government, seeing as they were looted from the old Summer Palace in Beijing back in 1860, when it was wrecked by marauding armies of English and French, trying to impose their imperialist agenda on China.

But that is not the issue that I wanted to dwell on here; rather, I am concerned with the outrage that there is someone still out there who is capable of phoning up an auction room and pledging €31m for these meaningless trophies. Are we faced here with a Russian oligarch? Or a junior member of the Saudi royal family? Or perhaps our own Seanie FitzPatrick has decided to switch some of his self-engineered loan of €89m into art? At any rate, the wide boys are still out there, plainly with hardly a feather knocked out of them. And these are the sort of people that poor Mr Lenihan is being urged by our major trade union leaders to track down and make pay for the debacle that we are in.

The only problem with that is that, first of all, they are not at all easy to catch, being hedged about with statutory guarantees; and secondly, there are not, after all, very many of them – perhaps 50 at the most – and their nailing would consequently not fill that much of hole in the exchequer returns.

Certainly they should be more heavily taxed, and their incomes severely capped, but, sadly, the real solution to the problem lies not with them; it involves, rather, recognising the fact that we have all been paying ourselves far too much, at all levels. For instance it is easily verifiable that (admittedly on the current exchange rate with sterling) the average nurse or Garda in Dublin is paid up to 40 per cent more than their corresponding ranks in London – and the same goes, I must confess, for higher civil servants and university professors. We have all been on a glorious binge, encouraged by dear old Uncle Bertie.

No wonder the trade union leaders loved social partnership. In its days of glory, the only issue was whether one would press for a ten per cent pay rise across the board, or whether, with great magnanimity and statesmanship, one would settle for, perhaps, seven per cent, offset by reduced hours of work and increased fringe benefits. The wretched IBEC would warn mournfully of the dangers of increasing non-competitiveness, but they were dismissed as grouches and bad losers. Now, however, the chickens have come home to roost, and the trade unions are faced with the unpalatable fact that social partnerships, like marriages, are entered into 'for richer, for poorer, for better and for worse', and we have now entered into the latter part of the bargain. But what do we find?

What we find is that something like the pensions levy – a most moderate and prudent proposal in the circumstances – is regarded as a gross imposition, an assault on public sector workers, meriting every sort of civil disobedience, up to and including a national strike, while what is put forward as an alternative, by the Great Beards, Messrs Jack O'Connor and David Begg, is a windy and vague 'Social Solidarity Pact', a set of proposals which amount to saying, "Let's you and him make sacrifices; we are far too stretched to make any contribution ourselves."

For what are they saying? We of course, they say, recognise the serious state of the public finances, and everyone must do their bit. But a pay cut for public servants is not on. A pension levy is not on. How else, then, one may ask, are public servants to contribute? A nation-wide novena, perhaps? That said, however, there is no denying that pain must be seen to be inflicted soon also on the better off. There must be a property tax, of some variety. There must be a higher top band of income tax, perhaps 46 per cent. And a whole range of fees to lawyers and consultants must be slashed. And lastly, I should say, a national government should be formed, for a period of at least two years, to push all this through. Only in this way can serious social unrest be averted.

The problem is that there is a plague of rats out there, and we seem to be trying to track them down with rabbits. What is required instead is a well-trained pack of hunting dogs.

Throw out the bathwater but save the Green Coalition baby

May 31, 2009

One untoward consequence of the vote on June 5 looks likely to be the decimation of the Green Party, purely as a result of contamination contracted from their larger partners. I recognise, of course, that there is something about the Greens that tends to bring out the worst in a wide swathe of the Irish nation, and correspondingly, of the Irish media. There is a composite image in the public mind of bearded, vegetarian, bicycling, tree-hugging moaners, shaking reproachful fingers at the fun-loving Celtic Tiger generation.

The decision to take part in government was also the occasion of much derision. It was indeed an agonising decision for a party of principle, with some high-profile defections, such as that redoubtable moaner Patricia McKenna. Trevor Sargent, while recommending the decision to go into government, felt in honour bound to resign as leader, because he had pledged during the campaign not to form a coalition with Fianna Fail. The media suspected hypocrisy. The truth was much simpler, really. The man is a Protestant. His word is his bond. He now believed this was, after all, an opportunity worth grasping, but he had earlier gone out on a limb against it, and that was that.

Not that Sargent's talents have been lost to the nation, I am glad to say. As Minister of State for Food, he has been able to pursue many of his favourite causes, encouraging farmers' markets, garden allotments, and, most charmingly, a scheme called Incredible Edibles, by which children are introduced to vegetables in the classroom. The department mandarins predictably declared there was no money for such a project, whereat he went out and raised the money himself.

Ribaldry also has surrounded his successor, John Gormley, for having to preside over the construction of an incinerator in his constituency against which he had campaigned long and hard while in opposition, not to mention the awful M3. At least he has been able to curb the activities of local authorities, and do something about the pollution of our water.

As for Eamon Ryan, he seems to have freed up the energy market, and to have begun, at least, to turn the sclerotic ESB towards taking renewable energy seriously. It may be true that wind, wave and solar energy can only be expected to provide less than half of our energy needs, and the Greens are surely going to have to overcome their aversion to nuclear power, but we should at least press ahead with developing what we have.

But all these things take time, and crusading ministers have to reckon with the enormous forces of inertia lurking in their departments, as well as the ambivalent attitude of one's larger partner. So I would propose that the Greens be given a little more time to show what they can do. This country needs to go in the way that they are pointing. The bathwater is certainly murky and should doubtless be poured out, but be sure to save the baby.

Greeks must be brave and get history to Repeat Itself

February 19, 2012

Contemplating the present crisis facing Greece, I am provoked to conjure up two notable occasions in its history – one from ancient history, the other from modern – on which the Greeks said No to a larger foreign power bringing pressure to bear on them, and got away with it, though in the second case not with such a fortunate outcome as in the first. I am not sure if any lessons are to be drawn from the examples or not, but it would not surprise me if they are passing through the minds of many of my Greek friends during this dismal time.

The first occasion takes us back to 480 BC, when the Persian king Xerxes, in the face of a series of provocations from this tiny, feisty and divided nation on his western flank, decided to bring the Greeks to heel once and for all, and add them to his empire. In preparation for an invasion, he sent a formal demand to all the Greek states for the forwarding of 'earth and water' in token of submission to his rule. A number of the weaker and more vulnerable island states duly sent in the earth and water, but the two main states, Athens and Sparta, proudly refused. The result was an invasion of Greece by an army of up to a million men, and the devastation of much territory, including Athens, but ultimately the expedition resulted in the defeat, in 479 BC, of the Persian navy at the Battle of Salamis, and of its army at the Battle of Plataea, by Greek forces that were much smaller, but vastly superior in terms of bravery and discipline. This in turn led to an outpouring of creativity in the arts, sciences and politics which constituted the classical age of Greece, and one of the great periods of the human race so far.

In this case, great danger and dire short-term devastation led in the longer run to great prosperity and self-confidence, and ultimately to the conquest of the whole Persian empire 150 years later by Alexander the Great. The decision to say 'No' from the modern era was equally brave, and was initially successful, but did not ultimately work out quite so well.

In the autumn of 1940, on the crest of a wave of Axis successes, Mussolini decided to pick a quarrel with Greece, and presented an ultimatum, calling upon the Greeks to surrender to him, in anticipation of an easy victory if they resisted. General Metaxas, Greece's dictator at the time (and not a very lovable figure, it must be said), to his great credit, told the Italians to get lost – enunciating the famous 'No' (*Okhi*), which is still vividly remembered. The Italians poured across the Albanian border, but, to their great surprise, were met by well-organised Greek resistance, and were soundly thrashed, being driven back in disorder into Albania. Unfortunately, however, matters could not rest there, as the Germans felt they could not leave their allies in the lurch, and they duly invaded, and occupied Greece for the duration of the war – committing a number of atrocities in the process, which are, of course, still remembered – and currently being highlighted by many indignant Greeks.

And so we come to 2012. Once again, Greece is threatened grievously from without, but this time by a foe much more intangible than before, though none the less dangerous and oppressive for that. A combination of banks and financial speculators have, admittedly with the connivance of successive Greek governments themselves, woven around the Greek nation an inextricable web of debt, guaranteed to bring the economy to a halt, depress living standards to an unbearable extent, and establish a debt repayment regime which will amount to a more or less permanent state of serfdom. To enforce this regime, a functionary from the ECB has been imposed on them as 'prime minister' who is himself Greek (it helps to be able to speak the language), but who is bound to find his loyalties conflicted between Greece and the EU.

What is to be done? Well, there are many Greeks who are prepared once again to say 'Okhi!', and take the consequences, whatever they may be. Unfortunately, though, to defeat this enemy ordinary old-fashioned bravery will not be enough, as its onset will be strangely intangible. No troops or military hardware will roll in. Instead, there will come about an absence; everything will just dry up. Money, credit, supplies of essential commodities will simply become unavailable. Such an enemy is almost impossible to defeat, but I am inclined to feel that even so the effort is worth making – and indeed that Portugal and Ireland should follow suit. The results will be apocalyptic in the short run, so we are promised, but I feel that it is our best chance to destroy the octopus of international finance that has brought us all to this crisis, and which, if allowed to triumph, will ultimately bring down the environment and civilisation along with it. I would go for it. *Okhi! Okhi! Okhi!*

This edition is printed in a limited run of 100 copies,
of which this is number:

99

KATOUNIA
PRESS